ALWAYS LEAVE AN AIRMAN BEHIND

A Real Story of Surviving The Crab Leadership Culture

By

Ellis Franks

© Copyright 2019 by Ellis Franks - All rights reserved.

It is not legal to reproduce, duplicate, or transmit any part of this document in either electronic means or printed format. Recording of this publication is strictly prohibited.

For all those left behind by a system that feigns leadership when the reality is a culture that's toxic towards anyone who seeks to achieve more than the status quo.

Table of Contents

I Was No Hero, But I Built Some	5
Homeless & Lost	16
Six Months For The Rest Of My Life	22
Stepping Out From The Crowd	83
I Hope You Like Cow Shit	99
Bulgogi, Bombs, & Bad Leadership	138
The Good Ole Boy Base	168
Searching For The Best Of The Best	201
Facing My Biggest Fears	293
What Do We Do With The Washout?	360
The Higher You Climb The Farther You Fall	399
Aftermath	463
From The Ashes	480
Acknowledgments	492
About the Author	493

Ellis Franks "Always Leave An Airman Behind: A Real Story of Surviving The Crab Leadership Culture

I Was No Hero, But I Built Some

The story of my life is not one about being a hero of the wars we have been fighting for the past few decades. I never accomplished anything as significant as many of the men I served beside who would earn bronze stars with valor, purple hearts, and other medals for their bravery. I served beside quite a few real-life heroes. I fortunately, I never had to endure the hardships that are required to earn those coveted reminders of selflessness, courage, and survival. My story is not one of kicking doors in on the battlefields around the world, but it is a story of survival.

Growing up I was the son of a drug-addicted mother who lived an impetuous life that created chaos for the kids that were unfortunate to be born to her. Surviving this chaos is a whole other story that may be told some other day because this story is the about how the Air Force saved my life and then discarded me as unceremoniously as I had started. The story was not a fairy tale, but the personal growth I experienced while serving my country created the character and work ethic I would need to become a successful entrepreneur and certified leadership coach.

My journey was not the easy path that most military veterans love to share. It is filled with a constant battle I waged against the mediocrity that the service I loved let settle into its core. I was on a professional development world tour looking for something bigger than I could imagine when I started. My journey had many disappointments. I made the mistake of caring too much about the Airmen I was charged with leading. I spent a lot of my career as the villain who pushed his people harder than they were comfortable but the results I achieved always led to a significant increase in my unit's effectiveness.

I was no hero, but I was a leader. My leadership journey took me to levels of success that a homeless teenager who did not know if he would be alive at age 18 could never have imagined. I mentored thousands of Airmen during my career who were also looking for something bigger than the lives they left behind. The memories of them are very vivid in my mind. The memories are so lucid I can still smell and taste the air in my mind from the several dozen countries I would visit around the world. I am reminded with each memory of the internal battles I faced in my quest to reject mediocrity.

I took an oath when I became a Military Training Instructor (MTI), the Air Force version of a drill instructor, and this oath I took serious for the remainder of my life. The oath was the Military Training Instructor Code and goes as follows;

The training instructor hat that I wear is a symbol of honor, integrity, and excellence in military deportment. My job is one of the most important in the Air Force and I will spare no effort to properly prepare young men and women for military duty. I am dedicated to the principles of fairness, firmness, and honesty in my dealings with those entrusted to my charge. I am pledged to strive for perfection and reject mediocrity both in my behavior and in the performance of those for whom I am responsible. I am an Air Force Military Training Instructor.

I spent my career trying to meet the obligations of this oath. I found that it was not the popular path to follow because most people are dedicated to making their jobs easier instead of pushing past their limits. I always believed that as I climbed the ladder of ranks within the military, I would be able to affect more change, but the reality is that the higher I climbed the more dedicated to the bare minimum the peers of each level had become.

Senior leadership tended to be at the ends of their careers and did not want to "rock the boat" to ensure they retired quietly. The Air Force contributed to this dedication to the status quo by creating systems of control that kept senior leaders from expressing their true thoughts on the status of their troops. I found the higher I climbed, the more likely I would be sitting in rooms with leaders who were not the top-quality people I expected but were rather the senior percent of those that remained at the end of twenty years of service. I was a rogue Airman who was detested by many. Many others were jealous of the successes I earned without the normal personal relationships that most Airmen believe is the only path to success.

The Air Force had created a vast professional development system that I rarely witnessed Airmen taking advantage of in their careers. The system was based on the intertwining of Air Force core values into every aspect of Airmen's lives from the very moment they set foot on the infamous "yellow dots" at their basic training squadron. Every Air Force instructor was trained to use a technique called the "schoolhouse weave" when teaching classes to ensure core values were part of every lesson.

Additionally, the Air Force invested millions of dollars into creating multiple levels of professional development courses for specific rank tier groups that taught the "expected" leadership, mentorship, and professional development for the Airmen these leaders were charged with leading. Attendance to these courses was mandatory to be eligible for promotion to the next rank. It was designed to give the leaders the minimum skills required to meet their new rank responsibilities.

Mentoring was the final piece of the Air Force's professional development program. It was mandatory per a general lawful order that required all leaders to engage in the mentorship of the troops under their charge. The Air Force took this program a step further by creating a system of mandatory mentoring sessions that a supervisor was given computer notification for due dates for each of their assigned mentees.

The system on paper was perfect, and it was nonexistent. The Air Force only required that a signed document be turned into the personnel department by the mentor but did nothing to ensure a session had occurred. This led to most leaders pencil-whipping the mandatory feedback sessions unless the leader wanted to document something negative to justify a lower rating than the expected "exceptional" rating that 99 percent of Airmen received regardless of actual performance.

Per the made-up version of the Air Force I lived within, my career would be judged as an epic failure by many people I served beside. This was because they did not realize the reality of the quest I had taken. Other NCOs took the easiest paths possible. They were rewarded with high ranking promotions, medals, awards, and a lifetime retirement check. I was fighting a battle against the tyrannies created by the status quo. Ranks and awards were always subjective in the Air Force. The system mostly awarded people who were popular and did not care if they were effective in their leadership. I even witnessed senior Air Force members take credit for accomplishments of their people for combat operations when they were not even involved in the firefights by claiming they "led the operations". The sad part was these ranking members were in the safety of their offices during the attacks.

The worst case I heard about was when I was in Afghanistan and a dozen insurgents breached our walls with explosives and a single Airman held his position until the Apache helicopters decimated the enemy. The leaders submit the actual combatant who killed a half dozen terrorists for an Air Force Achievement Medal "due to his rank". The unit then submit the Chief and Captain for Bronze Stars because they were the "leaders of the base defense". The supervisor of the Airmen confided his frustrations with me about this, but he knew there was no fairness in the organization. The politics of the system were corrupt to the point where a lot of leaders took credit for their people's actions.

I was different than these posers. I valued the rewards I received as more lasting because I changed thousands of lives by seeing each person's potential. I pushed them to meet my standards instead of lowering it for them to feel good about themselves. I also was not afraid to give them full credit for the work we did. I understood that every success for my people pushed us all forward. I was lucky to have been mentored by leaders from outside my chain of command who were legends from Air Force history who taught me to treat people fairly but to never be the soft leader who did things to be liked. I was the rogue leader who believed in the philosophical definition of the Air Force. I had a gift for pushing mediocre Airmen to levels of success they had long given up seeking. The path I walked was very lonely, and it attracted all the "crabs" attention who set forth to destroy any ideal that challenged the status quo they loved.

The crab mentality was a concept that I studied in my leadership journey and it represented the burdens an overachiever faced when they challenged the masses who were content on their easy paths. The idea was based on a metaphor that evaluated how crabs in a bucket do not require a top because if a crab attempts to escape the other crabs will pull it back into the bucket. The Air Force was the crab mentality in action, and poor leaders in all ranks held firm to policies or traditions that limited the productivity of the entire service. The military I served in was a precursor to society's desire to reward everyone just for participation. I witnessed NCOs being promoted who scored less than 25 percent on the supervisory and technical tests, but because they were liked by the management team they would be promoted under programs that were for "exceptional performers".

      I was appalled with the degradation of our nation's readiness level due to the sheer amount of incompetent higher-ranking individuals the Air Force's policies had created and this created two realities for the service. The first was a world where the Air Force spelled out every detail expected of leaders for them to be effective. The service created massive libraries of Air Force Instructions, Manuals, and other lawful general orders that were expected to be followed always. The philosophical version of the Air Force was perfect. The Airmen all were proud to earn the title and were selflessly dedicated to their missions. Every Airman was treated fairly and given the same opportunities. In this world, the Air Force core values were intertwined into every aspect of an Airman's life, and the competition for promotions, awards, and medals was very high pushing technological developments on all levels. Leaders took large amounts of their time to mentor their Airmen to be better than they believed they could become and ensured high levels of competence in the future leaders of the service. Airmen were experts in their professional military education and career field technical aptitudes, and the apprenticeship program all Airmen were part of produced the most efficient technicians in the world. This version of the Air Force did not exist, but on paper, the service looked like a force of 350,000 geniuses who were saving the world.

The real Air Force was a place where being called an "Airman" was viewed as degrading. Non-Commissioned Officers (NCOs) created a decades-long culture of shunning leadership development, detesting technical aptitude, rejected Air Force core values, and pencil-whipped their NCO responsibilities as the most common practice. The real Air Force was the bucket, and the leaders were the crabs that pulled anyone who tried to climb higher to escape the status quo of the bucket back down into their comfort zone. This real version of the Air Force rewarded laziness and incompetence if you accepted mediocrity as the first core value.

The results have created many higher-ranking people today that cannot tell you basic general orders for the job they have held for 20 years because they only reviewed the info sporadically over their careers for promotion testing. Many NCOs were falsely convinced they were competent because they confused the promotions they received with the fact they failed the tests of their readiness for promotion because they were incapable of knowing more than 50 percent of their supervisory and technical knowledge.

This was the Air Force that I left in 2009 after 13 years 352 days of dedicated service. I left a few days after being honored as the top Airman out of 350,000 who served when I was named the 2008 Air Force Sergeants Association International Member of the Year. I left the service forgoing the retirement for life that I had sacrificed the best years of my life to earn and had dedicated my life fulfilling the goals of an ungrateful service. I realized I had climbed the ladder of success and it was not in the correct place I was meant to be in the end. The Air Force had saved my life as a young teen and then discarded me abruptly throwing away everything I sacrificed in my career. The short-sighted crabs believed by destroying my credibility they could control me but the lessons I had promoted would forever live on in the thousands of Airmen I had instilled my values within through my mentorship. These Airmen are still affecting change in the Air Force today.

The crabs thought they could pull me back into their bucket to control me, but in the end, I would have the last laugh when I used the traits they deemed undesirable to become many times more successful than they could ever imagine. This is the story of that journey.

Homeless & Lost

It was a cold winter night just before Christmas in 1994. I was a senior at Jones County High School in Gray, Georgia. I was living with my eight-time divorced, drug-dependent mother in a trailer park outside of Macon, Georgia. The day was going well as some people I knew from school came over to hang out. We were enjoying our evening when my mother and her new boyfriend came home from an evening of partying. Everything seemed cool at first, but my life was about to change in an instant. I had no idea it was coming.

My mother was known for her temper, especially when she was intoxicated. This night was no different than any other over my 17 years I had been with her. She tended to start out laughing and antagonizing us. Then in a blink, she would turn insane on everyone. This time she was attempting to make fun of me in front of my friends and refused to stop. When we started arguing she abruptly left to go into her bedroom. She returned with her boyfriend's shoe then commenced to smacking me in the back of my head for no reason.

I quickly took the shoe from her and told her to go to bed. Unfortunately, she was only getting started this night. She went into a rage threatened everyone in the house. Her boyfriend, Vick, was a six-foot, five-inch-tall man in his late 20's-early 30's who weighed about 265 pounds. He had been coming around for a few weeks and he was an extremely rude, boisterous person. We had exchanged words a few days prior at the local Pizza Hut when he made a big scene because some homeless people paid for a meal and dined nearby. He demanded the homeless people be kicked out. When I disagreed, and he made a big scene making all the patrons inside look in our direction. He made threats to hurt me and cussed at me but never took the incident any further. Vick had not gotten over this incident. He was eager to have another opportunity to put me in my place.

He was standing behind my mother when I took the shoe away from her. He immediately jumped in threatening to hurt me if I didn't leave immediately. Unbeknownst to any of us, the two of them had spent the evening drinking, snorting cocaine, and they were highly agitated. They were getting more out of control by the second. That's when Vick escalated the confrontation. He grabbed me as I was walking towards my bedroom and I had to fight for my life.

I reacted immediately to attempt to free his grip but could not break free. I wanted to run to my bedroom where I had my firearms because this guy was almost three times my size. Luckily, he grabbed me first and saved me from a life-altering incident that could have potentially changed the course of my life in another direction. I didn't have time to think so my body went into action. I began punching him in his face as hard as I could. I can't remember how many times I hit him, but it was for what seemed like forever until he securely wrapped his arms around my neck. He firmly began to attempt to strangle me. I had no other option but to bite him until blood came out. That made him release me due to the pain.

I ran out of the door to a friend's running car as this behemoth chased me out the door. I narrowly escaped Vick's cocaine-fueled rage as he dove through a window to pull me out of the car to continue our fight. All the while my mother was screaming in the background that she was calling the police to arrest me. She kept saying that I was no longer welcomed at her home. I had gotten away, but I had no money, no clothes, and no idea where I was going to stay. This night I was lucky because the friend that drove me away let me sleep on his floor but reminded me it was only for one night.

The next day I went to school not knowing what I would do when the final bell for the day rang. I didn't have any prospects on a place to live but I guessed things would work their way out. When the bell rang to end the day, I walked out of the school. I looked each way down the road to consider the path I would take, and finally decided I would walk towards the small-town center of Gray, Georgia. I knew that if I traveled in that direction there would be more traffic than the back-country roads in the opposite direction. All I could hope for was someone to see me and ask what I was doing then maybe offer me someplace to stay. Unfortunately, I was not in luck this day as I watched all the people I knew from school, the teachers, coaches, and everyone else drive past me without stopping to check on me. I was saddened by this but had to keep moving as it would be dark soon.

I spent several hours walking to nowhere in particular. I finally stopped at a place to borrow their phone. This was a time before mobile phones, and the only choice of communication was a landline phone. I borrowed the phone of the stranger to call a friend who a beeper to send a message with "911". He graciously took me in for "one night only" but this saved me from sleeping outside in the cold. I was relieved. That night I used his phone to contact a girl I had been dating for around two years and lined up a place to stay for a few nights. Nothing was permanent, and I had no prospects for finding help.

I would spend the entire Christmas break bouncing from one couch to another as I wore out my welcome repeatedly. I had a big decision to make about the upcoming school start date after the holiday. I didn't know where I would be staying or if I could be able to return. I contemplated many options to include dropping out of school to join the Army. Now due to my living situation, I was not sure what to do. That's when I got super lucky by running into one of my football teammates while loitering in the local area. He talked to his father and they took me in a few days after school started back. I didn't have to drop out of school.

Going back to school was the best decision I could have made. I would end up being the only one of my siblings to receive a high school diploma. The question now was what path I am supposed to follow. I grew up the grandson of a professional baseball player who passed on the talents of playing the game to me. I always thought I would just play baseball. My failed beliefs were that my talent was going to open doors for me. This made me a lazy student that just skimmed by barely passing each class. Plus no one cared about whether I went so my attendance was abysmal. I was not even sure if I would be able to play baseball because I had no ride from practices to my temporary housing that was over an hour away.

Shortly before baseball season began my grandmother mediated my return home with my mother. I came home reluctantly. I knew I had to stick it out until after graduation, then I would be on my own forever. Our relationship was very rocky throughout this period. She continually threatened to kick me out again. Her biggest complaint was that I had been attending baseball practice. Due to the distance I had been getting home late each day, especially if I had to make the trip on foot. The stress of trying to play baseball became too much. I had enough after a team member named Bryan Gattie told me off for being a burden to my teammates. I had to make the decision to walk away from baseball.

This was the most devastating decision I had ever made. Baseball was the only talent that I thought I had. Now it was gone. I started to work 7 days a week at a grocery store my mother had a friend who was the manager, and he agreed to hire me. I had started down a path of underachievement. I had officially landed my first "dead-end job". I felt deep inside there was something bigger that I was supposed to do but the barriers in front of me were too much to overcome. I was lost and had no inclination of how to correct my life's path.

Ellis Franks "Always Leave An Airman Behind: A Real Story of Surviving The Crab Leadership Culture

Six Months For The Rest Of My Life

I had contemplated joining the Army out of desperation a few weeks before returning to school, but this was not something I had ever seriously considered. I must have looked like a big target to the abundance of military recruiters that visited our school weekly at lunchtime as they all got my information and began calling me. The most tenacious was a wiry Marine sergeant who was the most persistent person I had ever met. I never considered the Marines, mostly because I doubted I would survive boot camp at Parris Island. I had seen the movie "Full Metal Jacket" and this was not an experience I wanted. The sergeant recruiter was like a bulldog. He was unrelenting until I agreed to have a meeting at my home with my mother present.

I was very hesitant to bring this sergeant to our home as my mother had a bad reputation when it came to men. She had already been divorced eight times. She had about 20 times that in deadbeat boyfriends. I knew she would jump at the opportunity to take advantage of this man's stable career. Hesitantly, I invited him over one evening to discuss the Marines. He presented an exciting sales pitch for enlisting. He sold me on the idea of being self-reliant as well as the ability to travel the world. I was only 17 years old and to sign up I required my mother's signature. Her speed at signing that document mirrored my feelings. It was time to leave. I passed all the testing to qualify physically and was set to leave for boot camp several days before I was to walk down the aisle for graduation.

Meanwhile, I enjoyed the camaraderie of the Marines recruits. I attended all scheduled events. I was excited to leave for boot camp and begin my life on my own. During this period my fears were realized as my mother began dating the sergeant recruiter. Then after a short time period, they were married making him my ninth stepfather. My relationship with the recruiter turned stepfather deteriorated mainly due to my mother's negative influence. Before long we could not be in the same building together without arguing. I was out with a friend one day and expressed my desire to get out of the contract with the Marines. He informed me that he had joined the Air Force and was set to leave for basic training in December 1995. I asked him to introduce me to his recruiter to weigh my options for getting out of the Marines contract.

Master Sergeant Rosa was a character I will never forget. His no BS approach to his job stood in contrast to the Marines sales approach. He was a consummate professional. He also exemplified military dress and appearance. What I respected most was MSgt Rosa called me out on anything. He didn't sugar-coat

23

the situation. He gave me the first true example of the Non-commissioned Officer I would attempt to emulate later in my career.

He gave me detailed instructions on the process to which I followed exactly. Before I knew it, I was released from my commitment with the Marines. For a short period, I considered foregoing the military idea as I was not sure how I would make it. I was very undisciplined. I had been taught very little in the ways of commitment or follow-through. I feared the unknown of what would happen to me at basic training. I also wondered how I would react to someone in my face screaming at me. The only consolation was that my closest friend at the time, Razzy Lavender, was going to be with me on the journey.

We were set to leave for the Military Enlistment Processing Station, known as MEPS, on December 11th, 1995. We left on a bus to Atlanta, Georgia. I nervously spent the evening trying to not think about the events that were set to take place in the next 48 hours. The entire day at MEPS I kept thinking the drill sergeants were going to come out to start yelling anytime now. But the staff remained focused and aloof to our presence throughout the long day.

Ellis Franks "Always Leave An Airman Behind: A Real Story of Surviving The Crab Leadership Culture

    MEPs is an experience every military trainee undergoes to ensure they are fit for military duty. The process is a cattle call for recruits where they are put into groups then are ushered from one room to another to be tested from head to toe. The tests required a lot of poking and prodding from doctors or medical technicians over the entirety of your body. The MEPs building was cold, smelled of medical supplies, and the staff was not very friendly. We were all treated like work. They were just going through the motions no matter if it was painful to the recruits or not. The worst part was that each recruit was required to partake in this torture twice to enter basic training. The first trip was initial qualification and then a second time to ensure you still met requirements before shipping off to training I would end up doing this ritual three times since I left the Marines for the Air Force.

    The first MEPs trip for me was completed under for the Marines. I was aware of the long day to expect the second trip. The best part for me was the testing for qualification mostly needed only to be verified. I did not have to do all the tests like the first trip. I easily passed all the testing. I was set to join the Air Force in a few months.

    While I waited for my ship date to Air Force basic training I permanently moved out of my mother's home. I got three jobs at once to pay for the bills I would have for the next few months. Then I moved into a friend's studio apartment. The apartment was quaint because the friend was never home due to his work and school schedules making it a quiet place to stay.

I quickly realized leaving the area was the best thing I could do. I needed to go as soon as possible. My mother's reputation led to people I knew contacting me to connect them to buy drugs. I would be contacted several times a week by people who heard that I could connect them with the drug dealers. I had met several through my mother, one of her deadbeat ex-husbands who mostly sold drugs, and the kids of those people who were joining the family business. I could have easily made thousands of dollars a week selling drugs to these people. I could have fallen into the same cycle of failure that everyone I had ever know growing up seemed drawn towards. I never made those mistakes. Instead, I tried to work as much as possible to pass the time until I shipped out for training.

Finally on 11 December 1995, I took a bus to Atlanta for my final processing into the military. The day was very long. We were awake for what seemed to be 20 hours on my third trip to MEPs when we were gathered in a room. We now took our final enlistment oath to the Constitution. We were $_{\text{quickly}}$ given plane tickets for a flight to San Antonio, Texas. The staff pointed us to a Marta train, the Atlanta version of a subway, and a group of about 30 Air Force recruits was on our way to the unknown. I remember thinking I had made a huge mistake.

The flight to San Antonio was very unnerving. I had never been on a plane before. My anxiety about the events about to unfold was enough to make me physically shiver. I occupied my time reading a book by Terry Brooks called "Magic Kingdom for Sale", though I vaguely remembered the reading. I went through the motions with it but had to re-read it later. The flight seemed to last forever but finally, we arrived in San Antonio later in the evening. We had all been up since about 3 am. Many people in our group had spent the night prior partying making everyone exhausted before the stressful part of our day began. We were corralled inside the airport by the first military members we saw. Once again my mind raced thinking the yelling would begin immediately but the rollcall was peaceful. The Air Force sergeants grouped us then put us on more buses that drove towards Lackland Air Force Base. The scene was ironic for me as I journeyed on a dark bus towards an unknown future. I was leaving a sad, dark life behind.

The gates of Lackland AFB were bright when we arrived. When the bus stopped at the gate several heavily armed military police searched the bus and checked our IDs. Afterwards, we were driven to a building where we were greeted by the first Air Force member with the "Smoky the Bear Hat". My heart sank again as the stress from the anticipated yelling crept up. Once again, the sergeant sternly ordered us off the bus but refrained from screaming at us. I was relieved to simply offload the bus to sit in a big room awaiting our fate. An hour or two later our group was ordered to stand up to board a bus destined for our new home. We had been assigned to the 322nd Training Squadron located on what we learned to be called the famed "Hotel Row".

The bus ride to our new home for the next seven weeks seemed like an eternity. We were all apprehensive about what was about to occur. No one knew what awaited us when the bus doors opened. The uncertainty added to the nearly 20-hour day we had endured made it more stressful. The bus pulled up to our building stopping with the screeching of the air brakes. When the door opened a small-framed man entered the bus to give us instructions. He explained that we were to get off the bus with all our possessions, quickly form-up on the four dots that were near a wall and keep our "dirty pie holes shut". I was lucky that I had nothing really to bring with me. My small bag was very light. Some people packed several bags worth of gear that they now had to hold for an extended period. The instructors ensured they were in for some torture for the next hour.

The bus unloaded in a frenzy. As soon as the group made a very unorganized formation that was four people wide by about 20 rows. The doors to a hallway opened where several instructors exited slowly. The anticipation was like how you feel when watching a horror movie when the psycho murderer is stalking their prey just before they killed them. The one in charge took his position in front of the group. He began to go through his process as he read instructions from a sheet of paper. The instructor commanded all our attention with his booming voice as he lit up his first victim who had dropped his gear on the ground when he got into the formation. He made several clever remarks about the trainee's mother not loving him enough to teach him to follow proper instructions followed by a few other shrewd comments about his intellect. Then we proceeded to play a little game that was part of what every person who entered the Air Force got to experience where we picked our bags up and put them down for an extended period. This wasn't a big deal for me as I only had one bag. Some people were picking up two or three heavy bags then holding them at odd heights or angles all while two or three instructors constantly screamed in their faces.

This game seemed to last for an hour but may have been shorter. Soon the instructor in charge completed his role call seemingly satisfied that this part of our welcome was complete. The two groups were told to follow our instructors up to the stairwell. I can still remember the smell of the stairwell as we climbed our way to the top. The stairwell smelled of dirt and bleach. This was more than likely due to the fact the building was constructed in the 1950s, and it had an aged smell to it. The instructor screamed at someone in the front for not complying with his instructions for everyone to say aloud "walk don't run, hand on the handrail" repeatedly as we entered the area. We would be required to repeat this mind exercise for the next week each time we enter the stairwells or face a frightful dressing down from any instructor that was nearby. The intent was to instill safety into us from the beginning as I am sure a scared trainee more than likely took a tumble at some point prompting a smart-aleck instructor to create this clever fix.

When we reached the top of the stairs the line stopped for a short period as the Airmen inside the door verified the instructors' access the dormitory. This security position we would later learn was called "Dorm Guard". Many of our trainees would be recycled in training due to improper security procedures at this position. The next few minutes were a blur as we snaked our line around the dormitory near our wall lockers. A few sleep-deprived trainees made a fatal mistake of not walking near the lockers. They were greeted by an angry instructor who moved them by the force of their voice out of the "center aisle" which we learned was for instructors only.

The Air Force has a specific method of making a group of people lines up by sizing the tallest people to the right and the front of the formation. I ended up in the rear as most of my group, now known as a flight, was taller than I was. This meant I was in the first bay in the back where the only four bunk beds were located on each side. I stopped at the locker that fate chose for me. I stood there with anticipation for whatever came next. The instructors chose a few early targets to challenge their will to be there by gang-yelling at them for their incompetence for things like standing in a corner instead of in front of a locker, putting their bags on the ground again after being schooled on this infraction for an hour, or once again taking a shortcut down the center aisle.

Thus far, I had escaped any attention from instructors, but it didn't give me peace of mind that I would skate through this night without at least one encounter. It was about this time when my opportunity came. The lead instructor for our team the first night, I cannot remember his name from the stress of the situation added to the sleep deprivation, but I will never forget his ability to cast his voice through you when you screwed up. The trainee standing next to me was about to find out screwing up would be met with a fierce counseling from this instructor. Our next instruction was to set our bags down, take a knee in front of the wall locker facing it, and placing our finger on the number where the locked drawer was located. I followed these instructions then waited. I noticed the type of lock that was on the drawer was a brass military issue lock that required a little bit of finesse to operate. I knew this only because my Marine recruiter, now stepfather, had a dozen of them at our home that I had a chance to use. The guy next to me wasn't so lucky as he fumbled for minutes trying to unlock the lock.

    The instructor came out of nowhere knocking me forcefully out of the way. I crashed backwards into my own locker. He ripped this trainee for minutes about his lack of intelligence before turning to me to rip me for not displaying any leadership traits by not assisting my "wingman". Before leaving for basic training, MSgt Rosa had last told us all to refrain from "volunteering" as nothing good ever came to those who did so in the Air Force. These words echoed in my mind throughout the night. Now his advice was the very reason I was being screamed at and battered against the locker. I took my first screaming better than I thought I would. To be honest it was nothing considering the things my mother used to say to us in one of her intoxicated fits or her general negative ways she addressed us even if she was sober. I took the hint and immediately got the guy's lock unlocked. I returned to my spot as quick as possible, with my heart pounding.

The next few hours seemed like a haze as we secured our valuables inside the locked drawer. We then received a briefing about things that I did not understand then, but later would learn when I became an instructor that this was called the "24-hour briefing". It covered basic training rules, personal hygiene, safety, and security within the dormitory. After the briefing, we implemented the "personal hygiene" requirements where we took showers and shaved. In normal life, this is a simple task but in Air Force basic training it was more like a Quentin Tarantino movie scene. The feat of getting 60 individuals through the latrine in under 10 minutes would be impossible in any other setting. However, in Air Force basic training this took less time. The carnage was evident all over the "latrine" as one trainee was corrected when he referred to it as the bathroom.

The instructor took good care to brief verbatim the instructions for what everyone was required to shave and not shave. It seemed common sense to me, but I would learn that not everyone possessed the same level of common sense. I could list at least 100 now humorous things that happened in this time period but my top two are, one trainee shaved all the hair off his face – eyebrows, peach fuzz, everything. A second trainee shaved the tip of his nose off which earned him the attention of several instructors who ridiculed his stupidity as he spewed blood all over the floor.

The memory is hazy and chaotic. The instructor team was all inside the latrine yelling. They had about a half dozen trainees from later stages of training helping them. The instructors were well versed in this ritual from the extensive training and experience they had from pushing flights. The senior trainees were not attuned with the rules of the job. They just took pleasure in harassing the newbies, or "rainbows", as they referred to us.

The senior trainees were obviously not well briefed about their roles. They were very unprofessional. They said very unprofessional things to us, physically assaulted a few slower "rainbows", and made our life hell long after the instructors had left us alone that night.

After the chaos of shower time was finished, we finally got to lay down in our racks, but we were instructed that we should remain at the position of attention while laying. This was not a real requirement we later found out but was just more hazing from our instructor team. Regardless, I never slept deeper for the next hour and a half than I did that night.

As quickly as I fell asleep, the lights came back on. A new, fresh instructor was in the dormitory screaming at us to wake our "lazy, dumb asses up." He was a Senior Airman (SrA) accompanied by a half dozen Airman First Class (A1C) who had just graduated. They were replacements for our senior trainees who had harassed us throughout the night. These Airmen also abused the privilege of being chosen to assist. We spent our time playing petty games for the sake of hazing rather than training.

I was not a leader at this point in my life. I had led baseball teams as the best player, but I was never taught anything about being a leader. I had been chosen to be the captain of teams because I was the best player, but I had no inclination what to do with this privilege. I did recognize a lack of leadership immediately in our lead instructor, Senior Airman SrA Seabrooks.

SrA Seabrooks was a young man when I met him. His appearance was extremely crisp, and he carried himself with arrogant confidence that many Air Force Military Training Instructors (MTI) displayed. He had a distinct command voice and led us around the installation with confidence. His shortfall was that he was a young leader in the Air Force. He lacked the experience required to perform the duties required of an MTI. His shortfalls were not because of capability, it was due to maturity. I would later learn that a seasoned leader can utilize techniques learned through experience, but a new leader will react emotionally to situations that occur.

I later studied a metaphor about leadership that taught a lesson related to this issue. The idea was that leaders carried around two buckets with them. When a situation arose that required their leadership the experience of the leader would determine the best one to use. In the metaphor the buckets each contained either water or gasoline, using each one would produce a different result. This was especially true if the wrong bucket was used. Sometimes the leader would need to use the gasoline to motivate his people to achieve a success that they may not think is possible. Other times the leader is required to use the water to put out fires due to negativity within the organization. If wrongly deployed the gasoline can easily turn a small issue into a blazing inferno or using the water bucket could destroy all ambitions within the individual or unit.

SrA Seabrooks did not understand this metaphor. His primary response to all situations was to dump gasoline on it causing small issues to become out of control. He was also not a leader at this point in his career. SrA were rarely official supervisors in the Air Force as NCOs fulfilled this position both legally and customarily. The maturity of this instructor was evident, and he made our life hell for the next full week.

I survived the first night of Zero Week in Air Force basic training mostly because it was a blur. I rode the wave of anxiety straight to that bunk. I had enlisted with my friend Razzy, but due to our height difference, he had ended up in a different area of the dormitory surrounded by other guys who were not good influences. The first night I didn't see whatever Razzy had endured but I am sure it was equally scary. I had accepted that this was the path I was on because I had no plan B. I had no other choice but to make it. Failure for me would mean returning to the poor, drug-infested mindsets that I surrounded me back home. I knew my life would not last very long in that environment.

Razzy had a very different life than I did. He found our new environment to be too overwhelming. He immediately began to breakdown. He had been a popular guy in high school. He was also very popular with the girls. He was not rich but had all the material possessions he ever needed. Razzy had a fiancée whom he planned to marry soon after he finished all his training. He was used to things coming easy for him. Now he faced one of the first real challenges of his life. His vulnerability must have been visible because for the next few days the instructors paid him close enough attention that the stress was unbearable. He completely broke.

The first days of basic training consist of constant running from appointments to the dining facility and back. In between appointments we had a bunch of classes on common tasks like how to walk, fold clothes, and use a toilet. These tasks were taught from the official Air Force method with cheesy lessons filled with moderately inappropriate stories so that it had an impact to ensure it was remembered. The instructors are required to teach a few hundred official classes that were supposed to be learned over a few weeks but instead were taught in three days. The group would then spend most of the time applying the lessons learned, which meant we were constantly practicing how to walk or fold stuff to the "Air Force Standards".

Ellis Franks "Always Leave An Airman Behind: A Real Story of Surviving The Crab Leadership Culture

The classes all had a hundred references to the Air Force core values integrity first, service before self, and excellence in all you do. It seemed like they were trying to brainwash us with it. I could not understand why folding a sock was related to becoming a good person or having integrity. I rejected it all at first because for my entire life I had been shown the opposite of everything I was now being taught. My initial plan was to lie, cheat, or steal just to graduate. The goal was getting through this uncomfortable time at all costs. The first real challenge was coming fast. I was about to lose my friend I was depending on for support to make it through this insanity.

The problem started because the instructors are required to allow phone calls within 72 hours of arrival to allow the families of trainees the peace of mind that they arrived safely. It was also to give the families the contact information at our new home. This call was not a pleasurable one. It was business with an allotted two minutes maximum. The calls had an unexpected effect on many of the trainees as they became homesick. Most trainees were faced with the reality that they were on lockdown for the next seven weeks.

Razzy was clearly upset about his call. He retreated deeper inside of himself. I tried to cheer him up unsuccessfully. He told me he was fine, but I could see he wasn't. I was concerned about how he was acting. The day's activities all ran together where we received painful haircuts, got military issue clothing, and a bunch of other mundane training activities that became our routine. Then on the third day, we were surprised when we got our first mail call. I didn't receive any mail that day and SrA Seabrooks made a point to tell the guys "If you didn't get any mail from your girlfriend it's because she's back home taking turns with all your boys..."

The statement was just another inappropriate one made by SrA Seabrooks, but it didn't bother me as I had no girlfriend or close family who cared. Razzy had a meltdown that night. His mind must have been racing at the thought of his fiancée being unreachable by phone when he called. Now the statement pushed him past his limit. We were only three days into training, but he had already quit in his mind. The next day we were surprised to not awake to SrA Seabrooks at the door as our official instructor made his entrance.

Things were looking up. I was particularly happy as the day prior SrA Seabrooks had unprofessionally choked me with my locker chain when he felt I had not properly secured it under my shirt. He had made a point of embarrassing me as much as possible by making me stand in the dayroom in front of my flight mates for an extended time choking myself with the chain and repeating, "This chain is a choking hazard…", while pulling the chain hard as SrA Seabrooks monitored me while making rude comments. I was lucky in the big picture as SrA Seabrooks tended to be a little "rough" with other trainees that he thought he had to bully. We had wasted most of the previous day marching us in circles in the San Antonio 100-degree sun while wearing our duffle bags, which contained our entire newly acquired collection of military gear.

SrA Seabrooks took this torture to the next level by making us wear our cold-weather field jackets. We were all drenched a few minutes into this nonsensical activity. He had decided this was punishment for all of us for not making sure our "team" was squared away. He was just abusing us because he was young, unsupervised, and in charge of 60 uncertain new trainees. This "wing-it leadership" style would be a common theme I would encounter for the rest of my time in the Air Force. It was common because supervisors tended to not take their leadership development serious if they did it at all. Even worse the SrA instructors mostly had not even attended any leadership course until they were promoted to Staff Sergeant (SSgt). Lucky for us

SrA Seabrooks was now gone. We could focus on learning the things we needed from a much better instructor.

SrA Jokie introduced himself to us with a thunderous wakeup call this Friday morning. He was an intense, stocky young man but unlike SrA Seabrooks, he was very fair and professional. SrA Jokie had zero tolerance for deviation from his rules. He did not waste our time with the games, also known as "maltraining", that SrA Seabrooks seemed to enjoy very much. SrA Jokie set the example in every aspect of military professionalism from the crispness of his uniform to the mirror-shined combat boots he wore daily. His personal example of leadership would stick with me for the duration of my time in the Air Force.

Our first day with SrA Jokie began with him reteaching the methods that SrA Seabrooks had taught us to ensure it met his stringent standards. He assigned us to our permeant duties inside our dormitory. I was assigned to the "latrine crew". This job consisted of cleaning up the mess that 60 men created when they used the showers, sinks, and toilets. The job was less than glorious. It was disgusting as we had to clean up after every use as the facility had to be in inspection order always or we would pay a big price.

I kicked myself because I had the opportunity to volunteer for a leadership position, but I remembered the words of my recruiter about never volunteering. I had thought about stepping up at first but decided to remain anonymous for the time being. The decision has always bothered me because I had a natural tendency to take the leadership position on the teams that I had played, but I let fear guide me in this case. I had always feigned humility about it, more out of shyness and inexperience. But I always wanted to be the leader. Now I was stuck cleaning toilets for the next seven weeks. I decided to just make the best of it.

The latrine crew was a ragtag group of guys from all over the southern United States. The Air Force sends trainees to San Antonio all day Tuesday each week. The groups, called flights, loaded 60 members at a time. This meant most of us were from the southern US because we all arrived at relatively the same time until our flight filled.

The group that traveled from Atlanta together mostly made it to our flight except for several who were assigned to the Air Force "band flight". These trainees would learn Air Force music in addition to the military training we all did. They would also be performing at our graduation parade in seven weeks. That meant several of us made it from Atlanta to this latrine crew together. We were now a janitorial "band of brothers" and would keep the latrine spotless 24 hours a day.

I vaguely remember the team I was assigned to for these tenuous weeks of training. I have several memories of confrontations in the beginning as we processed through the steps of group dynamics from the "polite phase" to the "why are we here phase" to the "bid for power phase" as I would later learn when I studied Cog's Ladder in my first leadership course the Air Force, before I was promoted to Staff Sergeant. The first few days everyone was uncertain about the routines of our new lives. Also we were cautious due to SrA Seabrooks torturing us constantly no one really stepped out of line. The team dynamics began to form at a quicker pace once we all had our duties set. We now knew our place on the team. This is when most of the trainees let their true personalities show. Many would attempt to relapse into their lazy civilian ways.

The military is a cross-section of society that represents all demographics. The diversity of our flight was slightly limited to the geographic area we all came from, as stated previously about how the Air Force fills training flights. We ended up with a lot of guys who were apt to not put in much effort because they were content to let others bear their workload. I saw this play out many times over at all duty locations, also in a variety of career fields, I was associated with later in my career. The Air Force spent a lot of time training the trainees to meet Air Force standards. Then when they showed up to their first duty station most of the motivation they brought with them was squashed by the personnel stationed there that were content with the status quo. The latrine crew was my first experience with this Air Force norm. It bothered me from the beginning.

   I was not a motivated person when I landed in San Antonio, Texas. I had only put effort into playing baseball but hardly gave it my full attention. I had also barely graduated. I had set myself up to have no opportunity to make anything of myself with that mentality. When I entered the room at the Basic Military Training Processing Center on Lackland I made an internal commitment to give this opportunity my full effort. My alternative was to fall back into the family trend of being a loser drug addict who made just enough to score another hit of whatever they could find. I had no option but to adopt a "burn the ship" approach. I needed to fully engage my duties to make the best of my opportunity.

I was adapting easier than I had expected. I handled the stress of having a crazy Military Training Instructor in my face screaming for any errors I made. My friend Razzy, on the other hand, was going in the opposite direction. By the fourth day of training, his motivation was completely gone. He broke down in tears several times about missing home and his fiancée. He had still not gotten any mail by the time the weekend rolled around when I had gotten my first letters from home. Seeing all his flight mates enjoying letters from home pushed him to the breaking point. He was broken from the torment of SrA Seabrooks and the unknown from home. I tried in vain to get him to commit. I told him he needed to push through because it would get better. He seemed like I had reached him as he agreed to not leave me. Then as soon as I had sat down in the dayroom from speaking with him, I heard a knock at SrA Jokie's door. Razzy was reporting to him to quit.

Knocking on the instructor's door was not off-limits but it was highly discouraged. We were told that all issues should be passed through our flight leadership. The instructor would schedule a meeting with each trainee. Razzy had just broken this protocol. Also he was speaking to Jokie not at the position of attention due to his nerves. All hell broke loose in a second as Jokie jumped from his desk. He got in his face correcting his lack of military bearing. Razzy reacted with more nervous energy. He began to sob loudly that he "missed home" and "couldn't do this…" Jokie took this opportunity to light him up with fury to make an example of him. He began by asking "How old are you!"

Razzy answered "20 years old" and sobbed uncontrollably.

Jokie responded, "You're 20 years old and crying like a baby…" Then went on a tirade that was very intense. It only made Razzy cry louder. Jokie told him that there were only three ways to leave basic training – ambulance, cop car, or graduation – and explained the fastest way to get home was to graduate.

SrA Jokie then scolded him "Do you refuse to train?"

Razzy sobbed "I just want to go home…"

The flight was all in the dayroom, a common area with couches we weren't allowed to ever sit on. There was also a desk for the instructor. The second Razzy knocked and started crying all the Atlanta people looked at me in disbelief. I had failed to convince him to stay.

47

Now he was being removed from our flight under bad conditions. He had refused to train which meant he was now in violation of his enlistment agreement. The instructor team initiated their checklist for this scenario. The recruiters told us that if we did this we would end up in jail. This was going through all our minds as we sat there listening to the yelling from the flight office.

SrA Jokie burst out of his office and slammed through the dayroom door asking, "Who does this clown, cry baby belong to…who is his wingman?" I just sat there frozen thinking that if I answer then I would be screwed too. I did not respond. Jokie had a few trainees pack all Razzy's gear into his duffle bag. When they finished he all but threw it down the stairwell.

Razzy was gone. I had only come to the Air Force because he was joining. Now, I was alone. My mind raced about what this meant for me. I had made a pact with Razzy seconds before his meltdown that if he quit, I would follow him. He'd be throwing my opportunity away with his lack of commitment. I thought that if I placed my wellbeing in his hands, he would decide to stick this out, but his mind was made up regardless of our supposed friendship he had made his choice.

Once he walked out that dormitory it would be several weeks before we would see him again when he had come to our squadron to pick up his dry cleaning. I got a chance to speak to him for a second. He said his new situation was worse than what he had been facing. He explained that life in the administrative hold was almost like being in jail. He would still be at a Lackland well after I had graduated as he awaited his legal fate. He ended up staying in basic training for nearly double the time that he would have been required if he had not quit.

My first night alone without anyone I really knew was filled with the same latrine crew duties as normal. I spent more time perfecting our cleaning routine to ensure we had the place in perfect condition always. I used the duties to not think about the situation I was facing as my confidence was shaken by Razzy's abrupt departure. Finally, I hit my bunk for Taps and the day's letdown faded behind me. My last thought was, "I have nothing to return to back home."

I wish I could say I remember 100% of the details about what basic training was like but the full details have been stored deep within my mind. It was also within the character changes it caused. The things that I do remember are more related to the leadership situations that I observed from the trainees and the instructors. Throughout our training, many trainees never adapted to the "team first" concept. While the dedicated members of the flight engaged in our duties, these flight members would be working on their own inspection items only. The pattern of selfishness that began in basic training I would witness at every base I was assigned up until I finally separated for good in 2009.

The highlight of my basic training experience was the day I finally got to try out for Air Force Special Operations. The bad part was that I had not prepared at all for this rigorous test, but I knew I was meant to do this job. The Special Tactics recruiters briefed us a few days prior to our appointment for our test. I was excited for a break in my routine.

Our test began in the pool. I thought "Damn it" because I was not a good swimmer. When I was a small kid my mother's friends would all rent our rooms at a local Howard Johnson motel. They would drink tons of alcohol and do drugs for a weekend or more. The children that were dragged along were excited to be able to play in the pool, making it was a win for everyone. Then after a few hours of drinking the adults would turn to their favorite game of toss using the small kids to play catch in the water. Yes, I mean they used the kids as the ball to toss back and forth in their drug-fueled stupidity.

I remember them laughing as they threw us from one person to the other without letting us catch our breath. I always felt like I was going to drown. After this played out multiple times I became extremely scared of swimming. I never really liked to go to the pool.

Now here I stood poolside at the infamous "Skylark Pool", where thousands of Combat Controllers and Pararescuemen started their journeys, ready to be evaluated by some of the most highly trained Special Operations team members in the world. My only skill for this test was a desire and heart. I began my swim with a very inefficient stroke. Added to my challenge was that the pool had only 6-8 lanes to facilitate the testing for over 100 swimmers. The swim was a nightmare that reminded me of being tossed back and forth as a young kid.

My pace started out a sprint then ground to just a little more than a doggy paddle. I continued because I had no choice as several trainees attempted to exit the pool before they were finished only to receive a swift kick right back into the water. The cadre evaluating us made everyone swim until the time was maxed out for qualifying. As the horn sounded, I found myself less than five meters from completing the impossible swim.

I failed. When I joined the Air Force my goal was to be a Combat Controller. I had taken the next available departure slot thinking it wouldn't matter the job attached because I would be joining Air Force Special Operations. Now I faced a regretful reality that I had no idea what I would be doing as I entered the active force. Looking back, I know I would have probably been drowned in training had I made that last five meters. I was ill-prepared to meet that challenge as I had not dedicated any time to prepare for the test.

Looking back leads me to a realization that most people think leadership or success is the accumulation of skillsets and practical experience. This is only part of the equation. A successful leader is someone who has trained for their purpose and has faced adversity where their skills are tested under extreme conditions. Any person can make decisions on tasks when everything is perfect. The real test is when you have less than adequate circumstances that cause the dynamics of the situation to deteriorate. A leader is a person who has prepared the most for the situation. It is the one who is emotionally, mentally, physically, spiritually, and technically prepared to meet the challenges they face. At this point in my career, I was not prepared in any of those areas. I had just failed for the second time in a few weeks to achieve the desired result.

I had lost the best friend I had and the job that I desired more than anything. Growing up with a mother who got married nine times teaches lots of bad examples about commitment. My failure in the pool tested me. I felt like my purpose was now gone for joining the Air Force. It took me several days to recuperate from the failure. Two members of my flight successfully completed the entire test and were reassigned to Pararescue for their technical training. They were treated like rock stars by the instructor team for the duration of their training. Meanwhile, I envied their success. I was forced to await my fate to the unknown again as I had no idea what training I would get since my attempt at Special Operations had failed.

I got my answer in the 4th week of training when we received our career counseling. I had been assigned to begin training at Sheppard Air Force Base, Texas to learn to be a Fuels Management Apprentice. I had no idea what that meant as I had not researched the job. It was randomly selected for me. The remaining weeks were spent at the Confidence Course, Firing Range, Final Fitness Evals, and getting fitted for our service dress uniforms. The days crawled by as we rushed from one appointment to another every day.

Our instructor was one of the strictest. We saw very few liberties while in training. We would be doing our duties while other trainees spent time making phone calls and eating candy on the patio. This was an open area with phone booths and vending machines that were previously used as the smoking area before it was banned in training. What I learned from this fact was that leadership is an individual choice. Each person can develop their standards. Their individual choice will reflect in their approach to how they lead. Jokie instilled a strict military bearing, professionalism, and adherence to standards in many of the trainees in our flight. This was contrary to our brother flight who spent endless hours being rewarded for doing nothing more than being average.

I would grow to despise the mediocrity that was prominent in the Air Force at all levels. The higher I climbed up the chain the more evident the dedication to the status quo had become. I would become disenchanted with the leadership norms of the service. For now, I had gained some very important skills that would lead to my success later in my career that I picked up by taking the lessons of my instructors to heart.

I was always a highly capable, unmotivated student throughout my school years. The Air Force changed this bad habit for me by teaching me a foundational set of core values and instilling self-discipline deep within me. All Air Force trainees are overwhelmed with academic courses throughout training. We were required to be studying every second that we were not actively engaged in our duties or training. I had never studied anything before. This was a new habit I was creating. The Air Force required that each trainee be tested on these academics as one of the graded areas for graduation. My motivation was to be free of the prison-like atmosphere of basic training where you are locked inside your dormitory for most of the day. I studied very hard for the first time in my life.

I was blessed in life that I always had an excellent mind. When I read something the information stuck easily. I was inspired to do more than the bare minimum for the first time in my life. I set a goal to score 100% on this test and to have the highest score in the flight. I ended up with a score of over 90%. I had earned the fifth-highest score in the end because my testing skills were not yet to the level required to be the top.

I was laying the foundation for success. I was unaware of these changes inside me at the time. The Air Force promotions system was heavily weighed by testing in two areas – career field and general military supervisory knowledge. I was developing a skill set that would power me ahead of my peers in the future. I learned that studying leadership concepts is a foundational skill that gives leadership tools to deal with situations as they occur. The time between recognizing leadership issues and creating a solution is directly related to the amount of time the leader has dedicated to the study of the craft. Leaders rely on decision making to ensure the organization maintains a positive path. Studying leadership strategies reduces the amount of time it takes for a leader to make decisions. This is because a leader who has taken time to engage in professional development has studied situations and solutions ensuring when similar opportunities occur the leader has the knowledge to compare the situation. Contrarily, a leader who has not trained will not have a mental database to compare their situation. They will have to react solely on innate factors to provide a solution.

I had started down a path I did not realize at the time. I was creating my personal leadership database by creating foundational habits that I have refined for use today. Seven weeks earlier I had arrived at Lackland Air Force Base unsure if I would make it through this unknown task. Now it was time for me to graduate and become an Airman. Most importantly, I was starting a path dedicated to leadership development.

Time away from home was good for my relationship with my family. I had nothing much to do at night, and I wrote letters to everyone I knew in the hopes of getting letters in return. My philosophy was the more people I wrote the more letters I would receive. I enjoyed a steady stream of the daily mail. Sadly, the day after Razzy's meltdown in the first week of training he received numerous letters. I am not sure if these had come a day earlier would have saved him, but I found it very ironic.

My mother even wrote me letters of support which were very unlike her. We reconciled. She decided to bring the family out to Texas to see me graduate in January. I am sure it was more for the trip than to see me, but it was nice to know at the end of graduation I would not be the one Airman who was hanging out alone.

My family arrived just before our Retreat Ceremony on January 11th, 1996. Our flight had spent endless hours perfecting drill movements every day of training for the graduation week activities. This was the first time to show off was the Retreat Ceremony. The retreat is the customary call for the end of the day and retirement of the colors, US flag. The ceremony is performed by a mandatory formation led by a Non-Commissioned Officer. The playing of the National Anthem and the customary salute of the nation's flag was performed flawlessly by several thousand trainees in front of their families who were seeing them for the first time in about eight weeks.

Even today nearly 25 years later the thought of it gives me chills because it is an especially important custom the military upholds. There is nothing more inspiring than seeing several thousand troops snapping to attention and snapping a salute in unison on command as the flag is slowly lowered to the sound of our nation's anthem playing by a bugler. The sight must be unique for civilians who have never served as they witness the ultimate display of teamwork in action.

Once the flag was folded the commander of the troops gave the order to dismiss the troops. This is when each instructor takes a second to brief their flights on their orders before releasing them for the first time back to their families. These instructors had poured hundreds of hours into training the several thousand trainees. This was the first time our families would see the new us. Finally, after getting our orders for the day we were released with a thunderous mass of commands as each flight was called to attention then given the command to "Fall Out".

Seeing my family for the first time was a little weird. I had left for training assuming I wouldn't be returning home. I was sure no one would be coming to visit me no matter how cool of a location I was stationed. After we were released for liberties, I saw my family making their way towards me. It was good to see familiar faces weaving through the crowd. We spent a few hours exploring the base as I had not been on liberty for the entire time I was in training. We had the good fortune to get only three patio breaks to makes calls and eat sugar. The rest of the time we were in the dormitory or in training. I enjoyed being out and carried myself with pride as I had survived basic training. I would officially be an Airman in less than 24 hours. It was hard to sleep after I returned to the dormitory just before curfew.

January 13th, 1996 – My graduation day from basic military training was a clear, moderately cold day in San Antonio, Texas. We marched from our dormitory to the parade grounds early in the morning before waiting as all the flights showed up for Parade. The scene is something out of a historical military movie where troops form-up the lines on the battlefield. The military band forms the middle of the formation. Standing in a formation for an extended period is challenging as every muscle in your body cramps and falls asleep. We arrived early ensuring our torture was prolonged.

Finally, the ceremony began with the signal from the Commander of Troops. This prompted a massive chain reaction of commands. Every formation executed drill movements that we rehearsed for 100s of hours with perfection.

The first command was from the Adjutant, "SOUND ADJUNTANTS CALL!"

The US Air Force band thundered to life. On the first beat of the music the formations and all other key members move into formation. The thrill of finally executing this last evolution of our training was very emotional. I remember the pride I felt inside throughout the Parade. The most emotional was when we marched down the "Bomb Run". We executed a salute, called "eyes right", where every member of the formation except the fourth element snapped their heads 45 degrees to the right on command while the commanding instructor executed a crisp salute in unison with the guidon bearer snapping our unit colors in salute to the ranking Commander in the reviewing stand. The procession would include several thousand new Airmen in flights of 60 each executing the drill with precision.

The final task we had was to take our final oath to the Constitution. We were officially Airmen. We were released to find our families at the end for liberties beginning with a tour of our dormitory. The day was a memory every Airman will never forget for their entire life. I can remember it like it just happened. I was now an Airmen. My path had changed from the hopelessness I had faced a few months earlier when I was homeless trying to figure out what to do.

I had arrived at basic training a mess. I was one bad decision away from ending up in jail. In fact, several people I associated with ended up being put in prison for crimes to include murder, drugs, and armed robbery shortly after I left the area. I arrived there with the worst role models having taught me to be inconsistent, devious, and manipulative to achieve short-lived desires.

The Air Force spent seven weeks filling my mind with a foundational system based on the core values integrity, service, and excellence. I received a "Little Blue Book" of Air Force Core Values that detailed the service's philosophy of what was expected from each Airman. I also received another pamphlet Air Force Instruction 36-2618 The Enlisted Force Structure that detailed the requirements for every enlisted military rank. I studied those books daily and adopted the principles as my own for the duration of my career.

The "Little Blue Book" broke down each core value into several traits the Air Force expected all Airmen to embrace. Integrity first consisted of the following traits;

- **Courage**. A person of integrity possesses moral courage and does what is right even if the personal cost is high.

- **Honesty**. Honesty is the hallmark of the military profession because, in the military, our word must be our bond. We don't pencil-whip training reports, we don't cover up tech data violations, we don't falsify documents, and we don't write misleading operational readiness messages. The bottom line is we don't lie, and we can't justify any deviation.

- **Responsibility**. No person of integrity is irresponsible; a person of true integrity acknowledges his or her duties and acts accordingly.

- **Accountability**. No person of integrity tries to shift the blame to others or take credit for the work of others; "the buck stops here" says it best.

- **Justice**. A person of integrity practices justice. Those who do similar things must get similar rewards or similar punishments.

- **Openness**. Professionals of integrity encourage a free flow of information within the organization. They seek feedback from all directions to ensure they are fulfilling key responsibilities, and they are never afraid to allow anyone at any time to examine how they do business.

- **Self-respect**. To have integrity also is to respect oneself as a professional and a human being. A person of integrity does not behave in ways that would bring discredit upon himself or the organization to which he belongs.

- **Humility**. A person of integrity grasps and is sobered by the awesome task of defending the Constitution of the United States of America

The Air Force taught that integrity should be the foundation of all decision-making for every Airman. If all Airmen made every decision based on the integrity they personally displayed and in relation to the situational leadership requirements, then the service would be guided by a moral compass that would ensure our nation's objectives were always met with honor.

Integrity was also the basis for personal discipline. If all Airmen made decisions based on this core value, then they would always adhere to the regulations the service expected. They would always set a positive example for others. The core value, and it's specific traits, were all chosen to ensure Airmen made decisions at a higher level than their civilian counterparts. This was because our jobs directly led to the execution of war where poor morals could cause the deaths of thousands of innocent people, our teammates, or ourselves.

All the traits were important to ensure the Airmen were successful. I found myself applying accountability, courage, humility, and responsibility as my most important traits for success. Accountability was the cornerstone of ensuring mission success because no team could be successful if the common practice was to pass blame and hoard praise. This practice leads teams to break down as trust will become nonexistent over time. I would serve in many units that this was common practice at the expense of all the Airmen assigned.

I found that having courage was one of the toughest traits to consistently uphold because following it meant that you would face the wrath of higher-ranking individuals who controlled your future by way of performance reports, medals, and other administrative systems of control. Courage required individuals to stand up for the right thing regardless of the personal loss it may create. Throughout my career, I saw this as the least common trait amongst Senior Non-Commissioned Officers (SNCOs) because if they were faced with a personal loss in their career nearly all I served with would choose the easiest path at the expense of others.

Courage was not about facing down the enemies we deployed to engage, it was about facing your own personal enemies, bad habits, or character flaws. I served with a lot of brave Airmen who were not afraid to run towards gunfire but inevitably lacked true courage because they feared not being promoted or not being liked. I believed that this lack of courage was a contributor to the massive suicide epidemic our veterans face today because the veterans know there is no one in their corner based on the experiences of their service.

Humility was a trait that I personally struggled with in my career. I was awed by the responsibilities I faced but I found myself wavering in my personal humility as I earned awards or recognition for the things I did above and beyond the average Airman. I was always seeking something bigger. I always felt a pull for a challenge, leading me to lose sight of my personal humility at times. I was not an arrogant person, but the Air Force had saved my life from a nearly guaranteed life of poverty and criminal activities through my associations. I took everything I did very seriously. Some people I was stationed with thought I was an arrogant jerk, but this was because they never took the time to understand why I was so proud of the things I achieved.

Growing up in a house with the constant turmoil a drug addict caused gave me little hope that I would ever do anything of significance in my life. Every person that associated with us growing up was a bad role model who viewed all the kids in our circle as hindrances in their quests to get high. No one ever asked me about school and my sister signed our report cards from 5th grade until I graduated. No one ever asked about report cards for the next seven years of school. I rarely attended school because there was no incentive to go.

The only thing I ever did well growing up was play baseball. Playing the game was a break away from the reality of my life. Every time I stepped onto the baseball field, I was a different person. People looked for me to do something amazing. Then when the game was over, I went back to being the poor kid who lives in the trailer park with the slutty, drug-addicted mother.

I did not really have any friends growing up. The other kids who lived around us were a little older. They would only come around when they wanted to steal something I had, like baseballs or baseball cards. The rest of the time they would make up reasons not to hang out with me or worse the older kids would gang up on me in a fight. This was mostly because at a young age I had told on one of the popular kids for breaking into the other kids' houses. I had always had a sense of doing the right thing. I also always ended up paying a personal price for doing it.

I grew up in a poor area. I was one of the poorest kids. The other kids always had designer clothes and shoes growing up. I was the kid who wore other people's clothes. I would see the kids who lived in government housing, received welfare checks and food stamps, and then they would come to school the next day with new $200 Air Jordan shoes., $100 shirts, and $200 pants. I could never understand how these kids were poor enough to get tons of government money to afford these luxury items when my mother was always denied for government assistance. The system was rigged and only people who knew the people at the government office would be approved in our county. Unfortunately, we were not connected. I was forced to continue wearing the hand-me-downs I received. I learned that the only way to survive was to fight for yourself and not depend on others to assist.

    I did not really care about wearing labels, I just wanted to fit in with the other kids. Even at that age, I was different than my peers. I had shown a higher level of intelligence than the kids in my grade. The school tested me to move me up three grades. I knew that meant that I would be a lot younger than the other kids in the new grade. I decided to intentionally fail this test. I knew that being the youngest would get me beat up by the older, bigger thugs that attended our school. I also knew that if they thought I was smart, I would get messed with even more because most of the kids in the school could barely read, even up to the 8th grade they would struggle with their words. Then they would take out their embarrassment on the "smart kids" by beating them up at every chance.

    This started in the 5th grade when we would have a bathroom or playground breaks. There was a group of section 8 kids who had older siblings who were criminals. The younger siblings were trying to follow these role models by acting like them at school. These kids would gang up on the smart kids every time the teachers were not in sight. I overcame this problem one day by walking into the bathroom where I knew the gang was waiting and walked up to their biggest guy then punched him as hard as I could in his eye. I kept hitting him until he begged me to stop. The other kids took notice of their biggest weapon begging for me to leave him alone. The tables had turned on these racist bullies. They would mostly leave me alone, but other kids were always getting jumped, sometimes even with weapons. Many kids were hurt severely by these thugs.

No one in our family ever knew about this happening every day. Realistically they would not have cared. I associated school with violence. I dreaded going daily and in high school, I mostly stopped. I would skip the maximum amount of days each year and never turned in assignments. I would ace the tests because I had a good memory. It helped that I was an excellent test taker. I am sure that the only reason I graduated was that the teachers just did not want to deal with any students more than a single time. There were no teachers who took an interest in any of the students. They just processed us each year. This meant I squandered my intelligence growing up because no adult pushed me. I had no role models who could show me an example of how I should be performing. Everyone we associated with was a loser, a dropout, a failure. I was doing my best to follow their lead. Years later I would turn this all around and use my talents to test out of over two years of college work without even studying. For now, I was just a lost cause in the eyes of my teachers.

The sad fact is that most people outside of school did not even know my sister and I existed. My mother had an entirely separate life from us with her friends and carousel of boyfriends or husbands coming and going. She had a dead-end job that she went to every day, then after work, she did not come home to us, she would go to her friends' houses to party. She would bring us leftovers, food other people had eaten, for our dinner.

When you are hungry, things like that do not mean much. We would fight over the food then eat it in minutes of her arrival. We were just happy to have something to eat. A lot of times the food was leftovers from nice restaurants her friends had paid for her to eat. She at least remembered us to bring everyone's scraps.

Essentially, my sister and I were like dogs at the house. You pet the dogs when you come around, but they do not go with you when you leave to go places. Dogs are better seen and not heard. Dogs are sometimes hated by people and get treated poorly, and sometimes people hate dogs so much that they make the owner make them disappear in order to have a relationship. This meant we were left alone at our trailer park unsupervised most of the time.

Growing up in that reality you do not realize how bad things were because you were living it. A dog does not think it is a dog many times. This was how it was growing up. I was smarter than most of the low-life people that my mother surrounded us with. I would play whatever role they thought I represented as to not anger or bother them. I learned to survive by being invisible. I learned that ambition was punished. Therefore I never seized it.

The people I served with never knew how the Air Force saved me. They assumed I was some pompous jerk who was used to getting everything he wanted. They always believed this because I presented myself with extreme confidence and pride. I wanted to show them I was not a dog. I wanted to better than every one of them because we all had the same opportunity to excel but I took the chances when they hesitated to gain more opportunities to be recognized.

I rebuilt my entire self when I joined the Air Force. The service was a perfect place for someone like me because the entire path of success is completely spelled out for me to follow. I just needed to be informed of the expected efforts required. Then I could take actions to fulfill the requirements. The confidence that people feared from me was not out of arrogance but the individuals around me perceived it that way most times. Their fear was not about me, it was the fact that they saw the things I was doing and knew they were not personally doing their best. Some would in turn attempt to compete with me for awards or performance milestones that we earned in our jobs, but every time I controlled my destiny, I dominated the competition. The more I earned recognition I would be assigned special duties that other Airmen could not qualify to do.

The responsibility I was given during my career was humbling. I was initially responsible for $100,000s in personal equipment to do my job. I was solely trusted to later in my career with managing hundreds of personnel and million in assets. This was a source of pride that I took very seriously. I would always do my best to ensure I gave myself fully to the responsibilities I was given.

I took careful self-evaluations on each of these traits from the start of my career to the end. I found that these traits require constant work to ensure that they were adapted to the level of responsibility. The core value of Service Before Self meant more than just being willing to give your life for your fellow Airmen and nation, it meant subjugating your personal agendas for the benefit of the Air Force mission. The traits the Air Force highlighted to accomplish this included;

- **Rule following**. To serve is to do one's duty, and our duties are most expressed through rules. While it may be the case that professionals are expected to exercise judgment in the performance of their duties, good professionals understand that rules have a reason for being, and the default position must be to follow those rules unless there is a clear, operational reason for refusing to do so.

- **Respect for others**. Service before self tells us also that a good leader places the troops ahead of his/her personal comfort. We must always act in the certain knowledge that all persons possess a fundamental worth as human beings.

- **Discipline and self-control**. Professionals cannot indulge themselves in self-pity, discouragement, anger, frustration, or defeatism. They have a fundamental moral obligation to the persons they lead to striking a tone of confidence and forward-looking optimism. More specifically, they are expected to exercise control in the following areas:

- **Anger**. Military professionals and especially commanders at all echelons are expected to refrain from displays of anger that would bring discredit upon themselves and/or the Air Force.

    o **Appetites**. Those who allow their appetites to drive them to make sexual overtures to subordinates are unfit for military service. Likewise, the excessive consumption of alcohol casts doubts on an individual's fitness, and when such persons are found to be drunk and disorderly, all doubts are removed.

    o **Religious toleration**. Military professionals must remember that religious choice is a matter of individual conscience. Professionals, and especially commanders, must not take it upon themselves to change or coercively influence the religious views of subordinates.

- **Faith in the system**. To lose faith in the system is to adopt the view that you know better than those above you in the chain of command what should or should not be done. In other words, to lose faith in the system is to place self before service. Leaders can be very influential in this regard: if a leader resists the temptation to doubt `the system', then subordinates may follow suit.

I found this core value to be the most violated of the three, due to leadership not personally adhering to its principles. Senior leaders tended to treat lower-ranking Airmen with contempt because of their superior paygrades. They also consistently displayed improper examples for their people. Rule following was expected to be a "do as I say" concept where each individual senior member made up their own rules as they went. This created a disparity in all aspects of Air Force life because senior leaders refused to follow the dictated Air Force policies. They mostly created their own personal versions of them based on subjectivity and favoritism.

The Air Force culture itself also violated the core value of service because of its customs surrounding drinking alcohol. When I first entered the service every Friday evening our squadron hosted barbeques where the leadership would buy a few kegs of beer and food then drink into the early morning hours. They would start the day off by doing mass briefings in the morning where they would threaten all the assigned Airmen about drinking and driving or other alcohol-related incidents that may have occurred that week. Then late the very same night those same senior leaders would cause a scene when we attempted to not allow them to drive home drunk, having them personally violate several of the traits of service before self and losing the respect of their people.

These same leaders believed that the drinking culture was "mentorship". They instilled in their people the same idea where they tossed out the Air Force's expectation of mentoring and replaced it with a culture the revolved around alcohol abuse. They essentially created a culture that saw the rules as something only the lower-ranking people were required to follow. This created a cycle of substandard leadership across the Air Force. This type of leadership presented a poor personal example of the core value service before self. Though they achieved high ranks they did not truly embrace the core value of service before self or excellence in all they did.

The Air Force defined "Excellence in all we do" as the core values that direct Air Force personnel to develop a sustained passion for continuous improvement and innovation that will propel the Air Force into a long-term, upward spiral of accomplishment and performance.

General Fogleman, former Chief of Staff of the Air Force stated, "True quality is embodied in the actions of Air Force people who take decisive steps to improve processes and products; who capitalize on quality as a leverage tool to enhance products, achieve savings, and improve customer service; and who exemplify our core values of integrity first, service before self, and excellence in all we do."

Most people attempted to skip the other core values to jump straight to the core value of excellence. This is a common issue in society today where poorly equipped people become rich and famous but lack proper core values to guide them. I found the only path to excellence was to ensure the other two core values were consistently evaluated and adjusted to meet my objectives. Excellence meant more than awards or promotions, it was an accumulation of excelling in all aspects of life. It was the fruit of the labors each person had endured to achieve something bigger than themselves.

Excellence was more than just recognition and embodied the several important traits that included;

- **Product/service excellence**. We must focus on providing services and generating products that fully

77

respond to customer wants and anticipate customer needs, and we must do so within the boundaries established by the taxpaying public.

- **Personal excellence**. Military professionals must seek out and complete professional military education, stay in physical and mental shape, and continue to refresh their general educational backgrounds.

- **Community excellence**. Community excellence is achieved when the members of an organization can work together to successfully reach a common goal in an atmosphere free of the fear that preserves individual self-worth. Some of the factors influencing interpersonal excellence are:

    o **Mutual respect**. Genuine respect involves viewing another person as an individual of fundamental worth. Obviously, this means that a person is never judged based on his/her possession of an attribute that places him or her in some racial, ethnic, economic, or gender-based category.

    o **Benefit of the doubt**. Working hand in glove with mutual respect is that attitude which says that all coworkers are 'innocent until proven guilty'. Before rushing to judgment about a person or his/her behavior, it is important to have the whole story.

- **Resources excellence**. Excellence in all we do also demands that we aggressively implement policies to ensure the best possible cradle-to-grave management of resources.

- **Material resources excellence**. Military professionals have an obligation to ensure that all the equipment and property they ask for is mission essential. This means that residual funds at the end of the year should not be used to purchase 'nice to have' add-ons.

- **Human resources excellence**. Human resources excellence means that we recruit, train, promote, and retain those who can do the best job for us.

- **Operations excellence**. There are two kinds of operations excellence internal and external.

- **Excellence of internal operations**. This form of excellence pertains to the way we do business internal to the Air Force from the unit level to Headquarters Air

79

Force. It involves respect on the unit level and a total commitment to maximizing the Air Force team effort.

- **Excellence of external operations**. This form of excellence pertains to the way in which we treat the world around us as we conduct our operations. In peacetime, for example, we must be sensitive to the rules governing environmental pollution, and in wartime we are required to obey the laws of war.

I used the traits of excellence to measure my performance at every level. I earned an average of three significant awards per year over my entire career by following this principle. The Air Force essentially had mapped out the basic expectations for what it viewed as a success. The path was not complicated. It required the individual to embrace these values within themselves. They would then execute all responsibilities in accordance with these values and traits for all assigned missions. The sad realization for me was that most of the service could name the three values because they were forced to learn them, but few truly embraced the Air Force's vision for what the values meant more than just words.

I had incorporated these core values fully. I felt a change within myself. Over the course of my first seven weeks in the military, I studied those words and traits as often as I could. I adapted my lazy mindset using my new core values. This allowed me to easily complete every gradable area of basic training. I had strived for achieving "Honor Graduate" when we were briefed about it in the early weeks of training but would come up a little short due to a failed inspection in my third week of training.

The lesson I learned was that if you strive to meet the core values fully and commit yourself to live by them then you may not achieve your primary goal to its full potential, but you will find yourself achieving higher levels than your peers. I was graduating without any real difficulties, but the other trainees found themselves struggling at every turn because they chose to cut corners along the way, violating the principles of the core values. I had set a solid foundation for myself to move forward in my career. I was ready to move on to my next challenge.

The last two days in basic training were spent on town pass where we explored the San Antonio area just like millions of other newly graduated Airmen have done since the Air Force was created. I carried myself in a different way than what my family remembered as I marched instead of walking. I stood at ease instead of dumpily standing about. I addressed everyone with the disciplined courtesy that SrA Jokie had instilled in us from the minute he busts through the door early in training. I was not the same. I had my career ahead of me. This was an exciting feeling.

The day came when it was time to leave basic training behind. It was partly sad because we had come to call the cramped dormitory home. We had become a team. We had overcome our challenges together. We had watched team members leave and we had welcomed new teammates over the weeks. The experience was life-changing for me. I was anxious to learn more about the new career the Air Force had chosen for me. So early in the morning on January 15th, 1996 I boarded a bus headed north from San Antonio towards Wichita Falls, Texas where I would spend the next few months training as a Fuels Management Apprentice.

Stepping Out From The Crowd

My journey across Texas was my first exposure to anywhere outside of the deep southern US. The openness of the terrain allowed you to see the landscape for miles. The route we traveled lacked any trees as I was accustomed to seeing in Georgia. I watched the straggly trees as they passed by the windows of the bus noticing they all appeared rough and lacked color. The scenery changed minimally as we headed north from San Antonio towards Dallas and on to Wichita Falls. The ride gave me time to reflect on the experience I had just completed.

While you are in basic training the minutes fly by as the schedule kept us moving from one period of waiting to another, followed by periods of idle preparation for some inspection. Now as I rode on the bus, I had time to think about what all had happened. I started to formulate the leader I would attempt to become. I had been exposed to three different leadership types from our instructor team. I had seen examples of good and inadequate leadership qualities. Our team had consisted of SrA Seabrooks, Jokie, and Silva who tagged teamed our schedule with after the first week of training.

SrA Seabrooks had displayed an immature inability to lead the trainees he was charged with teaching. His methods were to intimidate and embarrass the trainees instead of motivating us with his example.

83

He also had shown a temper that bordered on dangerous as he frequently physically accosted some of the trainees in our flight. This included the chain choking instance that I received. I was a novice at leadership but knew this was not the example that was supposed to be followed. SrA Seabrooks showed he lacked several of the core values to include integrity and service, specifically violating the traits of accountability, discipline, respect for others, responsibility, rule-following, and self-respect. He would later be charged with maltraining and be removed from his position as an instructor.

SrA Silva had started with our flight before Jokie returned to full-time duty in Zero Week of our training. He was a tall, fit man that carried himself with a strong arrogance that he openly acknowledged at any chance. He was very tough in his expectations but unlike SrA Seabrooks he never had to raise his voice at us to get a reaction. His method was to whisper in your ear to make his message more personal. This left many trainees trembling and hanging on to his every word. Silva never showed any unprofessional behavior towards any trainee. He garnered our attention by his presence. I admired his ability to calmly strike the fear into our flight. I would attempt to emulate the confidence he portrayed always. I would use him as my model later in my career when I was meeting military boards for awards.

Silva was not perfect in all areas. He would later make national news when he was court-martialed nearly twenty years later when the Air Force led an inquisition on all former basic training instructors due to sexual misconduct in Air Force basic training. He was charged after he had obtained the rank of MSgt and his entire career was destroyed. His case was national news and the charges against him were finally dropped by the Air Force in 2017. The damage was already done because he had endured national humiliation, lost his career, and had been locked in a prison cell for years. If he was guilty of the charges by the three basic trainees it was due to his deviation from the core value of service before self, specifically his inability to control his sexual appetites. I personally never saw him act in an unprofessional way. After I became an instructor, I heard only positive things about him from all the instructors that knew him. His reputation with his peers was one of the best I heard out of anyone in the MTI corps. He had made a solid impression on the toughest critics in the Air Force. This fact was not lost on me.

SrA Jokie was the main influence I took with me from basic training as he spent most of the time with our flight. He never hesitated to get loud with trainees who got out of line, but he never crossed the line of professionalism by making personal attacks. He never used foul language. He did call us "clowns" and this pet name stuck with me for the rest of my life as a nicer way to tell someone they were being stupid. He epitomized all the core values which was a major influence on me. He would go on to retire after a long, successful career as an instructor, recruiter, and a positive role model for thousands of Airmen.

I did not know what kind of Airman I was destined to become but I knew I had no option but to make this life work because I had nothing to return to at home. I made a choice to take any opportunity to take leadership positions when they were available. I never forgot about the first day of training when the instructor had asked people to step up for leadership positions, but I shied away from it. I held my tongue despite my inner pull to be a leader. I made a pact with myself to not make that mistake again on that drive to Sheppard Air Force Base.

Finally, after many hours of driving, and a short stop at my first Piccadilly restaurant for lunch, we arrived at the gates of Sheppard Air Force Base in Wichita Falls, Texas. The area was mostly desolate as we arrived, just flat land with standard military brown painted buildings spread over the landscape. The bus pulled up to the processing center just as we had done at Lackland when we first arrived at basic training. This time there was no anxiety of the unknown. We had already faced the toughest challenge in basic training. Now we were just tired from the long bus ride. The night's events seemed like a blur. Before long we were assigned our dormitories then turned over to our Military Training Leader (MTL).

The training leaders were commonly called "blue ropes" because of the blue shoulder ropes they wore on their uniforms. The MTLs were responsible for the morale and welfare of the Airmen that were attending technical training. Overall, they lacked the intensity of the basic training instructors mostly they just inspected our living quarters randomly and doled out punishment for anyone caught breaking the rules. None of these supervisors made any kind of an impression on me. They never engaged in any type of mentorship with us to make an impression. I vaguely remember they existed. My training leader this night showed me to my quarters and then took off to let me settle into my room.

The dormitories in technical training were a big improvement over the open bays from Lackland. Now I had one roommate who was graduating in a few days. He was always gone doing out-processing for his departure. The room was more like an older hotel with two sets of beds, wall lockers, and desks with little more than a few feet of personal space. It felt like a mansion after living with 60 other guys lurking. The showers were still community ones located in a central part of the floor. It was shared by four hallways making morning details interesting as Airmen made messes then left it for the assigned hallway crew to clean.

The facilities were not as old as the ones at Lackland, which were all from the early 1950s, but they were still all dated. I did not venture out too much from my dormitory during my time at Sheppard. I did frequent the Base Exchange regularly. It gave me the chance to see the area as I walked back and forth. There was nothing exciting about this assignment. I was happy to bide my time until I graduated from technical training then moved on to my first duty station.

The daily routine was very different than it was at Lackland but the morning formations and marching to appointments were still required for most Airmen assigned. I was assigned to training that was on the flightline a long way from our dorms. I was lucky we had a bus pick us up daily to transport us to our training facility. This was a relief as the trip was long and the temperatures in the Texas panhandle were frigid for the duration of my stay.

The Fuels Management Apprentice Course training facility was one of the newer buildings on the base when I attended training. This building was home to training for most of my new career field's training for all levels. We were exposed to many higher-ranking members of that were active-duty members across the Air Force. I first noticed a trend with the people I saw who worked in the career field which included many sloppily dressed, overweight non-commissioned officers (NCOs) who spent many hours smoking and talking outside the building.

Our entire class was in awe of the NCOs at first, snapping to attention in the hallways each time one of them walked out of a room. This made most of them uncomfortable. They all told us we could relax a little, but we maintained our fresh military bearing as we were new to the military. I would not understand just how lackadaisical the standards were in the active-duty force for a few months when I finally arrived at my first duty station, but these first few NCOs set a very poor example in my eyes.

Our training days were long. we made it through the lectures by drinking large quantities of coffee at each hourly break. My days started at 0500 when we were required to fall out for morning formation. Afterwards, we would do our physical training. Next, I would grab a quick breakfast, shower, and change in time to catch our bus to the school. The classes were held in a building that had no windows as I supposed they thought that this would keep our attention more efficiently. I had not chosen my career field, making the lessons completely new to me. At first, the names of fuel system components, processes, pressures, and other information seemed like a foreign language.

    Our instructors were not military members but were rather retirees from our career field who now were civilian instructors at the Fuels Schoolhouse. Their teaching methods were not exciting. The instructors never gained much attention from the class. We were always rewarded with a heads up for "testable materials" when the instructor stomped his foot several times when he covered a point he knew was on the test. This gave the vigilant student a head start on the upcoming "Block Tests" we were required to take weekly. These tests were required to be passed to progress in training. Still many of my classmates spent all their time engaging in drinking at the Airman's Activities Centers in the evening and some had major difficulties with the course.

    Surprisingly, I had adapted my study habits from Lackland making the course easier. I passed each test we took but I sacrificed all the social activities to ensure I graduated on time. This made for my experiences at

Sheppard to be severely limited to dormitory acquaintances and schoolmates. I only ventured off the base one time to have dinner and go to a dance club. I only went after a couple of my classmates begged me for days to join them. The evening out was fun. But I worried about getting in trouble for being late for curfew which could cause me to be recycled in training. I did not want to do anything that would delay my departure. We made it back to the dormitory just as curfew time hit. The "Charge of Quarters" gave us a hard time but let us pass to our rooms. I was relieved and tired. So I went straight to bed. That would be my only trip outside of the base for the eight weeks I was assigned there. I would engage in more productive activities than partying like my peers. This is when I got recruited to be a student leader.

      I took my first leadership opportunity when the Military Training Leaders (MTLs) were recruiting student leaders to oversee leading the formations, physical training, and marching students to classes. I immediately jumped at the chance to take the leadership role. The MTLs sold me on the idea that the course was valid towards earning your college degree. I attended a week's training course for student leadership after I finished my normal classes. We were taught the expectations of the position and other leadership classes to help us transition to a leadership position. I graduated with ease. I was awarded a "green rope" that I could wear on my uniforms. It signified that I was a flight student leader. This meant I oversaw the Fuels Apprentice Course students where I was responsible for maintaining the discipline of the group. Also, I was required to organize my hallway details as well as be a liaison between the assigned Airmen and the MTLs. The best part about this training was that it was a certified course that I received one semester hour of college credit. This motivated me to attend more training to get more credits.

    The challenge of being a student leader was keeping the discipline of the groups I was assigned from deteriorating as many Airmen let their military bearing slip away after leaving basic training. Airmen were constantly getting caught breaking rules and even the law. This resulted in the student leaders being held accountable for their leadership failures. I ended up spending most weekends supervising punished Airmen for the training leaders. I made mental notes about the deviant behaviors that were causing these troubled Airmen to start losing their way. I saw that it was easy for anyone to slip back into old civilian habits if they let their guard down. This made me begin to formulate my own philosophies for what proper military bearing meant.

The major issue I found was that most of the troubled Airmen could not even name the three core values, much less fully understand the lessons of them. In fact, most of them openly mocked the rules. Many had almost completely reverted to their civilian bad habits. The training each basic trainee receives is supposed to be uniformly taught, but I found some new Airmen never were held accountable as their MTIs had just processed their flights through training with little efforts, but lots of rewards along the way. Now they were wasting my time since a student leader was required to monitor all troubled Airmen when they performed their punishment details.

I spent six weeks awaiting my final orders for my first base. I was disappointed daily when my classmates received orders to some very nice locations including overseas assignments, but I received nothing. I had only put overseas bases on my "dream sheet" but was warned the Air Force would send me whenever they needed me. Finally, a few days before graduation I was summoned to the CQ's office for an unknown reason.

I proceeded to the office with haste and reported in as required. The Technical Sergeant on duty took his time getting to the point of why I was called to his office. He attempted to tell me I was in trouble at first for something that happened over the weekend, but I reminded him I had spent the weekend supervising a hallway lockdown for a very unprofessional group of students making it impossible that I could have been where he claimed.

He laughed and said, "Ok you got me, I was just kidding". Then he looked at me slyly and asked, "Do you like cow shit?"

I confusedly replied, "Not particularly."

He then said, "Well you better learn to like it because you got your orders – Cannon Air Force Base, New Mexico. That place smells just like cow shit 24/7, who did you piss off". He then handed me my orders while still laughing at me about the assignment.

I had never thought about living in New Mexico. I had no idea what the place had to offer. Most people I knew thought it was a completely different country, to include my grandmother who asked me dozens of times where that country was located. I was disappointed because I had hoped to be assigned overseas to be able to experience a new culture far from the craziness of home. Instead, I was being sent off to the US version of Siberia, to a base that apparently not only had a horrid location but a foul smell always too.

I spent the first few hours after being notified trying to figure out what New Mexico had to offer but had little luck finding anything exciting. This was a time before Google. I was not able to do a search to find out information. I had to ask people at my schoolhouse. The look on 100% of their faces said it all, Cannon Air Force Base was not a good assignment, but it was mine. I had to make the best of it. The truth is that anything was going to be better than living in the training environment that I had lived for the last six months. If I adhered to the core value service before self, then I was supposed to put the Air Force mission before my own desires. I was going to get a big dose of this lesson over the next three years at this base.

I spent all my time in class, studying, eating, or working out. My schedule made the days pass by quickly. Graduation day came fast. Our class took our final exam to graduate which for most of us was an easy task. Our day was made longer as several students decided to party instead of study making the rest of us wait while they received remedial training before being retested. Finally, after everyone had passed, we were set for our graduation ceremony. Afterwards, we would be released to outprocess the base.

The schoolhouse's makeshift graduation ceremony was nothing like graduating basic training. The ceremony was mostly thrown together. We received our career field badges from the ranking member of the school. We were also told we promoted in our apprenticeship course from "helper" level to Fuels Management Apprentices. This meant we knew just enough about how to drive fuel trucks and move jet fuel in tank yards to be very dangerous but overall. We knew very little about what we were going to be doing when we arrived at our first base.

The outprocessing took several days to complete. After garnering all the signatures, travel tickets, and packing our gear I was once again on a bus headed to the airport for another adventure. I was selected for the Recruiters Assistance Program making my first assignment to work for MSgt Rosa in my hometown. The program required I show up each weekday and assist the recruiter's office with their tasks and be an example for the new recruits to see someone made it through the training. The assignment was easy and was the same as being on leave. I was very excited to be part of the active-duty Air Force finally and not be constantly monitored like a prisoner like the training environment required.

The visit home was final closure for several issues to include seeing Razzy for the first time since he was kicked out our flight and had to come back to get his dry cleaning from our squadron. The first thing that people asked me when I returned was "were you there when Razzy fought his drill instructor?" The question was shocking because he had not fought anyone and his time in training ended with him crying in the instructor's office. I did not say anything to anyone about the truth I just said no I was not there when that happened.

The lack of integrity with my old friend saddened me and I was implicit in his lie because I never told anyone I knew the truth. The fact was he quit on himself early in training and left me alone in his selfish, emotional decision. We would have spent the last six months together in training both at Lackland and Sheppard then on recruiting duty, but he had bailed. I never brought this up with him but the whole lie had bothered me and showed that I was not a real friend so after my time home I never saw him again.

Recruiting duty was fun and I decided during this time I did not like desk work. I did enjoy the travel around the area to the local schools to talk to potential recruits. The way they looked at us in our crisp blue service dress uniform was intoxicating and I grew to love the feeling over my career. The time passed by quickly and before I knew it, I was loading my truck with the few possessions I owned and started my first long road trip alone.

I Hope You Like Cow Shit

The drive from Macon, Georgia to Clovis, New Mexico takes just about 20 hours if you do not stop. I had never been on a trip more than a few hours on my own. It was a little exciting to hit the road. I was leaving behind a bad chapter of my life for good. I would not return but maybe 3-4 times over the next 14 years served in the Air Force. Once I left the city limits, I put everything behind me and drove west.

My trip took me through the deep southern states and then across the vast landscape of Texas finally arriving in Clovis, New Mexico. I drove as far as possible the first day. I stopped for the night in a small town in east Texas. The next day's drive would be nearly as far across some of the most desolate areas of the region as I made my journey up the high plains to my destination. The view was of flat farmland for miles with minimal amounts of vegetation making it a boring trip.

I had to pull over an hour or so after making my way up Highway 60-84 because it felt like the truck had a flat tire. When I tried to open the door, the wind was blowing so hard it was almost impossible to stand outside the truck. I found that the wind had been blowing so hard it was vibrating my truck making it feel like I had a flat. I took a moment to look around. I assessed this new frontier I was entering and shook my head. Thinking I must have really pissed someone off to get sent out to this area.

I got back in the cab of the truck and started the journey again towards New Mexico. Along this last leg, I would pass through several dozen small Texas towns dropping my travel speed from 65 miles per hour to 30 making the trip longer than it should have been, It gave me a chance to see the towns. Many boasted about their local football teams, though many were not full squads. I saw posters for teams that were eight or six-man teams because the towns were so small. The towns were dusty and looked like they might be stuck in the 1960s or 70s. There did not seem to be much in terms of opportunity other than farming. Now, this area would be home for the unforeseeable future. I already could not wait to leave.

I arrived at the gates of Cannon Air Force Base late in the afternoon. The base seemed to be an oasis in the middle of desolate plains. Driving through the town of Clovis it appeared that it only offered multiple restaurants, car dealerships, and what seemed like an abundance of religious institutions. The streets were poorly constructed making the drive very rough. It was like a rollercoaster as the roads were not flat at any point but rather had humps every 100 feet or so. I would later find out that Clovis did not get much rain but when it did it was prone to flash flooding. The roads were designed to help channel the water more than for driving. This made for a bumpy ride when traveling in town.

When I pulled up to the gate, I already could see my new duty section as the Fuels Management facilities were to the left of the main gate. This made checking in with my new unit very easy. Once I received my temporary vehicle pass from the Security Police, I drove straight over to the Fuels building to announce my arrival. I had arrived when the B-Shift was on duty. I met a bunch of experienced guys who were all SrA ranks or above. Everyone was curious about who I was. They curiously asked a few questions while I waited for the people in charge to sort out where I needed to stay for the night.

The first impression I got of everyone was that the place was mostly laid back. The Airmen all looked like they had different opinions on what the military standards were. Their uniforms looked anything between disheveled and crisp, but all smelled like jet fuel. The NCOs I met followed the same pattern of varying degrees of sharpness. Most of them sported fat midsections which I found to be very unprofessional. My image of military members was limited to the training culture where people were judged first by how sharp they were and secondly by how they performed. I saw an opportunity to stand out from the average assigned member immediately. I would take care to ensure I always was sharper than everyone around me.

    Finally, after what seemed like a few hours waiting, a Technical Sergeant (TSgt) came out to greet me. He explained he had been setting up my dormitory space for me. He then escorted me to where I would be living and checked me in with the dormitory manager who gave me my assigned room. I had arrived at the end of the week, and I was told to get settled. I was instructed to be back at work at 0600 on Monday morning to begin my inprocessing to the base. The TSgt showed me where the dining facility was located, explained how the process worked to use it, and then in a flash, I was alone in a dormitory room left to fend for myself for a few more days.

    The first night I was in my new room I was alone as the other person assigned never came home. I got all my belongings put away. I took a long shower before hitting the rack for the night. The drive across Texas was brutal and I was exhausted. The dormitory seemed to come alive after dark on this Friday as the Airmen began enjoying their weekend time off, but it did not bother me as I was too tired to notice how loud it was all over the dormitory area.

I woke the next day refreshed. I ventured over to enjoy my first breakfast at my first duty station taking notes of the people I saw as a walked to the "chow hall". The "Pecos Trail" was the dining facility on Cannon Air Force base. Early on a Saturday morning, it was nearly empty as only members with weekend duties seemed to be inside eating. The facility was mostly clean from my first impression. It had two lines that you could go through which offered varying food options – prepared set meals or grilled foods. I decided on checking out the grilled side which was like an express version of a Waffle House. I enjoyed one of the best omelets I had the pleasure of eating and some other side items.

My favorite part of the dining facility was the unlimited chocolate milk dispenser. It gave me a memory of my grandfather. He used to reward me when I was a kid with chocolate milk anytime I did something he approved. It was a reward I would get before my baseball games too. It was one of the few good memories I had from growing up and I still enjoy it today. I took advantage of it for many top offs. I thought if nothing else I will enjoy the free food the base provided dormitory Airmen.

After breakfast, I drove around the base exploring to see what it offered. The selection was not very good as the entire base hosted a shoppette (small gas station), Base Exchange, NCO Club, and a place called Amici's. The latter was like a pizza parlor where the Airmen hung out after work because it had pool tables and a bar. There was also a golf course that took up most of the landscape. I was not really that into playing the game, but due to the limited fun in the area I would learn to enjoy it. I ventured out towards the flight line to catch a glimpse of the aircraft I would be working with and saw we had F-16 Fighting Falcons and two older airframes that I could not identify but would later find out they were called EF-111s and F-111s. These aircraft were being retired as they were Vietnam era jets and we would become mainly an F-16 base for most of my time assigned.

I watched the weekend sorties take off and land for a little while before deciding to travel off base again to take a second look at the sprawling metropolis of Clovis, New Mexico. The trip reaffirmed my first impression that it was a desolate town that did not offer much in terms of excitement. I would find out later that the age for entering the popular night locations was 21 years old. I was now just about to turn 19. This made my options for doing anything to meet new people or have fun extremely limited. There were no Facebook or Tinder apps like there are today. If you wanted to meet people you had to get outside to physically do it. I did find a college located in the town where I immediately signed up for classes. I would take advantage of the lack of distractions to work on my college degree since my options were limited I made it my priority.

I spent the rest of the weekend getting settled into my dorm room. I made trips to the Base Exchange to buy items I needed, but otherwise, my first weekend in the active Air Force was uneventful. I did not know anyone and there seemed to be nothing much to do so I just got my uniforms ready for the upcoming week. I spent a few hours shining my boots to a mirror reflection. I starched my uniform then pressed it to the sharpest creases possible. I wanted to make the best impression possible when I arrived on Monday morning.

My first Monday in the active Air Force started at 0400 when I woke up anxious to get to work. I enjoyed an early breakfast, got dressed, then headed back to the Fuels shop. The night shift supervisors must have been messing with me because when I arrived the only people there was a skeleton crew that ran the C-Shift when there was minimal work. It consisted of about four total people for all areas. They informed me that A-Shift would not be in until about 0800 but were happy to occupy me with any questions about my background. Shortly after I arrived another new guy who I had known at Sheppard who had graduated a few weeks before I showed up. It was good to see a familiar face.

Airman Brown was a very laid-back guy who spoke softly. He treated everyone kindly and presented himself in an above-average appearance always. He was also always professional with the NCOs that presided over us. He liked the outdoors and over our time stationed together, we would take several road trips to visit the local sites. Everything in the area seemed to be at least a five-hour drive such as Carlsbad Caverns and White Sands. He would be a solid friend over the next few years, but we would lose communication after we were both reassigned.

I observed the Airmen who began to arrive at various times as they got ready for their duty day. Many came into the shop to drop their gear then they would go hang out at the pavilion where they would smoke and chat for an hour before the morning briefing. The morning briefing began promptly at 0800.

This was the first time I got to see our leadership. The flight was commanded by a Captain. His leadership team included a Chief Master Sergeant (CMSgt) and two Senior Master Sergeants (SMSgt). They led the morning briefings together. They would keep us informed about upcoming missions, the status of deployed personnel, morale issues, safety, and a host of other topics that they deemed important.

Now was my big introduction as the new guy who had just arrived. I was announced by one of the SMSgts. He called me up to the front of the room and told everyone my name. He explained that I was newly trained from Sheppard and then said something that I felt was very inappropriate. He told everyone that I was an "inbred from Georgia" to which everyone thought was hilarious but left me feeling a little uneasy.

This was a Senior NCO who was supposed to set the standards for the treatment of others. This was his responsibility per the core value service before self, but he had called me an inbred in front of all my new team members. My first impression of this leader was that he was very inappropriate, lacked core values and good judgment as nearly the entire flight had been in attendance. His actions were deemed acceptable for others to act the same. I had never interacted with someone who ranked as high as these guys. I just smiled and did not make a big deal about it. I did make a personal note to watch out for the leadership until I had a better understanding of how they worked.

The next few weeks were a whirlwind. I never got a chance to do my real job as I ran from appointment to appointment getting indoctrinated into my new base. I had appointments for anything you can imagine from chemical warfare readiness, deployment readiness, medical readiness, and a host of others that all meant I could be deployed in case of a conflict breaking out. I nearly tripled the number of possessions I had to store in my tiny dorm room with the equipment I was issued.

Finally, after a few weeks of inprocessing I was at my duty section ready to start to work. The A-Shift supervisors were a ragtag group of NCOs that did not seem to be organized. Several were borderline special needs by the way they carried themselves and their obvious challenges with performing their jobs. I was experiencing interactions with Staff Sergeants (SSgt) and TSgts daily for the first time. The expectations were high for what I was taught it took to be an NCO. I was fast learning that the standards that I thought were mundane parts of the military were subjective. Dealing with some of the SSgts was very frustrating.

The most frustrating was Staff Sergeant Howard. He was a seasoned NCO from the deep south, and he was also the dumbest person I may have ever encountered in life. His lack of mental capacity meant the Airmen assigned were constantly harassed by him for petty things. He would constantly bicker with people he outranked, but he lacked any credibility because of his actions. I cannot count how many arguments I saw when he would "counsel" someone for something he thought was wrong, but later we would find out he had misinformation. He always pulled rank on Airmen constantly, making threats and creating chaos daily. This was compounded by the other NCOs' open lack of confidence in his abilities causing him to be one of the most ineffective NCOs I ever encountered in my time served.

One example of Sergeant Howard's stupidity was the day he was doing a progress check on my Career Development Course (CDCs). He gave me a test to check how well I was learning the lessons I was assigned. After I completed it, he asked me to leave so he could grade it.

Then abruptly he screamed out of his office, "Airman Franks get in here now!"

He proceeded to tell me that I missed 100% of the questions. He then began to berate me publicly with all my peers standing around. After a few minutes of his constant yelling, another NCO inspected the graded sheet and found Howard had misaligned the grade key sheet. He then proceeded to mismark all my answers as wrong. I had scored 98%. The other NCO told Howard he was a moron, also inappropriate in front of the lower-ranking Airmen. Incidents like this happened daily with him for all the Airmen. His ineffectiveness made our work stressful for no reason.

Luckily, after about a year Staff Sergeant Howard was reassigned as a cook in our dining facility. We were freed of his antics but still had to see him when we went to eat. I did gain some satisfaction the first time I went to eat. He had to serve me my meal. He had some snide comments to make about all us "disrespectful Airmen" but I ignored him and sarcastically told him congrats on finding his rightful place. The comment was inappropriate to say to an NCO, but after his harassment, I could not resist.

SSgt Howard never displayed a single trait that the Air Force expected of an Airman or NCO. The performance of his duties was very far below the minimum standards, but he was never held accountable for his lack of efforts or lack of mental capacity to perform his duties. He was rewarded, like everyone else, with "exceptional" performance reports that caused him to be promoted to NCO status when he should have never been allowed to hold the rank above Airman First Class (A1C or E-3). He could not name the core values, much less adhere to the traits expected. He was placed in charge of the largest number of Airmen in our flight because he was senior to the other SSgt.

Howard was the extreme case of pettiness for the NCOs in our shop. Many of the others were not as bad, but few ever met the standard I thought an NCO was supposed to represent. The problem seemed to be a top-down issue as the SMSgts assigned, I witnessed engaging in the vilest activities that did not represent leadership. The worst thing I ever heard about from these two high-ranking men was when they purposefully embarrassed a Senior Airmen who had recently arrived from an assignment in South Korea.

The incident happened on Friday when our shop hosted our weekly barbeque for the entire Supply Squadron personnel at our pavilion. The events were attended by all the top-ranking officials in our squadron and lasted well into the night. I was hand-picked to work with all the SrA on B-Shift due to my performance in my first few weeks and this meant I was the lowest ranking. I was the one who ended up cleaning up the mess after the evening of drinking was concluded.

That night the SMSgts were drinking with the SrA. For hours they had rebuked him about his inability to hang with them drink for drink. The argument had started weeks back when the SrA was bragging about how much he alcohol he could handle because of his time in Korea. Now it was coming to a head this night. The SMSgts gave him drink after drink for hours until finally, this young guy passed on the ground.

The SMSgts took delight in their accomplishment and trashed talked the passed out SrA. Then one of them got the idea that they should piss on him for not holding up his word to drink them under the table. Both supposed leaders stood over the passed-out troop and simultaneously urinated on him in front of everyone present. The act was a testament to their lack of the core value trait "respect for others" and reaffirmed my first instinct that they were not trustworthy leaders. I knew for sure I should watch my back around them.

This was not the only saddening actions the top-ranking people took in our shop, but it was the most extreme. The other inappropriate actions were the NCOs constant talk of sending people who had wives they felt were pretty on deployment so they could attempt to take advantage of the Airman's absence. You could find these wives at our weekly barbeques being wooed by our management teams. I quickly questioned what type of organization I had joined as the leadership model I was seeing from some of the top people was less than appropriate on many levels. The unprofessionalism included our squadron commander, a Lieutenant Colonel who I believe was the source of the leadership culture issues.

The Lieutenant Colonel was an old school officer who had very little compassion for anyone under his command. He was a known alcoholic who was also known to have a refrigerator in his office full of beer and liquor that he consumed throughout the day. He was a big man who dwarfed most people in the unit. He was also not afraid to throw his rank around to get his way. He never looked sharp in his uniform, just mediocre at best. The worst thing about him was that he promoted the drinking culture and he was also a racist.

The Lieutenant Colonel was known to deny packages for all his black Airmen by default. He would deny them by telling them the reason was that they had not "done anything for his squadron" and he did not think they were a good candidate. I heard many stories of how he never would allow any black Airman to apply to become an officer. The worst part was everyone knew this, and no one did anything about it, including me. His leadership created the culture that empowered the "good ole boy system" at our base. My flight was well entrenched within his clique.

The flight did have some very strong leaders who were mostly assigned to the B-Shift. I met TSgt Hudson the first day I arrived. He had taken care of me to get settled. His number two was an SSgt and together this team of NCOs was the best in our flight. They would work together to shape us into the top Airmen in the flight as well.

TSgt Hudson was a sharp NCO that exuded military standards. He always led us by his personal example in all areas. He mentored us in the importance of preparing for military promotion testing. He would personally take troops who were not meeting physical standards to the gym to work out with them. He liked to incorporate promotion testing and fitness training making his favorite activity for us was to ride the stationary bike while reading our promotion materials. His study philosophies would shape my entire career. He helped me surpass my peer groups in rank easily because I had started studying the promotion materials as an Airman Basic (E-1) and continued studying daily until I left the service. He was also an avid wrestling fan which he passed along to our entire shift as a bonding activity. Many days were spent watching the nightly wrestling shows. TSgt Hudson enjoyed acting out the antics of his favorite character Teddy Long.

SSgt Widener was a lot more serious than TSgt Hudson. He kept us all in line with everything we did. He also took the entire team under his guidance for all matters. He also would have all his Airmen over for dinner with his family nearly weekly to talk about the things that we were having trouble within our lives. He always gave us the right advice, even if it was painful to hear. We appreciated his involvement with our issues. We were extremely lucky because the A-Shift had to deal with the antics of SSgt Howard at this time. We lived in a completely different dynamic that promoted excellence over pettiness.

Thanks to the leadership of TSgt Hudson and SSgt Widener I was able to create a baseline of success in the Air Force. I had a solid NCO example to compare my develop towards as I progressed up the ranks. I was lucky they took the time to reward our excellent performance and give us the tools needed to be successful long-term in the military. Hudson gave us all a copy of the "Promotion Fitness Exam" book that the NCOs were tested on for promotion. He told us it contained nearly all the questions we may have about the

Air Force. He made us first seek the answers to questions we had instead of just asking an NCO. This created self-sufficiency that we all used for success later in our careers. I was also honored to be selected to attend many military boards to be recognized as the best of the flight or higher levels. I attribute all the awards I earned to their mentorship. Thanks to their mentorship within my first few months in the Air Force I was recognized by my squadron for an annual award for academic achievement for completing my CDCs simultaneously while maintaining a perfect college GPA. This was the first of many annual awards I would earn in my career.

I also learned from TSgt Hudson and SSgt Widener that the best NCOs always had their Airmen's backs. I learned this lesson in a hard way one evening when I was hanging out with a few of the newly assigned Airmen in our flight in their dorm room. I had spent most of my time since being stationed at Cannon at the gym, work, or the dining facility. I never hung out with any of the other Airmen on my shift because they were either married or partied too much.

These newly assigned troops were put on B-shift with me. For the first time, I was surrounded by guys that were more relatable to me than the older SrA that I had worked with on the shift. This was the first time I had ventured out to hang with others. We planned to enjoy some movies while they drank some beer. I did not drink at all because I was dedicated to working out. I was also just 19 years old and feared getting arrested.

The night started out quiet but shortly into our first movie, "Goodfellas", there was a commotion in the room next to theirs that was unsettling. The noises sounded like someone was destroying their dorm room with a wrecking ball. Then suddenly it stopped.

The group looked at each other in confusion then relaxed to watch the movie. That was when the front door to the room crashed open and someone none of us knew stood in the doorway. The figure looked disheveled, angry, and he was obviously drunk.

He spoke mostly unintelligible words at us, "Garth Brooks fell off a mountain and has a scar just like mine on his face…. who wants to fight?"

I did not react at first to his threats. I wanted nothing more than for him to leave immediately because I was close to meeting my board for "Below the Zone" promotion, an early promotion to SrA based on performance. I did not want to jeopardize my chances of being selected. I stayed quiet as the other guys addressed the intruder.

Airman Wilkinson was a boisterous, country boy who likes to stir up trouble whenever possible. He was the first to provoke the guy standing in the door. He laughed at him as he said, "I will fight you, go meet me by my truck so I can get my ax handle..."

The intruder took his bait and began talking but his words made no sense. He rambled about some scar on Garth Brooks' face and about not being scared to fight us all. He responded to Wilkinson's heckling with growing anger, and the scene was very humorous.

I laughed out loud, drawing the intruder's attention and he walked straight up to me aggressively. He stood over me and asked, "Are you laughing at me?" He demanded I apologize and started to countdown from three. When his mouth uttered the word "ONE", I jumped off the bed kicking him in his chest causing him to fly backwards into the row of clothing drawers along the wall.

I was on my feet in a split second and engaged him by attempting to grab him to stop his insanity. The other guys also jumped up to grab this moron. After we wrestled a little, I noticed that my hand hurt bad. We all stopped in unison as we realized that the intruder was also bleeding heavily from his head.

Somewhere in the mayhem, I had cracked the guy in his head with a bottle. Now we were both injured severely. There was blood all over the place and the room was a huge mess. The awkward silence was broken when Airman Seaman, who's the room we were broke the chaos.

Airman Seaman gasped at the mess and proclaimed, "Damn it guys I just cleaned my room!"

His statement seemed out of place in the situation. He was not concerned with our injuries or the breaking and entering incident but was pissed because we made a mess. I would learn this was a typical Airman Seaman response later after we all became better friends. However, at this moment the out of place statement calmed the immediate threats from the intrusion and altercation.

I knew my career had just ended at that moment. I had not been drinking but hit the guy with a beer bottle.

I knew that because the intruder was drunk, we would both receive an alcohol-related incident on our records. I could kiss the "below the zone" promotion I had worked for goodbye. Worse yet, I probably would be in jail for assault. Maybe I would be kicked out of the Air Force.

I told the group, "Call the police, I will wait for them in my room because I know I am going to be arrested." Then I left to go wait for the police to arrive. I was bleeding and in pain but could only think about my career-ending.

The intruder broke from his slight moment of calm after I left. He started fighting with the other guys who tried to detain him. Three of my friends would attempt to hold him down until the police came. He broke free running through the dorms looking for me. While he ran, he punched out windows and broke machinery that was in the dorm. Then as he was approaching my room, I heard another voice yelled out at him.

The Security Police member yelled at him in an authoritative voice, "Stop, Security Police, put your hands above your head now!"

The intruder did not stop and yelled back, "Fuck you pig, I will kill you too…" then ran towards the officer.

I could not see the incident from my room, but I heard it clearly. The intruder ran towards the officer. I could hear his clumsy taken steps as he ran. The officer stood his ground with anticipation and gave him a final warning.

The officer stated, "Stop now or I will use force to detain you!"

Then the sound of the clumsy running steps changed to the sound of a one-sided struggle. The officer caught the bleeding intruder and slammed him face-first into one of the pillars of the dorm with a loud thud. The sounds became muffled as the two Airmen struggled on the ground for a moment. Then I heard the officer call for backup and announced the intruder had attacked him before he apprehended him.

The sirens of the responding Security Police caused chaos in the dormitory area as people came out of their rooms to see what was happening. The police all arrived on the scene ready for a fight. The intruder obliged them by consistently resisting, leading to a further beatdown by several officers he attacked. After a struggle they had him cuffed to a stretcher and officers escorted him to the hospital to treat his wounds.

      The officers then went to Airman Seaman's room to get statements and to locate me. I came out of my room to surrender to the officers peacefully. I had no reason to fight them. I had only fought the intruder after he threatened me. Still, I just figured the military would give me the boot for this incident. I was distraught at the thought of losing this life. I feared more being returned to civilian life to become a loser.

      I would spend hours at the police station being interrogated. Several officers came into my holding cell to try different methods of asking me the same questions to try to get me to change my story. They threatened to throw me in jail and a bunch of other scare tactics. My story was the same each time. Finally, after hours of being detained TSgt Hudson showed up to the station to take possession of me.

      He did not say much, he just stared at me and said, "Look at you, embarrassing." He then did all the paperwork to get my release. He drove me to the hospital since I had been bleeding profusely from my hand for the hours I was detained. We left the station very early that morning headed to the civilian emergency room in Clovis.

The wound required many stitches where the beer bottle had stabbed into the crease between my thumb and first finger. I took a mental note that hitting people with the bottle was only good in the movies. I decided to never try it again. The fact was that I did not even remember grabbing the bottle. Everything happened very fast. The adrenaline rush of the fight caused me to react, resulting in these injuries.

The wound was treated by the nurse who had also treated the intruder. She was fed up with Airmen this night by the time she treated me. This led to her just stitching up my wounds without cleaning it or giving me any pain medication. She grabbed a needle and stitches then went to work. Her lapse of judgment would cause me to nearly lose my right hand because the wound became infected in a few days.

The infection was very bad. It required me to be admitted as an inpatient for nearly two weeks. My dorm fight now had escalated because I was missing work This forced the chain of command to take actions for a "line of duty determination", which is an investigation into the incidents that led to an Airman missing duty. The investigation could have resulted in heavy fines and being kicked out of the Air Force if they found me negligent in my actions.

Worse yet, was the fact that we had to endure the intruder's court-martial. I also had to receive some type of punishment. I was surprised at how my supervisors stood up for me in this case. I had defended myself, but probably used excessive force with a weapon. This made my case sensitive. The chain of command could not just give me verbal counseling, especially when another Airman was formally being court-martialed in the same incident.

TSgt Hudson and SSgt Widener stood by my side and vouched for me to our leadership. I had worked hard and was the top candidate for being selected for "Below the Zone". They argued that I had defended myself. They told the chain of command that this was not my normal behaviors and that I was worth saving. I was lucky the chain of command heeded their words. when I was called to the Squadron Commander's office to face my charges. When I walked in I was greeted with our flight commander behind the desk.

The flight commander read the charges against me and the evidence. He also told me that my supervisors stood up for me which heavily influenced his decision. He had decided to give me a written letter of admonishment, but that I would keep the only hard copy of it for six months. I was ordered that I would always be required to produce it if anyone asked me to do it. He explained the decision was because of my supervisor's support and that I had shown that I was a hard worker. He also informed me that due to this incident I would not be submitted to compete for "Below the Zone". Though this decision hurt, I knew it was a small sacrifice to pay for not losing my career.

I was very grateful. I had never had anyone fight for me in my life. Mostly, I had been just a nuisance to my family, teachers, coaches, and friends throughout my life. I knew that I was being given a second chance and I would not squander it.

The intruder would not be so lucky. His charges were more severe due to his fight with me, assault on the officers, damage to government property, and his unprofessional behaviors after he was detained. I was forced to testify at his court-martial. The jury found him guilty on all charges. Though he was facing much harder sentencing the judge settled on him losing all his rank and pay while he spent a full month doing hard labor at Kirtland AFB in Albuquerque, New Mexico. I was extremely appreciative that I did not get the sentence he got for this incident.

The experience was paramount in creating the NCO values that I would later hold close to my soul. TSgt Hudson and SSgt Widener did not have to stand up for me. They saw the potential I had and did not let this bad decision destroy my career before it started. I was aware that if I had been on any other shift in flight I more than likely would have been left to fend for myself. The other NCOs on other shifts were not like these two leaders. I was very thankful they were my supervisors.

Overall, the leadership culture at Cannon Air Force Base was night and day depending on the shift that you were assigned. Most of the time I was assigned there the Airmen wanted to work with us on B-Shift to avoid the petty harassment they faced daily by the poor leaders that were on the other shifts. The long-term effects of the leadership seeds that were planted in our group would later affect thousands of Airmen across the Air Force. Our small group of Airmen on that shift would hold high-level positions and special duties that led up to 45,000 Airmen annually. Each one of us attributed our individual successes to the lessons we learned from TSgt Hudson and SSgt Widener.

After I recovered from the dorm fight, I was thriving in the Air Force compared to the people I knew back home. Those people were stuck in the same routines, dead-end jobs, and lack of opportunity. I had escaped. I was determined to make it using the foundation I learned in basic training. I decided to always look sharper than anyone in my flight. I gained a reputation where the flightline workers all knew me as "the office worker". The nickname came about because one of the crew chiefs asked me what office they found me in because no one that worked had boots that shined as nice as mine. I assured him I work 100 percent of my time on the line, but the name stuck. Over time more people began to remember me because of my personal appearance.

My efforts were rewarded when I was then hand-picked to represent our squadron on the Cannon AFB Honor Guard. This was a ceremonial unit that performed all the military honors at funerals and other military ceremonies around the region. I loved working with this team. I spent many days on the road for ceremonies. The biggest honor was when we were tasked for an active-duty military funeral for one of our brothers in arms that was recently killed. An active duty funeral takes a large team to meet all the formations that are required to pay proper respects. I served on the rifle squad for the ceremony. This ceremony required us to recruit Honor Guard members from nearby bases to assist us with honoring the fallen Airman. Our rifle squad delivered a 21-gun salute with precision and it will be something I remember forever.

Overall, I spent two and a half years at Cannon Air Force Base. I saw an improvement with the leadership after the SMSgts both left. The changes were due to a new leader who had arrived. He immediately set forth to whip the NCOs into shape. His name was MSgt Myles.

His leadership example was one of the most important ones to my overall success in my career. MSgt Myles was a no-nonsense SNCO that epitomized every aspect of being an NCO. He was the smartest NCO I served with. He made everyone around him better. He did this not because he was always people's friend. He was effective because he set the proper example, treated everyone fairly, and made us all reach our full potential. The flight dubbed him the "bad man" as he was consistent with his ability to correct any Airman regardless of rank. He set the expectations a lot higher than his predecessor.

TSgt Hudson found this out firsthand when he was caught smoking in an area where it was prohibited. MSgt Myles called him into his office and the sounds inside were as intense as any basic training counseling. MSgt Myles slammed doors shut on his desk cabinets while intensely letting TSgt Hudson know he was setting an improper example. Hudson came out of the counseling shaken up but took accountability for his bad decision. MSgt Myles was putting anyone who was deviating from the standards on notice. The standards were improving overall. The team was coming together after months of challenging the status quo. I saw for the first time what top-level leadership looked like by the examples MSgt Myles set. The Air Force was lucky to have a leader like him and he was rewarded justly by later earning the rank of Chief Master Sergeant (CMSgt).

We were improving as a team but were not perfect. One area we all failed was our team loved to give each other a hard time and talk trash. One of our teammates, SrA Dermeaux, received a lot of ragging by the guys because of his eccentric personality. Dermeaux had come to Cannon from overseas assignments. He was not accustomed to the life of a stateside Airman. He always talked about how great Europe was and how he missed it. He could dish out the trash talk as much as he took it. I believe people thought it was okay because he rarely complained. I always liked Dermeaux. He ended up being my immediate supervisor after he attended

Airman Leadership School and was ready to be promoted to SSgt, pending his promotion testing.

Dermeaux was always fair and friendly to me. He never treated me in a bad way. He took me out to Lubbock, Texas where we hung out in the town. We had a good time as he told me stories about his escapades in Europe. He never let on that the picking the other guys did bother him. I always laughed hard at their battles, and it seemed fine. Many years later, I would run into Dermeaux while I was a Military Training Instructor and I was dropping off a suicidal trainee's gear at the hospital mental ward that housed psychotic Airmen. He ran up to me with surprise and greeted me. He did not answer me when I asked why he was in the psychiatric ward. I would later find out he killed himself a few months later. I also learned he had suffered from severe mental illness.

I wondered immediately if the picking that we did had impacted his path to lead him to suicide. I thought that we may have pushed him into his mental illness by focusing on his differences. I was saddened that he thought he had no options left to him and felt remorse for not being a better friend. I think about this often wonder if there was anything I could have done to help him. Now we can only remember our brother and hope that we make better choices in the future when dealing with someone who is not fitting the group norms.

His suicide would not be the only Airman I knew that took their own life. I would have a troop I identified to the military doctors as a potential for hurting herself around the time I ran into SSgt Dermeaux at the hospital. I had done my job, but the doctors returned her to training resulting in her killing herself months later. I would also have a close friend take his life as a result of the high-paced special operations life causing marital problems that he thought too much to bear.

Losing an Airman, a friend, is never easy. With each one of them, I took a long time to self-evaluate how I had failed them or what I could have done better. I found there are many steps you can take starting with communicating with them. I realized that with each of my friends who died, I had also lost contact leading them. This added to their felling of isolation. These lessons I would later use in my own battles at the end of my career when I would be pushed to my limits by the crab leadership.

The Air Force defined the Suicide Prevention Program (AFSPP) as a population-oriented approach to reducing the risk of suicide. The service implemented 11 initiatives aimed at strengthening social support, promoting the development of social skills, and changing policies and norms to encourage effective help-seeking behaviors.

1) Leadership Involvement

2) Addressing Suicide Prevention in Professional Military Education

3) Guidelines for Commanders on Use of Mental Health Services

4) Community Preventive Services

5) Community Education and Training

6) Investigative Interview Policy

7) Trauma Stress Response

8) Integrated Delivery System (IDS) and the Community Action Information Board (CAIB)

9) Limited Privilege Suicide Prevention Program

10) IDS Consultation Assessment Tool

11) Suicide Event Surveillance System

The problem with the program was that the leadership never became involved in an Airman's life unless they were trying to kick them out for performance. The most common "mentorship" supervisors engaged with the troops was drinking or partying if they were involved at all. The stigma of mental health issues was nearly a career-ending revelation for any Airman who stepped up to say they had a problem. The leaders would feign support but would openly chastise the "weak troops" if they spoke up. Other times the leadership would not take the situations seriously or allow the Airmen to recant their suicide ideation statements and be returned to duty like nothing ever happened.

Even worse was in the units where the senior leaders were the actual problem. I served in multiple units where commanders or SNCO were engaged in toxic behaviors that pushed their Airmen towards suicide. These positional leaders would abuse their positions to create the very issues Airmen were having such as bullying, sexual misconduct, or other unprofessional behaviors. I personally experienced the hopelessness of this issue at the end of my career. When I approached all these listed agencies that were designed to assist distressed Airmen, I was completely blown off leaving me to deal with the stresses alone.

The suicide programs in the military fail because supervisors do not take time to know their people. Understanding subordinate's normal behavior allows you to be able to recognize when their performance deviates from the norm and being actively engaged with the Airmen also makes it more likely they will come to you if they have issues. During my 14-year career, I had many low points where I needed my supervisors to pick me up. I found that not even one of them ever noticed I was not acting like myself. Even worse, some of them took advantage of my weakened state to push me down even farther. My last supervisor in the service, who would later be promoted to Chief Master Sergeant, made a point daily to publicly humiliate me by screaming at me in front of the lower-ranking Airmen, stating negative comments out loud towards me in meetings. He seemed to take pride in trashing me every chance he got. This was the more common way the Air Force dealt with these sensitive issues. In the case of our friend Dermeaux the entire team failed him even if his issues came years after we were stationed together.

Despite the challenges I faced adapting to the Air Force, life was becoming mundane for me at Cannon AFB. I was in a routine of working out in the morning, working into the late evening, and then working out a second time after work. The job was not very hard to do, and I quickly became fully qualified to deploy. I was ready to go. The process for deploying at this time required the flight to be tasked with a mission request for personnel then anyone who wanted to go would sign up on the roster. The flight leadership would then handpick the personnel who they would submit for the deployment. This usually meant the "good ole boys" got all the good assignments while the rest of us got sent to the middle of nowhere in Saudi Arabia. I volunteered for assignment after assignment and never got chosen to deploy. I was at a loss for what to do next. I then started considering my options to retrain or change bases completely. I did not fully control either option at this point in my career.

The best thing about the Air Force was that no matter what you experience there were always chances for redemption. The lesson was clear when the Air Force Special Tactics Recruiting Team showed up on the base one day. I was excited to be given my second chance at joining Combat Control while assigned to Cannon. The recruiting team came out during the football season to recruit guys to try out the next day. I was the quarterback for our squadron team and during the game, I was tackled hard causing me to bruise my hip bone. The bruise made walking a little painful but once in a run it would subside for the duration of the workout. I decided to try out.

I showed up for the Physical Abilities and Stamina Test (PAST) eager to maybe make a change in my career. The one-day notice meant that just like my first PAST I was not prepared, especially for the swimming. I did manage to muscle my way through the 1000-meter swim but found it difficult to make the 25-meter underwaters. The anxiety I felt in the water was still there from the days my mother's friends thought the kids were pool toys. As I submerged all those fears of drowning rushed back causing me to surface and quit.

My lack of preparation had been the reason I had failed again. The recruiters allowed me to complete the run even though I was eliminated by the underwater failure so they could evaluate if I was worth working with to improve my water skills and try out again. My run time was one of the tops for the day so the Pararescue NCOs took my information for future recruitment. They told me to work in the water as much as possible then reapply when I could pass easily. I started planning for my move to Special Tactics when the Air Force stepped in and changed my career path again.

My plans to train were derailed nearly immediately as I received orders to South Korea within a few days. I was scheduled to deploy to a stateside mission and then a few days after my return I would pack my possessions to head to South Korea. I was very excited about leaving New Mexico but a little sad that I would not get the chance to complete my redo for Pararescue. The decision was made, and I had orders to a new adventure on my first overseas trip.

Bulgogi, Bombs, & Bad Leadership

My move to South Korea followed a short-notice deployment to Nellis Air Force Base in Las Vegas, Nevada. I was assigned to support the Air Force version of "Top Gun" called Operation Red Flag. The operation was a joint service, a multi-national exercise that practiced executing a large-scale air campaign against an aggressive enemy. The mission lasted six weeks and was an intense work schedule to support the hundreds of sorties we would have during the day.

The experience was very cool because I got the opportunity to work with aircraft I had never seen to include A-10s, B-1s, B-2s, C-130 gunships, F-4s, F-15s, F-117s, and other foreign aircraft. The exercise included foreign Air Forces from Canada, France, Germany, Japan, Singapore, South Korea, and many other nations. I was also exposed to new equipment and fuel systems that I had only read about in my career development training such as fuel hose carts and fuels hydrant systems.

The best part about being assigned to Nellis was that it was in Las Vegas. I was assigned to the night shift and from the flightline I could see all the action happening down on the famous Vegas strip. Growing up

I never thought I would visit the city because only rich people vacationed in Vegas. I was nowhere near being rich, but I was now living in the area for nearly two months and took time to enjoy the area. The only bad part was I was a few months away from turning 21 years old. This was a major buzz kill since all the fun things to do required you to be 21.

The Vegas strip is a wild place no matter if you are inside or outside people are partying all over. We cruised the area checking it out. We took pictures with our wind-up disposable cameras at the famous "Welcome to Las Vegas" sign, which was not as exciting as people make it out to be as it is randomly placed in an out of the way location. The casino sounds have changed over the years, and at this time the modern digital machines were very few so you would hear the clinking of coins pouring into the slot machine trays all over the places with a very distinct "tink tink tink" sound as coins hit the metal trays. I was never a fan of gambling or casinos because of the smoky atmosphere and the fact that I was never a lucky person. I limited my donation to the billionaire casino owners to a few dollars.

The best part of the trip was the food. Vegas casinos were world-renowned for their high-end buffets. I took advantage of it as much as I could afford. I have never eaten that much food in my life. This made the fact that I could not get into any clubs or other fun places bearable. I would visit in the area while the other Airmen with us partied and then be their designated driver at the end of the night. It would have been more fun had I been able to hang with the group, but I was used to being a loner. I took the time to explore all the sites on the Vegas Strip while they partied.

After six hard weeks of work, we completed our mission. We started the journey back to New Mexico. We had driven out to Nellis and the drive was an excruciatingly painful drive across some of the most desolate land in America. The maps do not accurately represent how big Arizona and New Mexico are and driving across there made me appreciate trees because there were very little along the route. The drive did give me time to think about my upcoming move and I had to decide of some personal things I had been considering over the past few months that would forever change my life.

While I was assigned to Cannon Air Force Base, I was talking to a girl back home that I had met days before I shipped out to basic training. We had a long-distance relationship for about two and a half years. We decided we would get married before I left for South Korea. I was now 20 years old and most of my friends were all married with kids now this seemed like the next logical step for me. The timing was not optimal since I was being deployed to South Korea for a year with a follow-on assignment to Turkey, but we decided it was time then took the leap so she could be added to my follow-on to Turkey.

The relationship was doomed from the beginning since her family freaked out and kicked her out. She was forced to get an apartment with a friend of hers. The stage was set for a stressful year in South Korea. We would spend most of the year fighting about her friend's constant partying and having guys over who expected to hook up with my wife. I was unaware of the real situations occurring or I would have signed the divorce papers while I was gone but would later receive a detailed letter from a third-party who explained all the bad things that occurred. The entire situation made my time in South Korea more stressful than it should have been, but I had made my choice, therefore, I was responsible.

Military marriages were like this often where two people rushed into marriage in order to be together. These arrangements rarely lasted very long and led to a high divorce rate in the service. The biggest reason many military members marry like this is that they are just lonely. Many times the military members are far away from home for the first time and think that marrying someone will fix everything. The idea is far from the truth and I spent a long time paying for this mistake. I endured a lot of unwarranted stress for my assignment to South Korea.

On May 6th, 1998 I boarded a flight bound for Seoul, South Korea with a single bag of uniforms and personal items. I did not own a lot of items anyway and my household goods had shipped weeks earlier from New Mexico. I hoped they would arrive quickly when I got there to make my transition as easy as possible. My first international flight was a long trip. I first flew from Atlanta to Seattle where I checked in with the military flight services. I was set to fly into a military base near Seoul then be bussed to my duty location. The travel time took nearly two days total. By the time I stepped off the bus at the welcome center on Kunsan Air Base, South Korea I was deliriously tired.

The welcome wagon was a large group of assigned military members who had been assembled to make a spectacle of our arrival and make us feel important. Each inbound Airman had a sponsor who was responsible for getting the new arrival situated with housing and scheduling of appointments. The welcome group had over 250 people present who cheered and high-fived everyone who got off the bus. The atmosphere was like a party at first. I wondered if every day was like this in Korea.

The wing commander, called the Wolf, welcomed us. He then gave us a serious intel briefing about the state of the country. I was surprised to hear North Korea had limited capabilities and used 1950s military equipment. The news agencies had made North Korea sound like an invincible war machine, but our in-brief was downplaying the threat. We were told that our tours would be spent preparing for the inevitable war could happen any day. Then we were released to our sponsors.

I was lucky that I was one of about ten Airmen that was reassigned from Cannon AFB to Kunsan. I already knew many of my peers. My sponsor was a guy I worked for at Cannon and he already had my dorm room set. He had also picked my radio call sign, "Disco" after the wrestler The Disco Inferno. It was a joke from our B-Shift wrestling days. No matter what I said I was stuck with it. I did not mind because it was also a fine tribute to our mentor, Johnny Hudson, and I decided to use it proudly.

My sponsor got me settled and told me I had 2 hours to get changed because I had an appointment to meet up with the guys from our shop and it was mandatory. I only wanted to sleep but he insisted that it was mandatory, and I could not skip it. I took a long shower and changed then met the guys where they asked me to meet. Everyone introduced themselves before we caught taxis to "A-Town".

A-Town is the local South Korean community located outside Kunsan City that caters to the US military personnel stationed in the city. The area is full of restaurants and bars where the local Airmen spend their off-duty time. The purpose of this trip down was explained to me on the ride. I was considered a "green bean". The ritual was to take the green beans down to A-Town and get them drunk off the local specialty drinks made from soju. Soju was a Korea liquor, most like vodka, except it had no real taste when mixed with juices making it extra dangerous. The liquor was poorly regulated. One drink may knock a man out or it may take ten and the drinker never knew what batch they were drinking.

The group gathered near our dorms in a group of about 20 people waiting for taxis to arrive to take us to A-town. I took in the surrounding scenes and realized that Kunsan was the opposite of Cannon. The area had lush vegetation compared to Cannon's desolate landscape. The weather was hot, humid, and the grounds were saturated with water all over the area. The smell of South Korea is one that I cannot really explain in full details, but the best I can describe is that smells pungent, sweet, wet, and foreign. The sensation is best explained as a combination of the smell of human waste that was being dumped into the surrounding rice patties, mildew, and an unknown sweet stench. The sensation was nothing like I have ever experienced anywhere else in the world.

Finally, our taxis arrived, and we were on our way to A-Town for the "green bean" ritual. I did not drink and was not that excited about the prospects of drinking a foreign liquor that may knock me completely out. I went along with their plan all the while thinking about how I could save myself from getting trashed. The first place the group leader, Draco who was my sponsor, took us was the "Soju Tent". The Soju Tent was a famous location for anyone who had been stationed at Kunsan. The older Korean woman who ran the small single room establishment welcomed us and took Draco's order.

He decided that the group need three full-sized "green slime" bowls. I was unsure what that meant until the owner returned with giant Tupperware bowls filled to the top with a green liquid. The substance inside looked better than the name would indicate and tasted very sweet. The bowls each had a half dozen straws in it. They explained to me that they were all going to drink the bowls through the straws in a single attempt. I decided this probably was not the smartest idea for someone who did not drink. I decided to blow bubbles while they drank the liquid through the straws. The plan worked. I consumed a very small amount of the green slime bowl that was surprisingly very tasty.

The group members who were trying to haze me had consumed all the alcohol. I was still standing as we got up to move to another bar. The drink orders at the new place were essentially the same as Draco ordered multiple "combat bowls" at each location we visited. I continued my bubble blowing to trick them into thinking I was drinking. By the end of the night, my hazers were all trashed from drinking all the alcohol. Most of the guys were blowing a ton of money on "juicy girls" who merely sat next to you, kind of talked, but ran up a big tab for overpriced pineapple juice. I saved my money and just took in all the action happening around me. I was still feeling good and we ended my green bean night out by eating at what would become my favorite restaurant in A-Town called "The Log Cabin".

The Moon family owned the Log Cabin restaurant. It was known to serve the best spicy bulgogi in the area. Mrs. Moon attended to everyone as if we were her family. She loved talking to us for as long as we stayed. I would meet her entire family over the next year. We all became close with them all as they welcomed us as their family anytime we were in the area.

Korean food can be one of two extremes – very delicious or extremely putrid. The Korean dishes tended to be a little sweet with a mild spiciness that complemented the dish. The most common dish served was spicy bulgogi, a sweet and spicy beef dish served with rice. This is still one of my favorite meals to eat twenty years later. They also served lots of spoiled vegetables called kimchi that I was not a fan of at all.

The group I was with ordered large amounts of "yaki mandu", a fried dumpling that we call "potstickers" in the US, that was a favorite snack for drunken Airmen. The drunks would eat this snack late at night than pay a price for it with various stomach issues the next day. The reason for these issues was in Korea there was no health department to come around to check on food quality. The Korean restaurants would pre-fry the yaki mandu then place them in a container in the window of the restaurant for many hours. When someone ordered them the cook would scoop them out to re-fry the order. This led to many Airmen getting sick when they first arrived. The new Airmen's stomachs were not used to the local germs which was made worse by the food sitting in the hot window all day. I played it safe and ordered steamed mandu and Mrs. Moon made it fresh for me each time I visited her.

    We returned to the base on the last bus out of A-Town. This part of the trip was the most interesting. The last bus from A-Town always would include the drunkest people. You never knew what would happen. I learned to avoid this bus at all costs to avoid the chance of trouble as many fights broke out with the drunks on the bus. I was always sober, and this made me a target for the idiots who could barely stand but believed the soju made them invincible. If something crazy happened in A-Town, it probably happened on the last bus back to the base.

    We dubbed the weird activity that people engaged in when drinking soju a "soju experience". The results were more likely attributed to the unregulated nature of the liquor that tricked some people into believing their tolerance for drinks was higher than it was. This would lead to someone drinking their normal amount but drinking a stronger form of soju and chaos would ensue. I cannot count the number of people I saw end up arrested for being naked in the streets or trying to sleep in a benjo ditch, a shallow, gently sloping ditch that funnels water and human waste from the cities out to the fields for use as fertilizer. Sleeping in one was not an idle night, but it would be one that would be remembered for the rest of their life.

I had survived my green bean hazing but many of the hazers did not fare so well. My roommate was one of the totally trashed hazers and he spent the night in the bathroom on the floor. I would find that Korea was a "work hard, drink harder culture". All levels of the chain of command followed this philosophy. The flight leadership that I would meet in the next few days had several openly alcoholic members that I am not sure how they could work most days.

Monday morning came fast as I settled into the routine of Kunsan life. I spent the weekend navigating myself around the base to find the amenities. The base had a lot more to do than what we had at Cannon, and I was happy with the change. The dining facility was an upgrade where were daily rewarded with random Korean inspired dishes that were amazing. Most of the dishes I never have seen again after leaving the country. There was a Base Exchange that was center of the base, a shoppette, NCO Club, and a multitude of other services. The best place to spend an afternoon was at the Barber Shop because for $10 you could enjoy a nice haircut, massage, and manicure from the local Korean women who worked there. This would be the highlight of my weekly routine.

I spent most of my time at the base gym lifting weights, running, and playing the Korean soldiers in basketball. My routine was to work out anytime I was free to stay away from the party culture that consumed everyone else on the base. I would spend hours in the gym. I also started training in martial arts that the gym offered daily. The master instructor was a famous Tang Soo Do black belt who had pictures of himself and famous people like Chuck Norris. He had trained with him at Osan Air Base when the actor was in the Air Force assigned there many years before. I used these activities to try to stay out of trouble since I was newly married and was trying to lessen the stress of being separated for an extended time.

I would also travel the South Korean countryside using their public transportation. The country was very beautiful. It included a variety of options for scenery from beaches to ski resorts and anything in between. I became an expert of traveling in the country. I found routes for all the cool local sites where we would visit navigating through the area by bus, taxi, ferry boats, and other local transportation.

My experience in the country was a lot different from the other Airmen I worked with because their routines were always the same. They would work all day, drink all night, and then repeat the process seven days a week. I was not into drinking and took the opportunity to experience local Korean culture. Sometimes it was not always good such as one afternoon when a few of us got caught up in a massive protest by a Korean group. Riot police were deployed as we watched. The Korean police beat the protesters in front of us. The scene was intense something I had only seen on the news. Now I was an active participant in the mayhem, and we survived without any issues to report to our unit.

My first day at work I was introduced to everyone at the morning roll call though I had met or knew most of the crew already. I was happy that this introduction no one made any offensive statements about me to the group. After roll call, I met TSgt Epps, who would become second-worst NCO I ever served under in my career.

TSgt Epps was from Georgia. He spoke an indecipherable dialect that was worsened by his constant drinking of large quantities of gin. Epps would drink all night long then come to work to sleep in his office for a few hours. When he finally came out with his daily hangover looming all hell would break loose.

TSgt Epps was consistent in only one aspect of being an NCO, he treated everyone completely unfairly. He would make mistakes on his reports then rip the Staff Sergeants or Airmen who he blamed for the errors. He never showed one ounce of accountability. Many Airman were subjected to unfair punishments due to his drunken wrath. I did my best to stay out of his way to avoid being targeted unjustly but it was a challenge as he intentionally tried to find something wrong with everyone. Looking back, he was probably acting out as a cry for help because his alcoholism was raging out of control. He would consummate his tour in Korea by drinking several bottles of gin on the bus ride to Osan to catch his plane. He ended up passing out in the boarding line.

His fall was an epic event that quickly made its way back to us in Kunsan. Had it occurred today it would have become a viral video, but this happened in 1998. Still, the rumors spread fast. The result of his fall he knocked out all his front teeth and was required to stay in Korea for an extended time to have surgery. I always thought it was karma for how he had treated people. I felt no sympathy for him.

I could never understand how TSgt Epps had been placed in charge of the greatest number of Airmen in our flight. He was the most incapable NCO and created drama constantly with his harassment. There were better-suited NCOs that could have been better role models for us, but the management team just stuck with the status quo. They did not make any changes even after numerous complaints. TSgt Epps was worse than SSgt Howard because he was not stupid. He intentionally tortured the Airmen out of spite. I could never understand how people like him could be promoted to higher pay grades. It seemed like a failure of leadership to allow him to remain as the head of our section.

TSgt Epps' consistent behavior was in direct violation of all the principles of the Air Force core values. He did not display a single trait of the values that the Air Force had identified as important for all Airmen to follow. He consistently displayed the opposite of integrity by not possessing the traits of accountability, self-respect, or humility. He also did not show a single trait of the core value service before self. This can be mostly attributed to his lack of the trait self-control, specifically regarding his inability to control his appetite for drinking that significantly affected his duty performance. The culmination of his lack of core values led to the entire flight of lower-ranking Airmen feeling isolated and threatened the entire time he was in charge. This prevented the entire flight from achieving a sense of the core value excellence.

The reason why these types of NCOs were in the positions they held was because of the Air Force's culture of not providing accurate performance report ratings. The common knowledge about TSgt Epps was that he was incompetent, petty, and a drunk. His performance reports should have rated him marked down in these areas, but instead, everyone got an "exceptional rating" and people like TSgt Epps continually got promoted through the ranks. Guys like him should never have progressed past SrA because of their consistent mediocre performance but the leadership's inability to hold people accountable allowed these poorly equipped NCOs to thrive.

This common practice was also in direct violation of Air Force Instruction 36-2618, the Enlisted Force Structure because every NCO in the flight observed his actions, some may have counseled him about his actions, but no one corrected his actions. TSgt Epps reigned by fear and bullying for the entirety of his tour at Kunsan. No one did anything. His actions were illegal, but he was still considered an "exceptional" performer on paper. His performance reports were rated "exceptional" and he was given a medal for his tour just like everyone else. He would also retire honorably from the service several years later.

The person who could have effected change in the unit and dealt with Epps was the Fuels Management Flight Chief, an SMSgt we called "Gasser". He was a very likable, fair-minded SNCO that always took an interest in me. He always chatted with me about how I was doing, and we had some good laughs in our year spent together in Korea. His example should have been the one the other NCOs emulated, but he did not influence those people below him to step up their game. I believe it was more due to his erratic schedule where he was constantly working with the higher-level parts of our chain of command and the flight leadership was being deferred to the MSgts in our flight.

Our team had two or three Master Sergeants coming and going always. I vaguely remember these guys because they were like ninjas for much of my tour. I do remember one guy who was a MSgt who was a tall, strong-looking Senior NCO that at first appearance seemed to have his act together. I learned later through interactions that he was just biding his time and would cut corners if he felt it was necessary. I only remember him because of two incidents where we had direct interactions.

The first incident was during an exercise when the flight had an emergency. None of the senior NCOs could be found. The entire base was in MOPP 4, meaning we had full chemical gear on and were responding to the combat scenarios that were unfolding. I happened to come across the MSgt while doing my duties. I told him the Control Center was looking for him and the other SNCOs. He told me to tell them I had not seen him. He was not in his MOPP gear and appeared to be drinking. The situation never sat right with me. I believed the leaders should be out front leading the troops, but here was an SNCO blowing off a base exercise while more than likely being drunk. Those leaders never faced any punishments. If the situation had been flipped around I have no doubt I would have been arrested and charged with some crime.

The second reason I remember this SNCO was because of an operational issue. I was assigned as part of the Fuels Hydrants team where we maintained the hydrant servicing systems and fueled the combat sorties daily. The fuels hydrant systems are like the systems used by modern airports when trucks can attach a nozzle to the ground outlet for a pressurized fuel line that is directly connected to the fuel source. The major difference is that the military version is in a hardened shelter to protect from enemy attacks. The aircraft can drive through the fueling area and receive new ammunition simultaneously.

Our team found discrepancies with the accounting totals for a hydrant system that was showing that each time our fuel pumps were run we lost a significant amount of fuel per the physical inventory we would receive. The MSgt then ordered me to perform an operation that did not have a checklist. I argued to him that I could not operate the equipment legally to perform the operation because if the operation failed and I had not followed the checklist I would be punished. He lit me up like a basic trainee telling me that I would do what I was told. I insisted that I could not do the operation and refused to follow the unlawful order. I knew if it failed and I initiated the operation I would be screwed. Even as he pressured me to follow his orders, I refused them outright.

I had displayed the core value of integrity, specifically the trait of courage, by standing up to the MSgt. The decision to stand up for the right process was not an easy one. My responses were met with anger and discontent. I was threatened and ordered to do the illegal operation, but I held firm to the right thing to do which was make the SNCO get out of his office to take accountability.

I took the angered counseling and finally he replied: "I am a Master Sergeant I don't need a checklist…"

This statement was not correct as all military personnel are required to follow all checklists when performing all operations. There is no differentiation for rank. This was a lawful general order and if this operation caused a tragic result due to there not being a proper checklist then the guilty Airman would be subject to court-martial regardless of their rank. He was confusing the requirement with the fact MSgts did not require training records, but this did not eliminate the requirement for a checklist to be followed. I was punished for refusing but did not take on the accountability of creating this new operation. My refusal made the leader get out of his office to lead the operation himself as it should have been from the start. He did just that while displaying an exceptional knowledge of his job as he created this process from scratch. His actions were impressive for a young Airman, even if I had endured the stress of his counseling.

The common mistake many managers make is they delegate orders to their people, and they try to delegate accountability. This is most done so that when something goes wrong the leaders can maintain plausible deniability to protect themselves while having an easy scapegoat to blame. A true leader will lead their people from the front, accept accountability for the outcome no matter if it is good or bad, and give full credit to the subordinate for the success.

I already knew that the MSgt maybe a cool SNCO, but his prior interactions with me showed he was selfish. I knew he would not hesitate to pass the buck if I messed up. I may have trusted him to have my back had I not previously been told to lie for him when he was drunk during the exercise when he could not be found. The decision to refuse the orders was scary. I learned that as a leader you cannot always play it safe. Sometimes the price of being in charge is taking the risk of standing your ground if it is the right thing to do.

These interactions were the extent of my experiences with the entire SNCO group at this base. The only other times I interacted with them was at official roll calls where most of the time they were engaging in drinking activities. Everything in Korea revolved around drinking and Airmen from the Wing Commander down drank ridiculous amounts of alcohol daily. I never really fit in with this culture in Korea. I met some of the best friends I would ever have in my life but the binge drinking always made me feel uncomfortable because the NCOs would not take control of their people when they had too much to drink. This resulted in a lot of fights, property damage, and even petty crimes being committed by the Airmen I worked within the flight.

The drinking also made mentorship from our supervisors impossible because of many times when you needed something they were out drinking or passed out drunk already. This led most Airmen to take an introspective approach to deal with their long-term absence from their families. I knew of dozens of guys having marital problems, but no one really had anyone to turn to as drinking took precedence over all other things. Drinking was also the main solution to all problems for these misguided leaders.

Drinking was not going to solve my issues. I just dealt with it. I spent a ton of money on phone cards trying to work out issues that had arisen from my departure. Over time my wife began dealing with her issues through another man. I attempted to talk about the issues with some of the NCO but their only gave bad advice or did not even care enough to give any at all. After nine months without drinking I got a new roommate named A1C Aguilar, call sign "Aggie", and he would break my sobriety by keeping me out in the bars for the next 90 days straight without a day off.

Aggie was the most dedicated partier I have ever met. Each day he would strip his uniform off as he ran up the stairs of the dormitory yelling "tear the club up!" over and over. He refused to let me be a homebody and persisted on me being his wingman for his nightly partying. His party ritual was a seven day a week operation. Many nights we would return just in time to shower, change, and grab breakfast before heading to work.

The next three months were a blur as we blew through more money than I can even count on drinking daily. We made up for the other nine months where I never went out within days. I nearly forgot about the troubles that waited for me when I was reassigned in the next few weeks.

I may have forgotten about the issues, but they never disappeared. My reassignment became a major issue as I got nearer to my departure date. I still had not received an official assignment. Originally, I was supposed to be moving to Turkey, but a mix up got this assignment canceled. Now I was left in limbo. I was more than ready to leave this Korea by now because our

Wing Commander had tortured us for the past six months by conducting weekly exercises where we performed combat operations 24/7 all the while wearing chemical suits, gas masks, and worked extended hours. His constant pushing of the readiness levels was taking a toll on everyone. We were all burned out. Staying extra time was not the option I wanted but I was at the mercy of the Air Force. I waited patiently.

I was finally given the option of going to three bases – Mountain Home in Idaho, Seymour Johnson in North Carolina, or Moody in Georgia. I choose Moody because I thought that I could work things out with my wife, and she would be happier being closer to her "home". I got my orders and was out processed in days. Before I knew it, I was at Osan Air Base awaiting the "Freedom Bird" back to the US.

I had survived one of the toughest years of my life in a country that was always one wrong move away from a major war. I had resisted the drinking culture for much of the year but in the end, failed to resist for the full time. I became just one of the guys by the time my "brown bean", the celebration of the outgoing troop's end of the tour. This time I was not blowing bubbles in the combat bowls as I did with my "green bean". I had turned to alcohol, like many others, because the leadership above me failed to provide any resemblance of a support system. The leadership mentality was every Airman for himself while I was in Korea. I believe this culture is the reason there is such a high suicide rate for military members. In the end, the crab culture had pulled me down to their level. I was no better than anyone else.

Had our leadership provided more activities to promote positive mental and spiritual health then there would have been a decrease in the drinking culture. Many Airmen turned to alcohol when no one would listen to their problems. My experience with the military culture is that someone in a high position makes up philosophy, then forces a lower-ranking member to make a computer-based training about it. Then high-ranking official would make the training mandatory for everyone to complete all the while patting themselves on the back for "creating a solution" to the issue. Supervisor involvement was never truly addressed. Airmen were left to fend for themselves. The Air Force preached a lot of valuable philosophies, but the front-line supervisors made up their own versions or did nothing at all. This lack of buy-in was the reason for nearly all the problems the military still faces today.

Somehow, I made it out of Korea in one piece. My last night was a blur. I awoke to find I had no wallet, no identification, no money, and no idea what happened. My old friends from Cannon who were now stationed at Osan had taken me out for a second brown bean and this time we got some high-quality soju. I do not remember anything about the night and ended up getting my stuff stolen by the Korean taxi driver that took us home.

I jumped up in a panic when realized I had only four hours to figure out how to get a military ID as it was the only way I was getting on the plane. I ran to the security forces desk to report my stuff stolen. They gave me some paperwork to allow me to get an ID. I quickly got my ID and then ran to a phone bank. This was a place to purchase long-distance calling cards and make calls. I had to make a call to my grandmother to get her to wire me a few hundred dollars to travel on since my wallet was stolen. She got all the details then wired me the money with just enough time for me to arrive with my gear at the terminal a minute before they closed. I was lucky to have made the flight. I was glad to be flying out of this wild country for good.

The flight back to the US took nearly 20 hours. I was relieved to be putting the tempo of Korea behind me. We had been in wartime postures for the past six months with little downtime to recuperate. I now had a chance to decompress for a few weeks before heading back to work. The time off was much needed. I took the opportunity to rest. The constant preparing for war in Korea was taxing mentally. I found myself having dreams that I was still there or gunfights breaking out around me. The realism of the training we continually engaged in was hard to forget. I cannot count the number of firefights I was caught in or the total that occurred just outside my dorm room when I was supposedly off duty. The training had worn me down and I needed the break.

Now was the time to face my personal issues directly. The most often forgotten casualty of military life is the military family. Military members are deployed on a constant rotation to bases around the world to support the many missions that we have been engaged for several decades. The deployment workload was constantly increased while manning was steadily decreased. This led to families who spend most of their careers separated. The result is a high rate of marital issues and divorce.

I did not leave Korea unscathed from this relentless cycle. I still had a decision to make on moving day about my marriage. My wife had spent the past year I was away "dating" some guy who nearly lived in the apartment I had paid for her to live. The relationship was no secret to anyone local, but I was lied to about it for the entire time I was gone. I was made aware of the truth by an anonymous letter in the mail that detailed the entire situation.

I was devastated and had successfully lived the entire year without making a similar mistake. This was hard because the opportunities were abundant in a place like Korea. I was tired of the dormitory life and decided to forgive the mistakes that were made. I thought I could just forget it all happened, but this was just the beginning of our end. I prolonged this relationship for selfish reasons. If I had the hindsight now, I should have walked away. I tried to stick it out, but it would be a tumultuous next five years until it finally ended officially. The only valuable thing of it all was my amazing daughter was born which is the greatest achievement I ever had.

The average civilian does not understand the stresses of military life. People have no clue about what it is like to have a family but to be deployed for years at a time to foreign lands. Every member of my flight from Korea completed or was facing a divorce leaving their tours. The military is unforgiving in that aspect. Many times the people who were supposed to have your back are the very reason family units were destroyed. I had seen how the older NCOs at my first base had preyed on deployed spouses. The problem was systemic. Both the deployed and non-deployed parties were guilty of contributing to these divorces. We were all just casualties of an unforgiving system. It was an issue no one ever discussed outside of the NCO Club, a military version of a sports bar. This was where the fraternization of military members and spouses took place most times. The Air Force ignored this unspoken custom leaving the Airmen to deal with it on their own. I was burned out from this year's stress and ready to just move on with my life.

I was now a seasoned SrA as I reported in to my third duty station in four years. I had experienced one of the most intense training environments for a year. I was one of the more competent of my peer group due to the experience I had gained on my tour. I was not a real leader though I tried to set a proper example. Many times I failed in my attempts to set a positive example. My time at Moody Air Force Base would be a major learning curve for me as I had come there with the intentions to separate to go help my father run his business, but circumstances would change my fate suddenly.

The Good Ole Boy Base

Moody Air Force base is in South Georgia just near the Florida state line. The local area consists of several small towns to include Valdosta, Georgia which is the nationally known as "Title Town USA" due to the abundance of high school National Championships the local school has earned. The base was in the middle of the South Georgia swamps where it was always very hot and humid. It was not uncommon for us to have to remove small alligators from our facilities. Sometimes we would have to call the professionals to remove extremely large ones that would get trapped inside our fuel tank farm. The small-town feel made the base a homesteading location for many people who would arrive as a new Airman then retire 20 years later without ever leaving the base. The culture that was created by these long-time inhabitants of the base promoted the worst "good ole boy" system possibly in the entire Air Force.

Moody Air Force Base had its own culture that was not exclusive to our units. If your spouse wanted a job but was not related to someone in an organization, the job office would only provide information about the jobs no one wanted like janitors, laborers, and other low-level jobs. The military units were run in the same manner where personal relationships had more influence than the rank structure. It made it nearly impossible to change the standards within a unit. The management of my flight was filled with this cancerous mentality led by substandard NCOs who protected their drinking or fishing buddies while killing the careers of anyone they did not like.

The first year I was assigned I had little prestige as I was just a lowly Airman in their eyes. I had tested for promotion to SSgt while in Korea after I was notified last minute that I was testing. I had not studied, but I missed the promotion by three points. At first I blamed my "Below The Zone" loss on it because the added six months' time in grade would have given me the needed three points. The truth is that I did not deserve it because I had not opened the book one time.

This would be the last year the promotion cutoffs would be at a respectable level. The next year the Air Force began dropping the standards for what is required to become an SSgt. The required cutoff scores would be dropped by nearly 100 points making the barrier to entry into the NCO ranks not very challenging. This meant even for the worst-performing laggards would be only be promoted with scores well below 50 percent on their promotion tests. The long-term effects of this decision are still playing out as the crop of laggards they advanced are just now becoming the highest-ranking members of the service, and most are poorly prepared to lead the Airmen. I do believe that this degradation of quality NCOs has greatly contributed to the rise in veteran suicides. This is due to NCOs not being competent enough to take care of their people.

At this point, my missed promotion was outside of my circle of control. I spent the next year as a fuel truck driver working for some NCOs that were new to the base like me. They had yet to be pulled into the "good ole boy system". This made my time bearable.

However, the Superintendent of our section was fully inducted into the system. His leadership style was petty, racist, and retribution was common for anyone who stepped out of line. One example of his petty leadership was when I spoke up about the NCOs gossiping about the Airmen constantly. I had decided to separate from the military and had only weeks remaining in the service. The NCOs constantly, openly gossiped about if I would stay or go. I had made up my mind to separate to assist my father with his company. Barring a major setback in his business I was getting out.

The NCOs could not leave me to my decision. They made up stories amongst themselves that turned to rumors. These rumors always came back to the person they were talking about. Some things that were said about me were inappropriate. I decided to address the issue the next morning roll call because I was not the only Airman having rumors spread by the NCOs in our flight. I felt that this required the issue to be openly addressed, like an overhead correction for all members to hear. I openly addressed the petty rumors that they were spreading about me to all members of the flight with little success at coming to a solution. Afterwards, the Superintendent called his NCOs into his office for a meeting.

The conclusion of the meeting I reported into the NCOs' office. I was told I would be working weekends for the remainder of my time in the service. My duty would be to scrape the waxed floors with a single razor blade then re-wax it weekly. The task was daunting as the building had several thousand square feet of waxed flooring. It was quite a punishment. I was told it was not related to my comments about the gossiping issue, but everyone knew it was retribution for speaking up about it.

The Superintendent and his posse would stop in during the weekend to "monitor" my progress making malicious comments towards me. This included being told that the task was just a required detail and not retribution multiple times. I just did the work to the best of my ability and never let them know I knew they were unjustly punishing me for speaking against them.

Shortly after my proclamation that I was nearly 100 percent getting out of the military, my father called to inform me his business was facing some challenges due to large sums of money being missing from his business accounts. He advised me that I should consider reenlisting for a time to allow him to figure out the problem because he could not guarantee my stability if I separated. A few days later, I was notified that I was being promoted to Staff Sergeant, and I decided to reenlist. Once I notified my flight leadership I was reenlisting, they immediately informed me that I was being deployed to Operation Southern Watch. Within a few short weeks I was on a plane with my combat gear headed to the Middle East.

I was thankful to be leaving because it freed me of the culture at Moody. I also was ready to be part of more real-world operations in the Middle East. Tensions in the region were as volatile as ever when I received my orders to report for duty to a small radio outpost a few miles off the Iraqi border. I was part of a five-man team that was responsible for all fuels operations in the area. Our team arrived at Kuwait International Airport where we were transported by blacked-out buses to this remote location in the desert. The base consisted of several radar compounds, base support agencies, Kuwaiti armed forces, and the flightline area where we received re-supply missions.

Kuwait was a desolate place. Sand found its way into everything. The temperature at midnight when we arrived was still well over 100 degrees. The air had a distinct smell of dirt. It smelled familiar and foreign at the same time. There was nothing to do there except work, eat, sleep, and workout at the gym. The entire experience was very much like being a prisoner, including heavily armed guards holding us hostage inside our compound.

The team we were set to replace met us at the bus stop and took us to our assigned tents. The tents were a big step up from what our Army or Marines brothers were living in as the Air Force construction crews have made partitioned rooms in each one to give everyone their own personal space. The bed was a standard-issue military cot that was just comfortable enough to sleep on. We had a wall locker and a desk inside our small personal areas. The floors were very sandy just like everything else in the country. We also had a cricket lived in the tent walls for the duration of our time. This was a nuisance that I spent many hours trying to find but never did.

The outgoing crew seemed eager to turn the operations directly over to us and get on their plane home. The team leader spent three days showing us the required routes for delivering fuel and the location of the tanks we ensured were always fueled up. Before we knew it, they took off and we were on our own.

The chaos started immediately before the outgoing crew was not even out of our airspace. The team had only shown us about 1 percent of the total amount of fuel tanks that required fuel. There were units that were beginning to hit critically low fuel levels without our knowledge. The commanders of these units began calling us for emergency tank fills and our schedule was wrecked by the constant off-duty calls for fuel.

I was the third-ranking person on the deployment, so I had no official position. I waited for the MSgt that was our team leader to start taking charge of the situation. His reaction was unacceptable as he just instructed us to respond to the calls that were being made to fill the tanks as needed. The plan was ridiculous because many of these fuel tanks were only taking 10 gallons of fuel for a 500-gallon tank. We were wasting our team's time. I rejected this plan and without clearing

174

it with the MSgt I decided to conduct some research on the fuel consumption totals for each unit's assets.

I first drove the entire base to any location where US personnel were operating to identify 100 percent of the fuel tanks installed. The list I created added over 100 tanks to the small list the outgoing team had told us about. I took the time to create a mapping of the area which identified each tank's location. I made it part of the official continuity plan for our operation. I then took the map and researched the consumption for each tank. I broke each one down using its official facility number to identify the daily, weekly, monthly, quarterly, semi-annual, and annual fuel consumption for each tank.

I used this information to create a report that showed this data to create a full schedule to ensure all tanks were filled per their actual consumption. This report was sent to all the unit commanders and I included my team leader in my email. This was the first time he had been told about this report and he lost his mind when he read it. He was in my office within a few minutes and had me standing at attention while he dressed me down for my "blatant disregard for his instructions". I explained to him his order was a complete waste of time and resources because it implied a reactionary plan to just answer calls as they came in for fuel. The new plan proactively addressed all the negative calls and addressed the unit commanders' perception that our team had no clue what we were doing.

Our phones started ringing just as he was telling me off. He was forced to take calls from the highest-ranking commanders on the base. The first one was from the base commander who commended his report then assured him that the off-duty calls would cease because our thorough plan addressed all their concerns about our fuel support. The MSgt absorbed the conversation and ensured he took credit for the plan, though I was later given credit for compiling the reports. He was not happy with me circumventing his order, but the support of the base commander made him at least ease up about the situation. We were only a few days into our deployment, and we had already had a major conflict. I did earn his respect by the efforts, though I was warned I better not go behind his back again.

I was rewarded a couple of weeks later when I was hand-picked to have lunch with Whitten Peters, Secretary of the Air Force, and his staff. The staff talked with me for an extended time. They had a lot of questions for me to answer about various Air Force topics. I received some military coins from the members of his team for my candid interview and it was one of the highlights of my career.

These leaders asked me about my Air Force experience and solicited candid feedback on programs that they had implemented. I took the opportunity to address my concerns that in my experience SNCOs were not engaging effective professional development. This was especially true of the ones I had worked where none had taken any college courses. I felt it was causing them to stagnate in their effectiveness. I explained that the SNCOs I had worked under did not promote education and were not flexible with the Airmen who wanted to attend college. Sometimes they outright prohibited the Airmen from seeking any professional development.

The Secretary of the Air Force listened to my words and assured me the Air Force system for professional development was a sound program. He explained that there was no requirement for enlisted leaders to pursue educational requirements because this was a requirement for the officer corps. I did not agree with this because I had seen the pettiness these lowly educated SNCOs could dish out. I believed that education was the key to improving the SNCO quality across the Air Force. I do not know if my words had any impact on the decision, but shortly after my meeting with these leaders the Air Force implemented requirements for SNCOs completing their Community College of the

Air Force (CCAF) degrees in order to be eligible for promotion to the top two enlisted ranks.

I would not have been allowed this opportunity had I not challenged the status quo and took the initiative to create a better process. The risk was mitigated due to my thorough efforts that addressed every concern the outside units had voiced about our operation. The breakdown was the lack of continuity for our operation and the lack of character the outgoing team had displayed by downplaying the operation. They had intentionally omitted information just so they could catch a flight home leaving us to figure it out. This was probably the same situation they had found themselves in when they arrived. Instead of fixing the broken cycle, they paid it forward to the next group.

This type of leadership was very common in the Air Force and violated the very core values we were supposed to stand for as a service. The first core value of integrity, if employed, would have eradicated the cycle of intentionally screwing over inbound forces. Sadly, most NCOs in the Air Force created their own values systems which created a varying standard of performance on all levels.

I had garnered the respect of my leadership in a short time. I had also gained confidence in my ability to make sound decisions and create new processes. I was still only an SSgt Select, meaning I had been promoted but had to await my turn to sew on my stripe in just over a years' time. The Air Force had a strange promotion system where each member receives a score based on their testing, performance reports, medals, time in grade, and time in service that were totaled to give you a total "Weighted Airman Promotion System" (WAPS) score.

The Airman was also given a rank for the position they scored in relation to the others in their career fields. I would consistently score in the top 5 percent of my career field for promotion. After the promotions were released, the Air Force would throw out this career-field rank then promote all selectees based on seniority alone. This meant they rewarded all the laggards first. These were Airmen who had stagnated in their careers and had barely been promoted. Still they could sew on their stripes first.

My overachievement was punished by having to wait over a year to sew on my stripes. I was motivated and scored high on the tests that measured every NCO's knowledge levels on basic military supervisory and technical aptitude tests. Many of the promoted members who sewed their stripes on immediately had scored very low on the tests. This meant the least qualified of all those promoted. But they would remain senior in rank and fill all the leadership positions in each unit.

The challenge of being in this limbo period meant I was required to conduct myself on the level of an NCO, but I had none of the authorities that the NCO was granted. The Airmen assigned to our team were also SrA, and they mostly looked at me as their peer. This was true even though I was officially accountable for their actions. It was an awkward position. I had to walk a tight line to motivate them to want to do things above just doing the bare minimum as the previous teams had done without having the official authority.

The time deployed to Kuwait moved slowly as my new process streamlined our schedule. We were now too efficient for our leadership because we completed our entire routes daily before 11 am. The Air Force does not reward efficiency on any level and our reward this time was being "volunteered" to do some of the stupidest tasks I had ever engaged while serving. I always felt that the task given was the retribution for the previous incident of upstaging the MSgt, but I never addressed the concern.

The tasks began as routine "details", the Air Force version of busywork, but quickly grew into petty time-wasting activities. The first tasking we were given was to sort out the different barrels of materials we were storing such as Corrosion Inhibitor (CI), Fuels System Icing Inhibitor (FSII), and Aviation Gasoline (AVGAS). We were instructed to put all the like materials together in separate flow through revetments. The first time we accomplished the tasking the MSgt decided he did not like the order we put the barrels. We were tasked with moving them again. The second and third time he had us move the barrels we did not say anything, even though we grumbled amongst our group. The tasking came to a head when he demanded the barrels be moved a fourth time.

When one of the Airmen asked, "Why are we doing this again?"

The MSgt screamed, "Because I told you so!"

The answer did not sit well with any of us. The point was clear that he was just creating work for the sake of work. It was unnecessary as we had other operational concerns we needed to improve. The entire team decided we were not going to do it again. The MSgt went into a rage, jumped into the bobcat to move the barrels himself, but he misjudged the weight of a pallet. He ended up dangling in his seat helplessly as the machine tipped forward off its tracks.

Our team busted out in laughter as he sat there suspended by the seatbelt yelling at us to help him. We left him there for a moment then made him agree that the barrel moving was forever over. He reluctantly agreed and we freed him from his situation. He was not done coming up with asinine tasks for us and his creativity would only get bigger. The worst was yet to come when he decided we were going to remodel a blown-up bunker that had been in shambles since the original Gulf War.

I never agreed with the military culture of punishing idle troops by making them do random tasks. I had endured several popular punishments that were prevalent in our career field culture. Each base I was stationed had their own style of creating retribution taskings. The NCOs at Cannon were notorious for making Airmen separate different color rocks or taking this to the next level by making them paint rocks. This was also popular in Korea and Moody. The rocks could be substituted by grass or dirt as well. It was simply used to put Airmen in their places. Regardless of the punishment, it was representative of a cultural problem with the NCOs not spending time developing their supervisory skills. They were conditioned to rely on the untraditional, petty methods they had witnessed coming up through the ranks.

Most NCOs loathed any professional development and openly complained about having to attend the minimum training courses that are required for promotion to different ranks. The norm was for the returning, newly trained NCO to be told to "forget the schoolhouse lessons" and learn the real way the unit does business. The tradition of shunning professional development has been a factor in the decline of Air Force standards for decades. It has contributed to the major failures the service has endured in the past few years. It was clear the MSgt was a product of this non-official leadership culture. Unfortunately, we had an undisclosed amount of time remaining to put up with him.

On October 12th, 2000, the USS Cole was bombed by terrorists in the Gulf of Aden. The bombing sent all the bases across the region into heightened alert status. Our team was recalled to the main base for a briefing by the commanders about the situation. We were unaware of the incident that had occurred. The region was being rocked by false reports of terrorist activities and plans to attack other outposts. Our small base was one of the supposed targets. The base leadership took us into Force Protection Condition Delta, issued firearms to all the units, and ordered us to protect our assets.

The Army also deployed a unit of tanks around the area. This patrol made the threats even more real. I had never seen a battalion of tanks on patrol and the sight is humbling. Tanks are individually large machines and make unique sounds as they move. When there is an entire unit of them on the move it is outright frightening. The power of the machines is evident and made the situation very real.

The US Navy also began moving their assets around the region to safer locations. Within a few hours, we were called by base operations to standby for an inbound Navy P-3 Reconnaissance aircraft. The Navy P-3 would be assigned to fly missions out of our base for the unforeseeable future while the turmoil in the region died down. The new mission gave us relief from the stupid tasks the MSgt had been creating as we now had a real-world mission to attend.

Our workload got even busier when the Air Force chose our location to test out forward air supply by a C-17 Globemaster. We had to prepare for a large airframe's arrival as our fuel supplies were limited to handling occasional C-130 Hercules flights which took significantly less fuel. The biggest hurdle was the unreliability of the Kuwaiti military as they consistently, intentionally caused logistical issues and delayed fuel shipments out of laziness.

We were fortunate that we faced no setbacks readying ourselves for the mission. All fuel tankers arrived on time and we had our fuel trucks standing by to "quick turn" the C-17 when it arrived. The plane came over the horizon and dropped onto the very short runway at a high rate of speed. This base was not designed for aircraft this size, but we were about to find out if it was possible. The pilots worked their magic using the engines and the brakes to barely stop the aircraft just before it came to the end of the runway. They were required to put the plane in reverse to back into a small area to turn around and stop.

Just as the aircraft came to a halt a team of Security Force Airmen ran down the deck of the aircraft with their M-4 carbines raised to secure the perimeter. All the people on the flightline waiting just looked at each other in confusion as the perimeter was already secured inside several layers of security. It was an odd act by their team, but we figured they were doing their jobs. We then got on with ours.

The C-17 took several full fuel trucks to meet its mission fuel requirements. Just as fast as it had landed the crew boarded up and took off again to another location. The mission was a success because our location was approved to receive inbound shipments from the C-17s. The challenge was the runway length was shorter than normal as our base was primarily used for small fighter aircraft by the Kuwaiti Air Forces. The new missions had saved us from the busy work torture we were subjected to for the past few weeks. Now we had actual missions to take up our time.

The third mission that we stood up was the MQ-1 Predator site. The barrels of products we had stupidly been moving many times over included AVGAS. We were told this fuel was a sensitive asset due to its mission. We never were told what that mission was, and no one ever requested it for the first few months we were deployed. Finally, one day a small aircraft carrying civilians showed up on the base. Within a day or two, they had erected an odd-shaped building that looked like a giant Hershey's Kiss. They started requesting the AVGAS and we delivered it promptly. We still did not know what the mission was and never saw any aircraft. We would hear a strange buzzing sound at night but never caught a glimpse of what caused the noise.

One day we were introduced to the source of the noise, the MQ-1 Predator, the coolest remote-controlled aircraft you can ever imagine. The civilian team was prepping for a mission and pushed the Predator out onto the taxiway so we could view it. The size of the drone was bigger than I could have imagined. It was also quite loud when the engines ran. The drone missions were new then and this was my first time seeing the technology. I was in awe of the aircraft. The details of the mission for this aircraft was never disclosed though we assumed it was being used to monitor Saddam Hussein's activities in Iraq.

Our final tasking before leaving Kuwait was to procure additional fuel trucks from the seaports in Kuwait City. The average Airman in the country was never allowed off the secured base. This was an opportunity for us to see the country while we were completing this mission. The plan was to deploy four teams out to the port to get the equipment then convoy back to the base. Overall, Kuwait was mostly safe but there were a few Iraqi cities on our course to the seaport. These areas had the potential for a conflict with the locals.

My assignment was to be the lead fuel truck driver and I was assigned the refueling truck maintenance technician as my armed wingman. We were escorted by two heavily armored Chevrolet Suburbans with armed Security Forces members. The trip to the port was uneventful. The drive was across the most forsaken land I have ever seen. The view was for miles of brown sand in every direction. Randomly we would come across a small village before returning to the isolation of the desert landscape.

The port officials were supposed to have all the paperwork completed and our time there should have taken only an hour. When we arrived the port officials were nowhere to be found. We spent an hour trying to locate them. The Kuwaitis were known to be lazy, not punctual, and their absence was no surprise. The group finally arrived after a long wait then escorted us to a small shack in the middle of a dirt lot near the water. The office looked like a parking attendant stand in most American cities, and the officials took their time processing our equipment into the country. They were taking too long and the Security Forces NCO in charge began pushing them to hurry for security concerns. The longer we were in the area the more time any enemies could plan an attack on our drive back to the Iraq border.

The officials finally released our trucks to us after about two hours. A few of us who were not required to do anything for the paperwork took the opportunity to visit the local markets in the area to get

188

food. The Kuwaiti food was a little exotic, but extremely fresh. I chose a stand that sold vegetable sandwiches with a local sauce on it. This seemed like the safest choice, and my decision was a good one as my sandwich was one of the freshest I have ever eaten anywhere.

When we returned to the office hut the SNCOs told us it was time to move out. We performed our safety inspections of the fuel trucks, checked them for explosives, and then lined up in the preset order we had planned before taking off for our base. The lead vehicle was an armored Suburban, followed by my fuel truck and two more fuel trucks behind me. The last vehicle in the formation was the other armored Suburban.

The convoy was leaving right about the worst time for traffic in Kuwait City. The heavy traffic slowed our travel drastically. The Security Forces SNCO told us to not allow vehicles to break up our convoy and to keep moving at all costs back to base. Every vehicle wingman was also assigned as the radio operator. They were tasked with monitoring the area for potential threats such as aggressive vehicles, then reporting the activity to the Security Forces vehicles.

The traffic on the route was heavy. It was nearly impossible to stop smaller cars from cutting us off. One of our fuel trucks nearly destroyed a Kuwaiti car they cut him off. We drove for about 30 minutes with no issues when my wingman noticed an aggressive SUV blowing its horn and yelling out the window at us. He called the threat into the Security Forces team to which they instructed us to stay on course. The rear SUV sped up to intercept the threatening vehicle.

The SUV saw the Suburban racing towards it then immediately turned right into the desert at a high rate of speed with the Security Forces Suburban in pursuit for a short time. The scene was like a chase scene from a movie for the few intense minutes before they broke off and disappeared into the desert. This was a time before Improvised Explosive Devices (IEDs) were extremely common, but car bombs were always a threat. This SUV was acting erratically making the moments very tense. The rest of the trip was very quiet as we made our way back across the sandy landscape to our base.

We now had three full missions to keep us busy. Our time seemed to pass quickly. Before long, the incoming team arrived. Unlike our predecessors, we took the time to show them the full operation using my newly created continuity book. We spent several days training them all on the routes, tank locations, fuel ordering procedures, and any of the lessons we learned the hard way. Our goal was to create a new culture at this base to ensure the new troops were set up for success instead of being intentionally sabotaged for some sort of hazing tradition. Once the new crew was trained, we were ordered to pack our gear and we were shipped out to Kuwait International Airport for outprocessing.

    I had survived my first deployment to the Middle East. The experiences were valuable leadership lessons and helped me to develop my leadership approach as I was getting ready to transition becoming an NCO. My actions during the deployment were recognized with an Air Force Achievement Medal. I also received a Navy Commendation Letter from the commander of the US Navy's Fifth Fleet for our support of the Navy operations to include The Fifth Fleet, Joint Task Force Southwest Asia, and the USS Abraham Lincoln Carrier Battle Group after the USS Cole incident.

    Additionally, I gained very important mentorship from the Secretary of the Air Force and his staff which was also extremely valuable. Mostly, I had gained the respect of my peers and the NCOs above me from the actions I had taken on multiple occasions. These were the most important lessons learned. My final evolution as an Airman on my deployment was that I had also reenlisted for the next four years. I was committed to making the Air Force career.

My return trip to the US was interesting as we were allowed stops in Italy, Portugal, and Philadelphia. I had never visited any of the areas. I was excited to spend the few hours we got checking out the sights. The hardest thing to adjust to leaving the Middle East was the colors that were abundant everywhere you looked. Kuwait had been a bland, brown-colored country where no real colors existed. When we got off the plane in Italy the color of the camouflaged uniforms, even the sloppy faded ones, looked extremely bright. My senses took several days to adjust to the colors when I returned.

Before long, I was back in the mundane existence that I had left months earlier. The next challenge for me was my immediate assignment to Airman Leadership School (ALS), which is the mandatory course you must take to be promoted to Staff Sergeant. ALS was an eye-opening experience for me because it was the first time I was officially let behind the curtain to see the actual requirements for being an NCO.

I had watched many examples of NCOs who had been winging it in their duties. Now I was shown the real requirements for the job. I was reintroduced to Air Force Instruction 36-2618, The Enlisted Force Structure, and I realized that there was an actual lawful order that most NCOs I knew never followed. I decided that I would follow this instruction to the letter to ensure I always did my job the right way. I did not want to portray the haphazard leader qualities that many of my new peers projected.

My instructor for ALS was SSgt Bodge. He was the epitome of military image and professionalism. He taught us the Air Force way for being an NCO. He challenged us to reject the mediocrity that many of our NCO peers held so dear. He laid out the challenge and told us this path would not be an easy one. He explained that there were more people who refused to utilize the tools the Air Force gave them and insisted on creating their own methods.

I took the lessons I learned to heart. I decided I would be the NCO that based his leadership on the Enlisted Force Structure. I refused to make up my own version of it. I graduated ALS after six weeks of in-residence study. Then by the end of the I was sewing on my NCO stripes.

The ceremony is one I will never forget as my grandfather who was bound to a wheelchair was brought in to tack on the stripe for me. He was a major inspiration for me growing up. He trained me in baseball and gave me most of the common sense I possessed thanks to his mentorship. He was the only person I thought of to tack on the stripes and he was one of the few people who had believed in me in my life. I was making a major leap into the NCO ranks and it was a special moment. He was so frail that I had to take a knee for him to be able to punch me in my shoulder where my new stripes were placed. He did a good job and socked me hard considering his health challenges. The day was one of the proudest ones of my career. I felt being an NCO was a special privilege. The responsibility I faced was daunting. I was informed that with my new rank I had a new position as well. I was reassigned as a Fuels Bulk Storage Supervisor.

My new job meant that now I was responsible for babysitting the troubled Airmen we had in our shop. The leadership culture of Moody had spawned an Airman revolt of sorts where many of the troops were busted using drugs or worse. Most of the assigned Airmen ended up convicted of drug-related charges. I always believed the lack of leadership in the flight was the catalyst towards the epidemic loss of discipline. Our Senior NCOs prided themselves of the fact that in their 20-year career they had never given anyone any paperwork. They always thumped their chests about their superior leadership abilities.

The real outcome of these Senior NCOs refusing to enforce the general order of the flight was the Airmen did not fear the repercussions of their actions. The common reaction to an Airman doing something wrong was typically a public humiliation followed by assignment to do some demeaning task. There were no records of the infractions or the corrective actions being kept, and all the bad troops' records were squeaky clean.

I had conferred with SSgt Bodge about what I should do about this situation. He urged me to keep my own personal records of the behavior and actions of the leadership. I began keeping detailed memorandums that tracked the negative actions of the Airmen, what I had recommended, and the allowed actions from my leadership. These records would protect me in the future when the "good ole boy" leaders started attempting to throw NCOs they did not like under the bus to take the fall for the outbreak of deviant behavior.

My direct supervisor, a black Master Sergeant Select, would not be as lucky as I was. He would bear the entire weight of the discipline lapse when he was court-martialed for the issues our unit was having. The incident's severity was realized the day the Superintendent called all the NCOs into his office. He laid out the mass drug testing plan that was about to happen for the Airmen assigned to our unit. My supervisor was present at the first part of the meeting when the Superintendent explained that a list of Airmen would be recalled in the middle of the night to be tested via hair sample testing. Once the information was given out we were ordered not to tell anyone outside of the NCOs in that room. Then we were released for the day.

My supervisor left immediately for an appointment and the Superintendent then explained the reality of the situation to the rest of us. He explained that the briefing had been a trap to give my supervisor false information to see if he would warn the Airmen set to be tested. The entire thing was entrapment for this unsuspecting NCO because the flight leadership had decided there needed to be a fall guy. Their choice of a black NCO was no surprise to me.

The Superintendent professed, "When those Airmen come into work with shaved heads, we'll have his ass" referring to my supervisor. The situation was clear that this unsuspecting NCO was going to be thrown under the bus to save the other poorly equipped NCOs that created the issues. I was more dedicated to documenting the daily issues we had with the drug case

Airmen. Now I knew it was to protect myself because the next in line was me.

My relationship with the NCOs at Moody was always a little strained. I was an outsider who had come to the base after I had served at several other duty stations. I was also outspoken about things I saw were not fair. I spent a lot of time "waxing the floors" on the weekends. The leader of the good ole boy clique was a MSgt. This MSgt had served over 20 years and was getting close to his retirement. He prided himself in never giving paperwork to any Airman in his career. He chastised any NCO who wrote up people for blatant violations of the rules. If an NCO sent paperwork up the chain to be added to the troop's personnel file, the MSgt would block it from going then instruct the NCO to do their job instead of writing up the Airman.

The MSgt and I butted heads many times about this. He tossed out several dozen letters of counseling I had be forced to create, but I maintained a copy file of all the activities that were occurring. The conflict came to a head when the Squadron Commander rebuked the flight leadership for not having any paper trail on the Airmen's actions. I spoke up that I had kept a file. I was yelled at by the commander about not doing my job and withholding what was now going to be evidence in the trials of the drug cases. I informed him that I had attempted to do my job. I explained the flight leadership consistently blocked any paperwork from being given to the Airmen. I clarified that I only kept the file in case of an incident like this where I would require evidence that I had performed my duties as required.

Flight leadership was not very happy with my actions. I would pay a hefty price in the future for doing the right thing. This would cause the leadership to not submit me for an Air Force Commendation Medal, which would end up costing me two promotions in my future. The flight leadership also refused to submit me for NCO of the Year, even though I had won every quarter I was assigned to the base that I was an SSgt. However, I had done the right thing. I had provided much-needed tracking of the deviant behavior for the bad Airmen that was critical to ensuring they were held accountable for their crimes. But to my flight peers and leadership, I was a deemed traitor.

The Air Force feigns teamwork. The true nature of serving is that you have cliques and then there is everyone else. The cliques were predominant at all bases I had ever been assigned. They had their own sets of rules that they insist everyone follows. Moody was one of the worst cases of cliques running the show that I had ever been exposed to in my career. The reason was the homesteading that many NCOs did at the base.

There were friendships that had been formed decades earlier that were more solid than the official chain of command. I found it impossible to be effective under this type of misguided leadership. Now my career was in jeopardy if I did not make some moves soon.

  The flight leadership would eventually throw the black MSgt under the bus as the sole person responsible for the drug epidemic at Moody AFB. He would be brought up on court-martial charges shortly after I left the base. I would be required to testify at his trial. I testified that though the defendant was the supervisor in charge of the Airmen when they were arrested, he was not the cause of the issues. I testified about the restrictions the leadership in the flight placed all the NCOs and how they had refused to allow anyone to punish any Airman that did anything wrong. The trial ended with the MSgt being found not guilty for all the charges except one. He was convicted of "violating Air Force Instruction 36-2618, The Enlisted Force Structure, because the jury decided that he had observed the Airmen doing deviant actions and counseled them, but he did not 'correct their actions' as ordered in the instruction". He was given a dishonorable discharge and was reduced in rank to Senior Airman. The MSgt had successfully pinned the issue on this disgraced former MSgt. He had gotten away with his own failure to enforce the standards and was rewarded with a full retirement a few years later.

Luckily for me, I had already decided to apply for special duty to leave town as soon as possible before this trial occurred. I was potentially saved from being this clique's next victim. I began the process of becoming a Military Training Instructor (MTI) secretly to prevent the good ole boys from blocking my package. I completed all the requirements then submit it to the Air Force Personnel Center to await my fate. I did not hear anything for months, so I settled into my routine as I walked on eggshells in my unit.

Searching For The Best Of The Best

The impression an MTI makes on the flights they train is one an Airmen never forgets. My career was shaped by the lessons that I was taught in those formative weeks I spent in basic training. I had arrived in San Antonio, Texas as a person who had no other path forward. I was a lost soul that was looking for my purpose. The instructors shaped my mind into the beginnings of something that I had found myself constantly searching to figure out what my true purpose was supposed to be. I had joined the Air Force on the buddy system with a friend who was too weak-minded to finish. His moment of failure had taught me to never attach my success to another person.

I knew in my first few weeks in the Air Force that I would at some point serve as an MTI. I saw the impact that my instructors made on my basic training flight. They had the opportunity to shape the overall Air Force which was something that appealed to me. I knew how the Air Force had saved my life and I wanted to repay the service any chance I could get. Many people I served with believed I was too serious about the military. Many times tried to get me to lower my standards to meet the group norms at a base. I always refused this notion because my instructor team in my first few weeks had warned me that this would happen.

The instructors told us throughout our training that the operational Air Force was full of people who were dedicated to upholding the status quo or lower. They told us it was our duty to ensure we always followed the Air Force standards instead of the made-up subjective standards that some NCO created on their own. The words stuck with me at every level I served. I did my best to at least aim for doing the right things even if it meant it created personal difficulty. I did not always perfectly meet the high standards of the Air Force, but I was at least trying unlike most of my peers.

I was extremely lucky that my first supervisors had taken a real interest in my professional development. Thanks to SSgt Widener and TSgt Hudson I had learned the proper examples of what an NCO was supposed to be like. I was also lucky to have been assigned to the flight I was in basic training because I was a few people away from ending up across the hallway in a flight lead by a weaker NCO. I would have been handed rewards but never taught I needed to earn them. The examples of my basic training instructors and those first supervisors were part of what I would later learn in MTI School was known as the "Law of Primacy".

The law of primacy, as it relates to the learning environment, stated that the first impressions that are made create a strong, durable impression on the student. These first lessons were more easily retained by the students and would affect their long-term development. My first impressions of what a military supervisor should be were SrA Jokie, SSgt Widener, SSgt Bodge, and TSgt Hudson. For the entirety of my career, I always attempted to make supervisory decisions based on the lessons these leaders showed me by example.

SrA Jokie was my personal example for dress and appearance, customs and courtesies, and a deep appreciation for the history of the Air Force. He taught me to love the ideals of the service and to be proud to represent it as an Airman. He was also the perfect example of how an Airman should always look, as his uniforms were always perfect no matter the time of day, weather, or any other reason many members would us as an excuse for why they looked like they slept in their uniforms. My uniform standards were always many levels higher than anyone I served with. Many times NCOs refused to stand near me during uniform inspections because of how sharp my uniform looked compared to the average Airman.

I used appearance standards as one of the foundational things I did daily to ensure I separated myself from the other Airmen around me. My boots were always mirror-shined even at the end of the workday they would look better than the oncoming shift Airmen's boots. I also ensured my uniform was starched and crisply pressed every day I went to work. This was my first impression I presented every time I donned my uniform. I did it because it challenged the status quo.

SSgt Widener had instilled in me the value of showing compassion for the Airmen you are leading. He took a personal interest in every one of us that he supervised. He always had our backs, even if we made mistakes. His contribution to my professional development was that he created my concept of "true north" for how an NCO should seek to ensure the Airmen they lead are getting the support they require to be ready to fight a war. Every NCO decision I made I would think about how he would have dealt with the situation and tried to put my own spin on his example.

SSgt Bodge was not one of my supervisors, but he was a mentor that I emulated because of the strong impressions he made on me as my Professional Military Education (PME) instructor. He was even sharper than SrA Jokie, and he was a seasoned SSgt that was an expert on all things required to be an NCO. He volunteered to mentor me after I had graduated from ALS. He was the reason that I knew to keep records of the issues the Moody POL flight was having. This was important for protecting my career. He was critical to my personal formulation of my NCO example I would create. He taught me to use the actual Air Force Instructions as my guide for everything because most of the service did not follow the general orders as required.

TSgt Hudson was the most important of all these mentors because he taught me the importance of studying my trade to be the most knowledgeable Airman possible. He always said that knowledge was power then reminded us that all the information we ever needed to know was at our fingertips. Every Air Force Instruction was readily available for every task an Airman can do. He told us that there was no excuse for us making up our own versions of what was expected. He also led by example for studying and would make us study the PME all the time. He would personally take struggling Airmen to the gym for a "bike and study" session where he made them ride a stationary bike while reading the PME to ready themselves for their promotion testing. These sessions gave me strong insights on the military knowledge that was required for competing at military boards. Over my entire career I would excel at this earning several trunks filled with awards.

When I first arrived at my first base, I found out about the military boards that we could compete against our peers to earn recognition. I had a highly competitive spirit, even before I joined the military. The boards were a perfect outlet for me to indulge this desire. The flight leadership at my first base decided after many quarters that I had won too many boards. After a while, I was not allowed to compete as to let other Airmen have the chance to win. I believed that if I was the best then someone needed to beat me to prove they were better but the world we live in today likes to reward everyone to make them feel better.

The trend of being banned from competing at boards continued at other assignments as well. While I was at Moody, I began competing for Non-Commissioned Officer of the Quarter from the day I sewed on NCO stripes. I won every quarter I was an NCO at Moody for my squadron and gained a reputation outside my flight as a top NCO. Winning awards coupled with my sharp military image made people start recognizing me all over the base. People began to solicit me for doing special duties outside my career field to gain more insights on being an NCO and to continue my professional development.

I volunteered to be a professional development instructor for the new Airmen who were coming into our squadron. I taught several classes because I felt it was my duty as an NCO. One day while giving a lecture on customs and courtesies, as it relates to discipline, we were discussing my desire to become a Military Training Instructor (MTI). A female Airman laughed at the idea. She told me that I would be eaten alive at Lackland. The words stuck in my mind. Her words made me evaluate all the traits I possessed that would make the young Airman doubt my abilities.

I suppose my teaching skills were not at their apex as I had not attended the professional school that would teach me how to teach others, but the words seemed to mean a lot more. She seemed to imply that I was not worthy of becoming an MTI, or that I was not good enough to hold the job. I was extremely self-confident in my abilities. I took those words to heart to ensure I did everything possible I could do to be the best MTI I could become.

A few days later I was called to the commander's office at the squadron. He made me formally report into his office and acted like I was in trouble. He asked me if I knew why I was there and what I had done. I was oblivious to his reproaching and ensured him I had done nothing wrong. He laughed and then told me "Congrats, you are ordered to go to Lackland Air Force Base to become an MTI".

I was extremely excited that I had been chosen for this special duty. The total number of MTIs at one time is around 500-600 and represents a fraction of 1 percent of the active-duty and reserve forces. I had been found worthy of this elite duty. I was very proud of the opportunity. I would work hard to prove the young Airman who doubted me wrong.

The fun part was getting to go back to my flight to tell them I was leaving. No one knew I had applied for the special duty and many of them were shocked that I had been accepted. Most people told me I was an idiot for volunteering to do the job, but I felt it was my calling to be the first example the new trainees would experience to hopefully do a better job than had been done for the drug-charged Airmen our flight had failed. I had less than six months to outprocess the base and I was taken off my rotation to be deployed to the Middle East again. My group had just come eligible. I was ready to take another adventure but that would have to wait.

On Tuesday, September 11th, 2001, I woke up around 0830 to start my daily routine. I had been assigned as the NCO in Charge of Fuels Bulk Storage B-Shift and my shift ended at about midnight each day. My normal routine was to wake up before 0900 to eat some breakfast, watch SportsCenter highlights, and then go to the gym for my daily workout. This day would be a day that changed the entire world. As I woke up, I did not realize the events that would change our lives were already in action.

When I turned on the television SportsCenter was not playing but the screen showed the World Trade Center smoking. The news people were debating what had happened. They speculated that a small plane had crashed into the tower, but the details were still being processed. I made myself a bowl of cereal and returned to watch the news of what had occurred.

Just as I started watching a plane flew into the live feed of the burning tower. The second plane slammed into the second tower as the entire world was watching. I knew this was no accident. I remembered my friends from my first base who were blown up inside Khobar Towers in Saudi Arabia, and the promise our enemy Osama Bin Laden had made to kill as many Americans as possible. I immediately called into our control center for directions. The NCO on the desk told me to shelter in place to wait for instructions as the base was in Force Protection Condition Delta and no one was allowed in or out. I called my immediate supervisor and he told me to just stay by a phone for orders. He did not think the base would be open for hours.

The news was reporting that there were over 10,000 people inside the buildings and within a few minutes, the first tower collapsed. I knew there would be a massive need for blood. I packed up my gear and headed to the Red Cross. I was one of the first people at the location. They quickly got to work on getting the blood from me. The time it took to get my blood allowed the entire lobby to fill up with people who were there to help those in New York with the only method they knew how to give blood. The sight was awesome and showed what people could do to help each other if they put their minds to it.

I returned home to wait for a recall to occur which I expected to happen any minute. Finally, later in the afternoon, the Fuels Control Center recalled all our personnel. We all reported into work to find out our fates. We were now preparing for war.

We were very familiar with the enemy that we knew had sponsored this attack. Al Qaeda had blown up a dormitory in Saudi Arabi with several of my co-workers inside in 1996 and had blown up the USS Cole when I was deployed. We all knew they were in Afghanistan training new terrorists every day and it was the best guess that was where we would be heading.

My group was the next deployment package set to head out in case of war. I was ready to go. I had joined the military not to sit at a desk and was ready for real-world action. I was saddened to find out that I was not going to be deployed as the Air Force deemed my need at Lackland greater than the deployment. I was destined to sit out the war at a training location, but my purpose was renewed when I thought of my service as a force multiplier. I would train thousands of Airmen that would execute the war America was now about to fight.

My last few weeks at Moody Air Force Base flew by. Before I knew it, I was packed to leave for San Antonio, Texas. I was a little sad I was going to miss the annual awards banquet because I had won all the quarterly awards. I was the easy pick to earn NCO of the Year. I found out a few weeks later that they did not even submit me for the award I should easily have earned. Also, I was notified that I would not receive an Air Force Commendation Medal for my service at Moody. This was the final punch in the gut that the "good ole boy" clique would give me as I headed out the door. The annual award was saddening but the Commendation Medal ended up costing me two promotions as I would miss making Technical Sergeant the first time by two points, Master Sergeant by three points. The medal would have given me exactly three additional points. The final retribution ended up costing me thousands of dollars, and potentially changed the path of my career at the end.

I was now returning to the place where my career started, and my life had changed forever. Driving I wondered what this experience would be like. I reflected on how my instructor team had developed us all into a cohesive unit and pushed us past the minimum standards. The lessons had stuck with me and shaped my career. I was on a fast track well ahead of my peers. I had earned a lot of awards along the way, despite not being the popular Airman or being part of the good ole boy cliques.

The secret to my success thus far had been those lessons that my MTIs and a handful of mentors had taught us about always doing more than what is expected of you. I looked the part and I always set forth to outperform all my peers. Now I was taking a much bigger step by joining the ranks of the elite MTI corps. I would be doing a job most of my old career field peers could not even qualify. I was ready to make a difference in as many lives as I could and hopefully create some exceptional Airmen that would influence the future of the force.

When I arrived in San Antonio I checked into my hotel. Once I was settled I officially signed into the 737th Training Group, which was the command for all Air Force Basic Training. I spent half the day reading and signing Air Force policy letters concerning many topics that applied to our job. I was assigned to the 321st Training Squadron as my primary home for the next four years. I was sent over to check in with my squadron where I was introduced to our Master of Drill and Ceremonies NCO, Technical Sergeant Cabe.

TSgt Cabe was a very tall man with the loudest voice I had ever heard. He showed this off for me when we walked outside to find my temporary trainer where he found some trainees goofing off. TSgt Cabe lit these trainees up with a thunderous roar. His command voice had several of them physically shaking where they stood. After he was finished tuning these trainees up, we walked away, and he was smiling like nothing ever happened. He had set the tone for what was expected in the squadron. The reputation for the instructors assigned was well known across the base. I would later learn that our squadron was the most intense for training. Our leadership promoted this hard style while providing excellent top cover from the desk officers at the Training Group.

TSgt Cabe introduced me to my trainer who would be responsible for me while I awaited my official class start date. My trainer was an SSgt who had come to Lackland from the Civil Engineering career field. The career field was known to be very brutal matching the hard work they were expected to perform. This SSgt did not let the reputation down. He was very thorough in his lessons and performed every step with perfection. He took pride in the job he did while pushing the trainees with an intensity I had never seen before or after him.

My duty day started at 0400 when I would arrive at the office. I would leave most days after 2200. The instructor team was tag-teaming the training while I stayed the entire time. I would come in with one instructor then they would switch sometime during the day, but I was never told to leave. The schedule was packed with training from morning until night. I wondered at first how anyone could keep the pace up. The flight I was assigned to train was in their first week of training and most of the hardest training had already happened in Zero Week, making our focus on polishing up the lessons they had learned.

My trainer had been pushing this new flight for the last few days alone. He had already established his dominance over the group. I noticed immediately that whenever he moved towards a trainee they would immediately get out of his way, sometimes falling over furniture to do so. I never saw him physically grab a trainee, but I could tell that this group had endured some tough love from him in the early parts of their arrival. They wanted nothing more to do with him at this point.

Maltraining is illegal in Air Force basic training. Training is required to be professional in nature. It never should result in physical harm to any member of the service. Unfortunately, some instructors lacked the leadership skills to garner the respect required to train a group of civilians to be productive military members. When there was an immature instructor, and this had nothing to do with service length but meant their leadership maturity, then they often reverted to improper training methods that were not legal. The culture of Air Force basic training was supposed to be a team mentality that protected their ranks from these types of incidents, but I would find that many times this depended on who you were in the social structure more than an actual practice.

I would witness my first maltraining incident this first week I was assigned to BMT. The ramifications of it would stick with me for my entire tour. The incident occurred later in the week when our flight was eating lunch. My trainer had intensely ripped a few trainees that day and there was one that was still seething from his counseling.

The trainee finally had enough when he was yelled at while eating his meal. He stood up defiantly and exclaiming, "Fuck you my dad is a Chief Master Sergeant and I don't have to take your shit!"

My trainer did not hesitate and grabbed him immediately by his throat then pushed him roughly against the wall. His grip on the trainee's neck was solid and he choked him as he raised him off his feet against the wall. The trainee was no longer screaming, and my trainer was pulling back to smash him in the mouth with his fist. The commotion got all the instructors sitting at the "Snake Pit", the instructor dining tables, moving immediately to interject in the altercation. Several seasoned instructors arrived in time to grab the trainee and my trainer to prevent him from hitting the defiant young man. Their quick reactions more than likely saved my trainer's career because if he would have physically hit the trainee, he would have been subject to a court-martial for his actions. This did not mean the trainee was safe from being corrected for his actions because now he had a lot more instructors in his face yelling at him. The trainee was overwhelmed and broke down within a few seconds. He began crying uncontrollably.

My trainer was pulled out of the dining facility to our Section Supervisor's office to await his fate. I was still standing in the exact place I had been when the altercation started. The instructors that did not run to aid my trainer ran to me then pulled me out the opposite side of the dining facility. They interrogated me on what I had seen.

I explained that I was monitoring the drink line when it started. I told them the wall had blocked my view of what happened. The instructors told me that I hadn't seen anything at all, and I was on the opposite side of the facility when it happened. They explained that I could be in trouble if I had participated in the altercation. They said they wanted to protect me from having to testify against my trainer. I could tell they were concerned for his career and that he had made a major mistake that would be a lingering problem for the squadron.

The stress of the incident was high for the entire team. My trainer was a well-respected instructor and well-liked by all the other members of our squadron. His actions backed the squadron leadership into a corner. They had to act against him, especially because this trainee was already making claims that his father would take outside actions against the NCO for the incident.

The funny thing about basic training is that no matter what drama occurs the training never stops. A new trainer was assigned to me within the hour and we were back to business like nothing had happened. The incident was a surreal reminder that this job was unforgiving. It could destroy your career in a second. I tried to break down the reasons why the situation had occurred to use the knowledge to prevent making the same mistake in the future. However, I would find that the culture of BMT was nearly impossible to stay out of trouble no matter how careful you did your job.

My new instructor was a female Staff Sergeant named Lila Whitlock. She was a very pretty, hardcore NCO that was just as intense as my former trainer but had a lot more style with her approach. She carried herself with a confidence that made people take notice both for her physical appearance and the expertise to which she executed her duties. She would prove to be tough on me but fair and pushed me to be better than I thought I could be in my training. Her influence would be very influential in my development as a Military Training Instructor over the next few months. She was ultimately responsible for setting me up to earn the

Distinguished Graduate award I would later earn when I graduated.

The training atmosphere for becoming a Military Training Instructor was a lot like joining a fraternity. The seasoned instructors took every opportunity to haze the student instructors across an array of senseless activities. The first thing I learned was that student instructors were not allowed to eat in the dining facility while their flights were eating. The student instructors had to monitor the trainees like a prison guard for the entirety of the meal. Then if there was time after the last one had left then you would be allowed to grab a quick meal. Most meals were quick, and the flight would be off to the next appointment meaning the student-instructor was left to figure out where to eat later, if at all.

Military Training Instructors were also known for their giant egos. Many of them had a hard time adjusting to dealing with normal people. This led most instructors to attempt to "train" everyone around them regardless if they were trainees or not. The absolute power that a basic training instructor has over their flights is very hard to let go for many instructors. This caused them to think that everyone should bow to their every command. There were no formal rules that overrode the Air Force rank structure but informally there was a perceived set of rules that were enforced that put a student instructor as the lowest of the low in the squadron regardless of their rank. I played this game patiently appeasing the harassing instructors while biting my tongue more often than I wanted so I could graduate and do my duty.

      I adapted to the peculiarities of my new trainer as each instructor created their own daily routines we called "instructor preference". SSgt Whitlock's background was from the medical field prior to becoming a Military Training Instructor. She employed attention to detail that was never matched by any other instructor I served with during my tour. This meant that any mistake I made was quickly found. I spent many days fixing perceivably minor errors on the paperwork that had been made. Somewhere during the history of Air Force BMT, an instructor had decided that paperwork had to be completely perfectly legible to be correct. This meant every letter in a signature had to be legible or the entire form had to be redone. The reasoning was that when the flight was inspected by the squadron "Blue Ropes", a group recognized as the top ten percent of the instructor corps who performed quality control for assigned flights, everything had to be perfect or the instructor would be scrutinized by their leadership.

      Success was not measured by graduating Airmen from training but how perfect each instructor performed during these Blue Rope inspections. The instructor's reputation would be created based on how the flight performed in all the areas that were subject to inspection to include dormitory cleanliness, wall lockers, drill, and tests on the military bearing of the flight. SSgt Whitlock had a reputation as being one of the top instructors in the squadron, later earning her own "blue rope". She maintained this reputation by keeping standards many times more stringent than what was expected. This made my life miserable at first as I spent hours daily redoing paperwork that was immaculately completed in any other environment.

The training days were a blur. The days started early and ended late. The activities ranging from dark morning hour marches to appointments, inspections, physical training, and a lot of waiting around in between. The training schedule required several hundred classes to be taught to the trainees within the first three weeks. I learned that it was expected this list be completed before the end of Zero Week to be able to apply the lessons throughout the next few weeks of training. Every rule in BMT was expected to be completed to insane levels of higher expectation that exceeded the minimum standard as written in the training instruction books. If the instruction stated three weeks to be completed the leadership would impose a new standard that required it to be done in a few days. This was completely opposite of the standards that the operational Air Force maintained where most of the standards were barely met, and the standard was then lowered so all members could meet it.

BMT forced all members to meet seemingly unattainable standards. People who didn't measure up were treated with contempt. The culture of BMT was the most cutthroat environment I have ever endured. Seasoned instructors refused to speak to student instructors or rookies. They would address them by way of their more seasoned team members when they were standing beside them. These instructors also refused to assist the new instructors and would instead chastise them to the rest of their peers if they decided they were not worthy of being an instructor. The ego-driven environment made for a lonely assignment where you could only rely on your immediate team members to get through the long days.

BMT supervision consisted of several levels of NCOs and officers that had very little loyalty to the instructors that were pushing trainees through training. I saw my Section Supervisors only when they were counseling me for some random complaint from a trainee about their treatment in training. These supervisors were supposed to be active in the training of the trainees, but few ever ventured out of their offices to take part in the training.

The next level of supervision was the Training Superintendent, Operations Officer, and Squadron Commander. These positions were filled with Senior NCOs and officers that did not engage in the training of the trainees. The support received from these positions varied based on the member who held the slot. Your top cover support would change frequently as personnel changed. I experienced good leaders and bad leaders in these positions while I was assigned as an MTI.

The best leaders would set clear standards for what they expected and what training deviations were allowed. The discipline required for the average trainee to become a successful Airman in the operational Air Force was nearly impossible to be achieved with the watered-down standards that were created by the desk officers in charge of BMT. The good leaders would provide top cover protection for instructors who were accused of breaking the rules of training. This did not mean they promoted maltraining, but rather they were upfront with the trainees about what they expected from their instructor teams. They made it clear to both instructors and trainees that they had zero tolerance for breaking their chain of command. This ensured that if there was a problem everyone was expected to address it at the lowest level possible and not elevate problems that could be handled by the squadron supervision.

Then there were the other officers that took pride in taking Military Training Instructor's hats for discipline reasons. The most notorious was a Lieutenant Colonel who was assigned to the 322nd Training Squadron. He kept all the hats he took from instructors on his bookshelf. His leadership method was to screw over as many NCOs as he could while he was in command. There were many commanders who took this same leadership approach though not to this extremity. The assignment of a leader of this caliber would destroy the morale of a squadron in a short period of time as instructors would quickly learn that no one had their backs if something went wrong in training.

The BMT officers' approach to the chain of command defied the Air Force instruction that created it. Air Force members are required to handle all problems at the lowest supervisory level possible to ensure leaders have an opportunity to address the problem. However, in BMT the officers created a trainee incident reporting method that bypassed six levels of supervision because it went directly to the Group Commander. The Group Commander would then proceed to counsel every supervisor in the chain of command about the issue starting with the Squadron Commander and working their way down to the accused instructor. The instructor would be read their rights, they would have their campaign hat confiscated, and they would be removed from training until their case was resolved. Most times the reported incident would be found out to be something minor or a trainee attempting to get an instructor in trouble as a means of trainee retribution towards the instructors.

I would face about ten accusations during my time as a Military Training Instructor. I learned quickly that there was no one truly on your side. The best course of action was to invoke your Article 31 rights, like Miranda Rights, under the Uniform Code of Military Justice. I faced charges of racism, maltraining, and other false accusations from trainees that were not solid performers. The characters were products of the "trophy for all" generation that was becoming popular in American society and expected the military to bend to their wills like their parents had trained them to expect.

The racism accusations were from a trainee I had been hard on because he was not meeting minimal standards. He filled out the Group Commander's critique form and put it in the box for delivery to the Commander of Basic Training. The form stated that I was a racist because during a drill class I used an example of the cartoon character "Magilla Gorilla" when explaining a concept called the "long arm, short arm rule". This drill principle stated that when lining up in a formation the trainees who were in the front line would maintain exact fingertip to shoulder contact while the ones lined up behind them would be directly behind the trainee in front of them regardless of how long or short their arms are they would place their arms behind the trainee next to them.

    I used the cartoon character as a visual aid to help them understand the concept with a character they could envision who had arms that were excessively long. The trainee wrote in his complaint that I used the gorilla to represent all black members of the flight. They claimed they were offended by my "racist comments". The Group Commander took immediate, decisive actions against me without any investigation where I was read my right and removed from training. After a long investigation, it was found that the comment was not racist. The critique was only an attempt to have me removed from training the flight. The trainee was not held accountable and could stay in training. My reputation was damaged with the leadership and the stress of the situation was very high.

    This was a common occurrence in training across BMT. Many instructors were not as lucky as I was and faced UCMJ actions for similar incidents. I believe this was a big contributor to the later sexual assault epidemic that BMT faced because there were so many critiques filled out for issues that should have been handled by a Section Supervisor that the leadership could not see a real problem that was really happening. Had the officers in charge of BMT not circumvented the chain of command through policies that promoted micromanagement from the Group Commander's office then supervision at lower levels could have led their teams. Instead, these commanders created a culture of fear and reactionary supervision that isolated Military Training Instructors even further from their chain of commands.

My time as a student instructor was very long due to a backlog of new instructors reporting for training. The normal process for an instructor was to spend a week with a trainer before you started the intense academic program at the MTI School, followed by pushing a flight for seven weeks as a qualification evaluation where the student would receive their campaign hat at their flight's graduation ceremony. I ended up pushing an entire flight before starting classes and I gained a lot of experience that would be vital to my success in the course.

The Military Training Instructor School (MTIS) was a six-week academic course followed by a seven-week practical training qualification course. Our class included about 15 new prospects from various career fields who were all excited to start their new journey. After four years less than half the group would still be instructors as many would fall victim to violations of the rules of BMT or the corrupt leadership that preyed on the careers of these NCOs.

The academic portion of the training was a monotonous process where each of our classmates was taught how to teach courses in accordance with Air Force teaching methods. The classes were 5 days a week and no less than 10 hours each day located inside a classroom with no windows. The days dragged along as each student instructor sat through the classes and then also were evaluated teaching the lessons to their fellow classmates. Occasionally, we were taken out to various squadrons to evaluate training with real trainees to break up the monotony.

After six weeks had passed and we were qualified in the teaching methods we were released to our official trainers from our squadrons. My new trainer was Technical Sergeant Paul Julbes. He was a very laid-back NCO who did not have the intensity of the last two trainers I had recently been assigned. I found this a pleasant change after being in training for over 15 weeks. It allowed me to learn without the heightened stress level.

The flight I was assigned for my first official group of trainees was females. I had spent time training male trainees prior to my class starting. This was my first exposure to training females. The group dynamics of a female flight is completely different than a group of males. The motivators that drive the groups were completely opposite. Male trainees were motivated by ego and tended to not respond to training until their personal barriers had been broken. Males could withstand a lot of yelling but would breakdown if they were called out in front of their flight mates. Male flights tended to perform poorly at the start of training until their personal agendas were broken and they accepted the team goals as their own. Male flights' group dynamics would peak around the 4th week of training and they would strongly bond by the end of the training.

Female trainees would start training stronger picking up lessons a lot faster than males. The groups tended to start out working together faster but by the 4th week of training their group dynamics faced serious challenges as groups within the flight would engage in a bid for power creating tension in the ranks. I learned that during this period the females required a re-focus of their agendas. I would be forced to create an emotional experience for the team to re-bond around.

I joined my flight a few days after they had arrived during their Zero Week of training. The assigned instructor briefed us on what all had been accomplished and the classes that needed to be taught. He had already chosen the flight leadership and had chosen some very strong leaders to oversee their elements. We took accountability of the flight and he left us to continue their training. I was now in charge of my first flight.

All training in BMT is guided by training instructions that outline the time limits for teaching each lesson that must be learned. I had studied the training instructions thoroughly and could answer any academic question that I was asked. When you are placed in charge of 60 trainees knowing what to do and executing the plan can be a challenge. My trainer was very patient with me as I became overwhelmed with the gravity of the situation and fumbled constantly in my duties.

The combination of long hours and the gravity of the leadership responsibility were not a factor at this point in my training. I was excited to be finalizing my certification so working 20-hour days was just what seemed to be the norm for this job. I quickly learned that the training instructions only covered the basic requirements for the training that was expected. The real requirements changed with each flight depending on demographics and gender. For instance, I learned a hard lesson about ensuring the black females retained or purchased specialized hair products to ensure their hair did not become damaged. There was no mention of these diverse challenges anywhere in our instructions, it was something you had to learn, or it was passed on by a good trainer.

    I also learned the importance of thinking about the examples you used to describe things to trainees to prevent offending someone or creating an opportunity for a trainee to make an issue out of something that was said. This was when I received my first critique from a trainee and endured the process of being investigated by the BMT leadership. A student MTI who gets a critique usually will have their tour ended abruptly but I was lucky to have an active Section Supervisor who had my back.

    The previously mentioned hair products lesson was the source of my first critique investigation. The instructor who had been pushing the flight prior to me taking over had made the females put all their personal hair products in their baggage and stored it until training was complete. I had unknowingly inherited the issue. There was no mention in the training instructions about these hair products being needed.

My mistake was that during a morning inspection I mentioned to one of the females her hair looked like the dry stuff on the outside of a coconut. The statement was an observation. Her hair literally looked like dried coconut, but the trainee decided that it was meant in a racist manner. She did not say anything to me about being offended, but at lunchtime, she dropped a critique form into the Group Commander's critique box and the fire was lit for the investigation.

Racism was a trainee's go-to complaint when they felt offended or did not like an instructor. The critique program promoted circumventing of the chain of command and the trainee gossip network passed the technique to get rid of an instructor along very quickly. Trainees used the critique system as a means for retribution towards the NCOs that were above them. The system treated the accused NCO as "guilty until proven innocent". The fact that there was no accountability required from the accuser meant trainees could tie up good instructors for many weeks in an investigation and take them out of training.

My Section Supervisor was Master Sergeant David Duell and he was a very good supervisor who took care of his instructors. He called my trainer and I into his office then explained that there was a critique filed against me for being racist. He told us that I was not allowed to go around the flight until I was cleared. He then read me my rights under the UCMJ and began interrogating me about the incident.

    I had not intentionally meant the statement I made to offend the trainees. Their hair had literally looked like a coconut which concerned me for their welfare more than anything. I answered all his questions and he assigned me to an administrative position for the duration of the investigation. This was more stressful than anything I had ever endured in my military career. I was sure that I had already ended my time as an MTI without ever officially graduating.

    I was very lucky to have the Section Supervisor I had because most of the ones assigned to BMT rarely would stand up for their instructors. Most of the supervision was not willing to risk their promotions or careers for the instructors assigned. They had no problem making an example of one to instill fear in the ranks. MSgt Duell was a rare leader in this cutthroat world as he quickly investigated and ended the situation by having me apologize for the "insensitive comment".

    I was back in training and only missed a few days with the flight. My trainer had assumed command keeping their training on track while I was away.

Pushing a flight as a student is already a challenge because all the trainees can visually see you are different from the other instructors because you do not have a campaign hat until you graduate. Now I had a secondary challenge because I had already been investigated and another critique would more than likely end my tour. I had to take special care to not offend any trainees and could not fully engage them in disciplinary matters fully due to it.

I was lucky to have a very loyal group of student leaders that helped get the rest of their trainees in line for the duration of the training. The student leaders each had a quarter of the flight that they oversaw supervising. They reported all issues out of their control to me. They were my eyes and ears within the flight helping me to manage the internal issues that happened throughout the training.

The days were long, but the weeks of training flew by in a blur. BMT is one forever repeating day filled with the same daily routines for both the trainees and the instructors. The mornings start with an early 0500-0600 wake-up call, breakfast and dormitory set up for inspections. The flights are required to work in teams to complete the daily tasks as fast and perfect as possible. The student leaders drive their elements to get beds made then pushed trainees off to complete their assigned details. The scene can seem chaotic from an outside viewpoint, but the process is a very refined system that has been happening for nearly 100 years of Air Force basic training.

The rest of the schedule included morning physical training, classroom instruction, administrative appointments, drill, and the highlight for the trainees was mealtimes. Instructors are required to be present with the flight from the minute they wake up until the minute they go to bed. The Air Force is supposed to ensure that there are four instructors assigned per two flights who are within the same week of training. The reality of the job was that manning numbers were lower than 60 percent and we were always one instructor per flight.

The schedule meant that I was required to be at the squadron daily around 4 am then I would leave most days after 9 pm. My stamina was pushed to its capacity but all activities outside of work were put off. I cannot count how many nights I would fall asleep at the blinking red light or fall asleep in the movies because I was extremely exhausted. The schedule also meant that personal relationships were secondary to the mission. Within the first few weeks I was pushing flights, my wife left me because she could not understand why I was being required to work so many hours.

The worst part of the situation was the BMT leadership falsely reported our work hours to senior leadership. They showed we maxed out at no more than 12 hours. The truth was the average instructor worked no less than 16 hours in a day and closer to 20 hours during Zero and First Weeks of training. The hours worked took their toll on me and by the 4th week of training I had developed pneumonia and the doctor told me I needed to be put on quarters. I informed him there was no one to push my flight and I had no choice but to work. I would be sick for the next two weeks of training but never missed a day of work because I felt I was obligated to show up daily.

The worst day of this time was my final drill evaluation that counted towards my graduation. My academic instructor came to evaluate if I could safely control a marching flight. That day was one of my sickest. The temperature was mild in the morning when I was scheduled for the evaluation but as I stood there for the in-briefing I was sweating profusely to the point where my uniform was completely drenched. The evaluating instructor was concerned for my well-being, but I assured her that I was able to complete the evaluation and proceeded with her assessment.

I can only remember starting and finishing the drill evaluation. When I was finished, I was completely dizzy from calling commands. I was even wetter now after moving for an extended period and I was very light-headed. Somehow, I aced this evaluation and received the highest score in my class for drill. I had completed the last graded assignment for graduation and now I had completed my requirements for graduating. The remaining weeks included Warrior Week, the training evolution where trainees complete combat skills training, and the final week of training that included outprocessing and graduation parade practice. The hardest part of training for me had been completed. Now I was learning the basics of our parade sequence which all instructors were required to memorize.

Warrior Week was supposed to be a good change of pace for both the trainees and the instructors. This was the first time I was expecting to be given a break because the trainees are assigned to the Warrior Week Flight. We were only required to attend the scheduled events such as the Confidence Course and Field Training Exercise. Unfortunately, BMT leadership liked to play cruel jokes on instructors and during this week we were additionally assigned Charge of Quarters. We had to work 9pm-7am instead of being given the customary time off. This was common practice because the Warrior Week instructors were the only ones available besides Section Supervisors who refused to do the job.

When I was being recruited for Military Training Instructor duty, I was told that instructors were working seven weeks then would receive a full week off before receiving their next flight. The reality was even worse than could be imagined. The career field was so critically manned that there was only one instructor to push each flight. Since Section Supervisors were not required to do extra duties the workload was pushed off to the instructors that were supposed to be on their downtime to recuperate in between flight loads. This meant that instructors were not getting adequate time to rest before starting the hellacious Zero Week schedule where they were required to work 20 hours a day for the first 10 days the trainees were assigned.

The promised break into between flights was a myth. We found ourselves shipping a flight out early Monday morning then spending the next 24 hours preparing for our new trainees to arrive on Tuesday. This was our schedule for three straight years, and it took a serious toll on my body. One day while out drill practice I noticed I was having pains in my abdomen and I reported to the hospital to be checked. The doctors look me over but sent me home without finding anything. I would spend the next year with the pain occurring daily, but doctors could never locate the source. They concluded I was not injured. After a year dealing with the pain while working out and calling commands, a new doctor found that I had torn my abdomen in several places. This had resulted in multiple hernias on each side. The damage was bad enough where my surgery was scheduled within the next few days. I required bi-lateral hernia repair that put me out of action for the next two months. I was placed on leave and had my first break in over two years.

The tempo of the job was breaking my body down due to the daily early start and late finish my body could not recuperate from minor injuries. Our manning was not being increased because our leadership was actively lying on the reports about how many hours we were working. This created a deadly cycle for the instructor corps. It also set up the entirety of Air Force BMT for a national scandal due to numerous sexual assaults that I directly attribute to the manning issues we faced.

Instructors who were refreshed could make rational decisions about situations that occurred while in training. Chronically sleep-deprived instructors were more likely to make very bad decisions and engage in maltraining of trainees due to their irritated state. I believe the later sex scandals that rocked BMT was directly related to the lack of integrity BMT leadership showed in the reporting of man-hours for the instructor corps. The lack of manning meant instructors spent twice as many hours with their trainees than should have been required. This led some to engage in activities that were not appropriate and illegal. The failures of our leadership included the pencil-whipping of our hours, minimal involvement in the training, and a complete lack of adequate mentorship once an instructor was trained.

A new instructor could expect to be given the location of a flight, the flight book, then be told to get to work. The Section Supervision would be a ghost after that point who would only come out of their office when a trainee had critiqued an instructor. The lack of supervision inevitably led some instructors to make bad decisions as they felt their power grow in their isolated realms. I knew many instructors who reported to Lackland with one personality only to see them change to very arrogant personalities as they lost their way due to a complete lack of supervision.

The culture of BMT was to "eat your own" and instructors engaged in all types of petty behavior to discredit other instructors, especially new instructors. The program was the benchmark for military professionalism on many levels except in the treatment of instructors who were pushing flights on the streets. The Military Training Instructor corps were stuck in a training mindset where they could not transition from the training of trainees to having conversations or supporting other instructors leading to a highly cutthroat environment where the word "Sir" was used often in a condescending context.

I was not a fan of this culture from the start. I played their games up until a point when I had hit my limit. One morning our flight was going through their morning routine while awaiting the call to report for breakfast when the intercom buzzed me. The instructor who oversaw the breakfast board was a Staff Sergeant named Andrade. He was a student of one of the most hated instructors for students in our squadron. He had picked up his trainer's negative, hazing approach to dealing with student instructors. Our conversation was no different than the dozens of other ones I had endured over the last 13 weeks.

SSgt Andrade yelled into the intercom, "Hey student, where is your damn flight I called for five minutes ago?"

I answered, "Sir the chow runner just told them to fall out for chow and they are forming up as we speak on the pad."

Andrade yelled again, "I told you to get your damn flight in here and stop messing up my chow line, now get them in here now!"

This statement was my breaking point. I let him have it over the intercom. I rebuked him, "SSgt Andrade I already told you the flight was falling out and forming up, what do you want me to do Star Trek teleport them into YOUR dining facility?"

The reply I cut off and told him I was on my way to deal with him. I kicked open my door then stormed down to the dining facility. My trainer had been out dealing with some trainee issues and was not around when the incident began. He showed up as SSgt Andrade and I were in a heated discussion in the dining facility. I quickly entered the dining facility and from across the room yelled back at Andrade to "Chill out with his bullshit."

He responded by attempting to put me in my place as a student and tried to tell me to shut up. I countered his condescending remarks by informing him that our flight had followed the procedures as quickly as possible. He was simply being a jerk because I was a student instructor.

He stood up and aggressively stated, "Report to the Section Supervisor's office now student, I am not taking your shit." I was ready to fight if necessary, at this point because I was tired of the immaturity many of the instructors had shown me over the months I was in training. My trainer and I followed him to the office and the argument only got more heated.

I bust in the door and began saying, "I am tired of your bullshit, and if acting like an asshole is what it takes to be an instructor then you can shove that campaign hat up your ass and send me packing because I will not be talked to like you are addressing me!"

Andrade did not get a chance to respond as my trainer was the ranking member and he stopped us right there to mediate the discussion before it became a physical altercation. Andrade and I were both bullheaded NCOs who did not back down, and it took quite some time for us to reach a civil solution to the incident. TSgt Julbes told us that we were not setting the proper example for the trainees. He told us that we needed to remember that next time we needed to have a discussion like this.

Julbes was completely correct in his assessment. The constant arguing instructors engaged in was very unprofessional and presented an improper example. The fact did not stop other instructors from consistently attempting to embarrass another instructor for some infraction they witnessed, and this trend was not limited to student instructors.

I was unaware at the time, but I had reached a critical point in my training as an instructor. I would learn later when I became an MTI Trainer that each student instructor had a breaking point where they experience a breakdown just before their break-through in their evolution as an instructor. I felt completely released after the incident and after standing up to another instructor no other one approached me in the manner that Andrade had that day. We had disagreed about his treatment of student instructors but in the end, I consider him one of the best NCOs I served with while I was at basic training.

I was now ready to graduate and receive my campaign hat. My flight graduated a week earlier because we had picked them up at the end of Zero Week and we were a week behind for my graduation. I was sad that my trainer was the one that got to lead them down the bomb run for the biggest accomplishment of their lives, but I was proud of their accomplishment. We had grown together as military members. They taught me lessons I would use for the rest of my career.

My family decided they were going to be in attendance for my MTIS graduation and they arrived the day prior to the academic ceremony. My mother, sister, and brother were in attendance when the schoolhouse hosted the ceremony. I had mixed emotions about them being there as I had not been close to them due to me being stationed all over the world for the past few years. The ceremony was a big day for me as I was awarded the top honors for my graduating class being named Distinguished Graduate.

The award was a surprise and I was extremely proud of the accomplishment considering all the hardships I endured over the six months I was in training. The other instructors who had evaluated me always made me feel like I never did a good job and when the award was announced I had no expectations of winning it. The course had been the hardest thing I had experienced in my career, even harder than being a basic trainee or being deployed to the Middle East.

My mother began her antics soon after arriving and after the ceremony told me she was leaving to go meet some guy in New Orleans that she had been talking to online. I tried to explain to them that the real ceremony that mattered was the campaign hat ceremony at the parade the next day, but her need to find drugs overrode her rational mind. The family left immediately, and everyone missed the most important moment of my career.

I could hardly sleep that night with the excitement of finally earning my campaign hat and the annoyance at yet another slight by my mother. I decided I would not let her addiction mess up my achievement and moved on with the thoughts. I woke early on the day of the ceremony and reported to work. Everyone was going through the usual stressful final preparations for the parade. I was ready to be done with this chapter of my career.

The flight I was commanding was from another section in our squadron. Instructors and their flights create a strong bond while in training but this one was not mine. I just had to remember all the steps in the sequence of events. The instructor who had trained these new Airmen, unfortunately, had to watch their parade from the grandstands and I understood from the week prior how this felt since I had just missed my own flight's parade.

I had practiced all the drill movements to a high level of precision and executed all steps perfectly for the parade. The highlight was the hat ceremony when they called my fellow classmates and I to the reviewing stand where all the high-ranking officials were located. Our trainers presented each one of us with our fresh campaign hats before making us take the previously mentioned Military Training Instructor oath for the official time. We had made it through one of the mentally toughest schools in the Air Force, but our journey had only just started.

I reported back to my squadron after the parade to receive my official assignment to my own dormitory and a new flight. I was lucky to be placed in the same dorm I was for my student flight and the instructor I had worked with while training. We also gained a third team member, a female instructor, who would float between the two flights we were assigned.

I graduated at the top of my class. This gave me a boost of confidence that I already knew what I was doing. I quickly learned that this arrogance was wrong as training without my trainer present for the first time was a challenge. BMT leadership expects you to hit the dorm running once you are certified. They stand back to watch you fail as a lesson for new instructors. My experience would be no different. Just like the scene from the movie the Matrix, when I jumped off that building, I smashed right into the ground.

My first flight I did not know the unofficial timelines for completing all the required training. I found out quickly that the answer to this mystery was all training was expected to be completed immediately no matter what timeframe was on the training instructions. My Section Supervisor gave me a total of five days before he showed up to my dorm to fire me for not meeting his standards. My flight was way behind his schedule, a schedule that I had never been officially told but was expected to know.

I spent the next two weeks working a Charge of Quarters at night while another instructor pushed my flight. The flight was completely different when I returned to training. All issues that happened with inspections or evaluations were solidly placed as my failure. I vowed to never allow these instructors to embarrass me again. I made my own checklist for completing all training. I got advice from my former trainer SSgt Whitlock then set forth to building top-performing teams with my trainees.

I was a haphazard leader at best during this time, but I was willing to learn any techniques to make my trainees the best in our squadron. My approach at first was to be intense to create trainees with discipline and physical fitness as a baseline for their training. I believed that if the trainees were disciplined and fit then I could build in other areas around it. The only problem was that I had not engaged in proper professional development personally. I was limited in my team-building skills.

My first flights had excellent military bearing and could do hundreds of pushups. I was not equipping them the skills they would need later in their careers to be successful. Then one day at our lunch meal a sharp Technical Sergeant had a talk with me about leadership. He was one of the sharpest NCOs I had met in my career. He consistently earned recognition across the Air Force for his performance. He was a highly intellectual person, and many years later he would retire as a Command Chief Master Sergeant.

TSgt LugoSantiago talked to me about leadership and the importance of studying the craft to expand your effectiveness in building our teams. I had not had an NCO take time to mentor me about being an effective leader since I was a new Airman. I appreciated his counsel. We talked for the duration of lunch and at the end, he recommended a book for me to read and wrote it down.

The book he recommended was by John C. Maxwell and titled "The 21 Irrefutable Laws of Leadership". I found it at the local Barnes & Noble's bookstore and began reading it immediately. The book struck me like a bolt of lightning. The lessons were simple and connected stories to the leadership principles. I completed the entire book in a single day and was left with a thirst for more learning. I would re-read the book several times to try to absorb the lessons as much as possible. I also discovered that Maxwell had written several books and decided I would try another one.

I purchased my second leadership book by Maxwell. I chose another title "The 17 Indispensable Laws of Teamwork" and the book was perfect for my current position as an instructor. A training instructor is charged with training and developing civilians to become productive military members. The group dynamics of a training flight is chaotic at first because trainees come from all over the world with their own agendas. The training we received had little to do with group dynamics or how to create an effective team. I found this was the missing piece to the puzzle for my training and set forth to apply the knowledge I was gaining.

John Maxwell had also created audiobooks on tape of all his books. This allowed me to integrate the lessons into my training day. I set up speakers in my dormitory and while the trainees were working in the dormitory. I would play the laws of teamwork book as they worked. The trainees were not happy at first as most resisted the concept of having to listen to the training book instead of music. However, after a few days, the trainees began requesting the book be played if I forgot to start it when they were working. We would discuss any questions they had during our evening briefing when we were all in the dayroom for mail call.

The book became a bonding system for the trainees and gave us something we could discuss that was not part of the daily grind they experienced. The trainees all looked forward to the next chapters in the books. I would always hear them talking about what they had listened to previously when they were working in the areas or studying. I could see an immediate improvement with the teams as they progressed in each lesson and they understood what it took to be a good team member or leader.

I was also growing as a leader during this time. I had arrived at Lackland Air Force Base a new SSgt with limited experience as a supervisor. I had the intensity that my squadron expected when training and I could do physical activities longer than any of my peers or trainees. Therefore I made that my initial focus. I thought that I could instill discipline, have the strongest trainees, and that would be enough. My perspective changed with the leadership study I was engaging daily.

While my trainees focused on two books they would alternate listening to, I was reading about two books a week on leadership and team dynamics. I would test out the theories the writers had created. Some I to be of value and others were no better than theory. The most valuable lesson I learned was that I could force the teams through the phases of group dynamics by creating emotional events that anchored their learning process. The techniques we employed were in the gray areas of the training where there were no specific rules against them, but the Air Force tended to use the UCMJ Article 134 for anything that they did not have a specific law against to make their case.

I can honestly say I never engaged in any physical abuse of a trainee while I was assigned as an MTI with one exception. I had an Airman in his last few days of training smart off at me in the dining facility in front of the other instructors. I preached discipline and respect for NCOs as the core principles of my training. At the level of training this young man was at, I needed to permanently correct his attitude. He was feeling bold due to the freedoms he received in his final week of training while he was on base liberties visiting his family and let his discipline slip. I grabbed this young Airman by his tie and led him to a mechanical room just outside the dining facility to begin his lesson. I was not yelling at him when I explained that his actions were unacceptable and speaking to an NCO in the tone he had used would not be tolerated.

    I slowly removed my own tie and took off my blues tops hanging it on the only clean thing I could find, and I approached him closely. I told him now no one was around for him to impress with his smart mouth. This was his chance to take out his frustrations if he decided that was a good idea. His other option was I give him an "Unsatisfactory Core Value Rating" for this week of training and have him recycled for two weeks meaning he would have to complete the entire Warrior Week training again. The Airman was shaking uncontrollably as I stood so close he could not twitch without me sensing it. This was something I learned from another instructor when I first started training as a student. He began crying apologetically begging me not to hit him or recycle him.

    I had no intention of hitting him at any point. I immediately flipped the switch from being aggressive to mentoring him. I reminded him of all the hours I had spent preparing him to be a productive member of the Air Force only to be treated like an asshole now that he thought he had made it through. I reinforced the laws of teamwork lessons that we had learned over his training and counseled him on how he had failed his flight due to his actions. He was at rock bottom at this point. I then began building him back up by stating that I expected so much more out of him because he had been one of my top trainees in his flight and now he had let me down. I also explained that I believed in him and he could be one of the top Airmen in the Air Force if he never acted like that again. He had gotten the point and promised to fix his arrogant behavior immediately. I sent him back to his breakfast.

The incident was the closest I had ever come to having to be physical with a trainee. I knew the seriousness of the situation and I was always in control of my emotions while I was "re-training" him. I was prepared to take defensive actions if he lashed out at me to detain him and de-escalate the situation. My personal leadership training allowed me to create the emotional event then re-build his loyalty and confidence. My lesson was the leadership training gave me an edge and emotional intelligence that allowed me to manipulate the trainees' actions to the desired outcome without the need for maltraining.

I knew of instructors that had a reputation of being a little physical with their trainees, but I never witnessed anyone after my early trainer touched a trainee out of anger. I believe this was because our team would correct out of line instructors the moment they began using improper training techniques that were just being used to boost their own egos. Every training technique we used was done with a training purpose and was the repercussions of the bad decisions a trainee or the entire team made.

I had no problem getting into a trainee's personal space to make them as uncomfortable as possible to drive a point home. But that was as far as I would take it. I trained in the gray area more with the amount of physical training I would use to get control of the flight and establish my dominance as their leader. If a group was really performing bad, I would personally do the exercises with them. This was worse than if I had dropped them only as I could do all the exercises a lot longer than most of them could handle. I had begun training for Air Force Special Tactics to become a Combat Controller, and I was training seriously for the first time to ensure I made it. I could embarrass 18-year-old kids who were crying and trying to quit by doing pushups with them on my back while telling them "I had failed as your leader." The statement was worse than the activities as they felt like they had let me down and would then work harder to not let that happen again.

My tactics did not please some of the more egotistical members of the instructor corps, especially the Blue Ropes from our Standardization and Evaluations Team (STAN TEAM). I had run-ins with these cocky jerks more times than I would have liked. They never could do anything other than a complaint about what I was doing.

One morning as we were going to an appointment, the flight was marching like a group of "rainbows", what we called the new trainees before they received their uniform issues because of all the colors from their civilian clothes. I halted them for a lesson. When a flight is about to be punished for whatever reason we would tell them to turn 45 degrees to the right or left depending on where the sun was facing out of their eyes then drop them for exercises. The flight was expected to drop in unison with one sound as they assumed the pushup position as a team.

When they hit the deck, it sounded like a ripple of movement. I made them get up to repeat the action about ten more times. The act of standing up from the pushup position to the position of attention is a simple task but after a dozen times doing it fatigue will set in regardless of your physical conditioning. The flight was not focused this day. I decided that it was my failure as their leader to properly motivate them. I made them stand up at ease while I assumed the pushup position.

I began pushing and saying "My flight is a failure and it's all my fault" to chastise their actions. The embarrassment was worse than the pushups. After about 20 the student leaders screamed at their elements "If he's pushing, we're pushing so hit the deck". This time they did it as a team with one sound and no complaining. The flight fell into rhythm with my pushups and repeated what I was saying very loudly. I planned to drive the point home. I told them they are not required to do the pushups, and anyone could stand up to rest whenever they chose to do it. Everyone responded, "NO SIR!"

I never saw the STAN TEAM NCO approach as I was taking my punishment, but he ran up to me yelling immediately "SIR, MAKE THOSE TRAINEES STAND UP YOU HAVE EXCEEDED THE MAX NUMBER OF PUSHUPS YOU ARE ALLOWED TO GIVE THEM!"

I repeated my message to the flight without acknowledging the STAN TEAM SSgt "You are not required to participate in my punishment for failing you as an instructor and anyone who wants to quit can quit anytime."

The flight responded with a resounding "WE WILL NEVER QUIT SIR!"

The STAN TEAM SSgt attempted to order the flight to their feet and the student leaders responded that they were not getting up until I got up. The response sent the SSgt into a fury and he began yelling at them to stand up and once again they all refused. The Dorm Chief added a call for a "war cry". They all answered in kind with a loud scream that was the most intense I had ever heard from a flight. The SSgt then stormed off mumbling something about disrespect and talking to my Section Supervisor.

I was the first instructor around that began doing pushups with my flights when they were not performing well. Shortly after the incident, I began noticing other instructors attempting the same and before long you would see several instructors doing pushups with their flights all over the training base. I had done this initially to try to shake up the dynamics of the flight to make them use peer pressure on weak performing trainees. I did not condone trainees bullying others, but the team could use their collective influence to get lazy performers motivated or they would be recycled. I found that doing the pushups with the trainees created a bonding experience. The groups would push harder if they knew I was outperforming them. Most did not want to be outdone by an older NCO and others just wanted to show me they had my back. I was not attempting to create a trend, but it was so effective other instructors took notice and began trying it.

The older instructors were more egotistical and despised the methods because they felt they were better than the trainees they pushed through. They would make snide comments at me when I would drop to do the pushups. I mostly ignored these people having only occasional heated discussions with the most condescending among the ranks. I was not popular with the seasoned instructors because once I graduated, I stopped playing their childish hazing games. I returned their condescension with more smart-alecky responses.

One incident involved a newly promoted TSgt who had been in the service for nearly 20 years but had barely been promoted to paygrade E-6. He became more arrogant when he sewed on his stripes and began bossing the other instructors around. One morning he marched out to the training pad where I was doing evaluations for my flight and began "counseling" me about what I was doing wrong with my trainees. I had enough of his nonsense, and I threw him my flight book and said. "Since you're the expert and are so involved with my flight training then I am going home."

I walked straight to my truck, got inside, and drove away leaving him to take care of my flight for the rest of the day. He was so angry that he never spoke to me again for the next two and a half years. That meant he also never interfered with my training again either. I took that as a small victory.

I developed a reputation as an intense instructor that produced some of the most highly disciplined Airmen in the Air Force. I would routinely be cornered by an instructor that I had recycled a trainee to his flight, and they would tell me that I had sent them the best trainee they had ever had. They never could understand why I would have gotten rid of such a talented young trainee.

Technical Sergeant Eric Smith was one instructor who I got along well with, but we also joked about each other's opposite training styles. TSgt Smith was very laid back and sometimes it was hard to tell if he was awake because of how chilled out he acted. He would call me a tyrant and I would tell him he was so skinny that when he did an "about-face", drill movement to turn around 180 degrees while standing at attention, that he disappeared for a split second. We joked with each other out of fun and never any negativity.

TSgt Smith came to me one day and asked why I had recycled a trainee to him. He explained that the trainee was the best one he had, and he promoted him immediately to Dorm Chief because he was so far ahead of the others. He could not fathom why this exceptional trainee was sent back in training.

I responded. "You and I have differing levels of expectations on what we accept for performance and my standards are higher as this young man did not meet minimum expectations."

He argued that my standards were too high, and I disagreed. We debated the methods we used to determine a trainee's value and performance. He attempted to tell me that I should do more training with the trainees and less recycling, but he had no idea the levels of training that my flights were enduring.

I had a system I used for disciplinary issues with trainees. The system was progressive in how intense the penalties were for deviating from the standards. I did not allow a single deviation to go uncorrected because we were instilling the foundations of discipline in the trainees and they all tended to revert bad to their poor civilian habits after they left BMT if a strong foundation was not created. Therefore, I dedicated myself to intensely training each deviant to the extent the Air Force allowed and a little into the gray areas just to ensure I had done everything possible to train them before using the paperwork option for recycling.

My system started with intense yelling, followed by physical training and if the trainee was still unresponsive, they were assigned the most monotonous, dirty extra duty possible that monopolized most of their free time. The lack of time normally led to their personal areas lacking the appropriate attention and meant they had two choices –

1. Stay up after hours working to catch up

2. Ignore the responsibilities and face the next consequences.

If the trainee used his prized sleep hours to catch up, the efforts would be noted, and it was apparent they cared enough to sacrifice their sleep. I would spend more time with these trainees and try to mentor them towards making a change in their poor behavior. Most trainee issues were due to poor habits they learned from parents who did not hold them accountable for their actions. Many times, the trainees believed that if they just continued to act how they were that I would just keep making idle threats to take actions against them but never follow through. They would all learn very quickly that when I said something, I meant it to be done exactly to the specifications I gave them, and I did not lower the standards just to pass them. The lesson was hard for many to learn at first and I found that by the end of the first week of training nearly all the trainees would be eliminated from becoming an "Honor Graduate" because they had tested my will to hold them accountable.

The loss of this individual award opportunity had another effect on the group. The trainees who no longer were eligible for "Honor Graduate" no longer felt the need to seek self-preservation or do tasks that benefited only themselves first. They were more likely to bend to the team needs rather than their own and the result was a stronger bonded team due to the elimination of personal agendas.

I never sought to eliminate any trainees from becoming Honor Graduate, but I could not start their Air Force careers off with them thinking that the standards were an ever-moving target that they could manipulate.

They would all learn soon enough when they arrived at their first duty station that the average NCO lacked any real standards and it would be up to them to be self-disciplined to survive their first enlistment.

If a trainee chose the second option, then I would have no issue giving them an unsatisfactory core value rating for the week of training and referring them to my Section Supervisor for recycling. Not every trainee I sent down to the Section Supervisor was recycled, and I trusted the judgment of my supervisor to determine if a trainee needed a second chance. If the trainee returned to my flight, then I would not argue and reintegrate them back into the group with the understanding that they were on a short leash for discipline.

Trainees who were returned mostly became organized and ended up being top performers who never challenged any rules from that point forward. The lesson was instilled that we were not their mothers or fathers or teachers that would count down from ten then start over repeatedly. When I said something, they knew I meant it by the letter. I found that the trainees craved this structure in their lives. Many came from broken homes or bad situations where they had not faced challenges or discipline and they were looking for a change in their lives. The changes were not easy, and many struggled to adapt in the first few days. Their initial resistance would be overcome after they understood how things worked and the expectations for their jobs, and I found that if I gave them clear expectations of their roles they would perform well. I fully understood and related to these trainees' plight as my story was very similar, and the Air Force had saved my life, but it was not free and required dedication from their ends to secure their new lives as Airmen.

The intensity I displayed was due to how I felt about that fact, and I was lucky my instructor team was also very intense. We all trained within the framework of the acceptable training allowed by the Air Force with few exceptions. I cannot say we did not use colorful language to get our points across and I was probably the biggest violator of this rule. However, we did not abuse the rules and we never used language that demeaned any trainee directly.

I would always ask them a question like, "Are you a dumbass?"

The trainees would reply "No Sir."

I would then say, "Ok since you are not a dumbass, then you know better than to do…." and this would get the point across that they had messed up but were smart enough to fix it. Phrasing the statement in the form of a question helped prevent them from feeling like I was personally attacking them but allowed me to drive the point home in a forceful manner to make it a more emotional experience. Trainees learned faster through emotional experiences than they did from being told, and I was the Creative Director for emotional journeys for my flights.

I had a male flight that started training off wrong and they were learning very slowly. No matter how much physical training they received they were not responding to any corrective actions. The group had the most egos I had ever dealt with since becoming an instructor and I had to figure out a method to break through this barrier to begin their learning process. I decided I needed an extreme method to get their attention.

My teamie was training a female flight who entered training eager to learn and they were killing the males in every aspect of the process. Their dormitory was in perfect condition by the first day of the first week of training and all their inspections were nearly perfect. I decided I would use them as a training tool to wake up my male flight, and I formulated the plan with my teamie.

Ellis Franks "Always Leave An Airman Behind: A Real Story of Surviving The Crab Leadership Culture

The plan was to have the male flight stand on their chairs next to their wall lockers at attention while the female flight took a nap in their beds for a full hour. Then we would wake up the nappers and have them run through the proper dormitory set up while the males watched from their perches on the chairs. I would randomly command the females to face the males and give them a "war cry", and they never failed to provide the now sobbing males with the loudest screams you can imagine.

The females performed wonderfully, and they set a record for setting a dormitory up due to how pumped they were to show up their male counterparts. The entire process took about 1.5 hours, including their well-earned naps. The females filed out of the dormitory leaving the males crying on their chairs at the sheer humiliation of being shown up and their dorm looked the best it had ever looked. The group was devastated, and this gave me one last item to attend, and I gathered them around me in the day room to begin the learning process.

First thing I did was look at each one of them and make them tell me why they joined the military, who they were serving for, and who they were letting down back home if they failed. The conversation made them more emotional and by the end, the entire group was in tears. I took the opportunity to begin building them back up and instilling pride in their actions.

I began my motivational speech by stating, "Each one of you is important to the success of this team. You are all accustomed to your civilian lifestyles where the standards were lowered so you could all pass or earn a trophy, and those days are over. Your enemies are not lowering the standards, they are training and sacrificing 24 hours a day preparing to kill you if they get the opportunity. You must take your training just as serious, because in the next 12 months some of you will be face to face with our enemies, side by side with your wingmen, and you better be someone they can count on to do the job right the first time. I believe in each one of you, I know each one of you has 1000 percent more to give, and I will not let you just go through the motions of training to be ill-prepared for the challenges you will face soon. If you follow my lead you will become the top one percent of your peers and the future leaders of our Air Force…"

The flight had a renewed sense of pride in them. I gathered the student leaders and gave them instructions to take their elements down to the break area to make phone calls home and then prepare for the next day's activities. I left the flight to these instructions to give them time to think about what they had experienced. I also told the student leaders to talk as a team about their plans moving forward. The next day the team performed at a higher level and had more energy than they had previously shown, but they had a lot of training ahead to reinforce their new character habits.

I had essentially forced the group to move through the stages of group dynamics by creating an emotional situation that generated the "Why Are We Here Phase". Once the flight understood their mission and dropped their personal agendas, they were able to bond more quickly as a team. Their progress was outstanding, and they would become one of my "Honor Flights", the flights that were the top of their training cycles as graded by the Blue Ropes in many inspection areas over the course of their training, and they were honored in front of their families as the "best of the best" at their graduation parade.. I remember them as one of the finest marching flights I had ever trained, and they were known for their thunderous heel beat.

I also learned that not all training produced positive results and there were many missteps along the way as I tested various training methods to motivate the trainees. One failed training evolution resulted in one of my top trainees having a nervous breakdown and never graduating. The flight was a female flight and their

Dorm Chief was an older trainee who had said she was a business manager in her civilian life.

Since she was accustomed to managing people, she seemed like a natural choice for the Dorm Chief position which required managerial abilities to manage the dorm operations. She was responsible for managing the element leaders and all the detail leaders to ensure all dorm inspection items were always 100 percent compliant. She was also responsible for keeping the trainees aware of the upcoming schedule to ensure they were prepared for all the appointments and classes they had each day.

The Dorm Chief performed at an adequate level to start and I believed she had more potential as a leader. Unfortunately, she lacked self-confidence and as the training intensity increased, she collapsed under the pressures of the position. The final day she was the Dorm Chief, the team was being punished for failing an impromptu dorm inspection by my Section Supervisor.

I decided to conduct "Air Raid Drills" with the flight to enhance their productivity during dorm set up. The drills included the trainees starting in their beds under the covers as if they were sleeping and then the "air raid" sirens would go off and they would jump out of their racks to get on their uniforms and set up the dorm. I set a time limit of 30 minutes maximum for their time to be complete. Every time they failed, they were required to face extreme physical training regimen and then start over.

The dorm was rearranged in accordance with Air Force standards for training, but it was a mess when the air raid sirens went off each time. The instructors would trash the latrine, military term for the restroom and shower areas, by taking the brooms and wetting them with laundry detergent then scrubbing the mirrors, walls, doors, and all other surfaces we desired to be cleaned. The purpose was to give them something harder to clean, but also the laundry detergent thoroughly cleaned all the walls and floors making the dorm smell very fresh.

The trainees would jump out of their racks each time and go through the entire dorm set up from start to finish. The process was repeated for a full duty day with only breaks for the three meals of the day. The trainees were becoming very proficient at the dorm set up, but the Dorm Chief was crashing under the pressure of the air raid sirens and instructors yelling at them to pick up the pace.

Finally, after the dinner meal, the Dorm Chief collapsed on the latrine floor having a panic attack. She could not catch her breath and would not respond to our instructions. I had one of the element leaders call over the intercom to the front office that we had a trainee in distress from a panic attack and required an ambulance immediately. I had to think fast about the overall situation as the dorm was trashed from the drills and if leadership wanted, they could more than likely accuse me of maltraining.

Everything we had done was within the limits of the guidelines for training but overall the dorm looked like a warzone and I could not take the chance of losing this flight while awaiting an investigation. I got my element leaders together and explained I needed all the Dorm Chief's items she would need to be gathered for her trip to the hospital and I needed one very reliable trainee to be her escort. I then ordered a second element leader to get the Dorm Chief up down the stairs to await the ambulance to ensure they did not enter the dorm until it was in inspection order again.

The element leaders moved with a sense of urgency that I had not seen from them and this was the level of motivation I was attempting to instill with the drills. Unfortunately, now we were moving due to panic-stricken Dorm Chief and her training was now about over. The ambulance arrived and took her to the psychological ward of the hospital for evaluation. The flight completed the dorm set up in about 20 minutes and we all sat down in the dayroom to discuss the day's training.

I explained why we had trained hard and that we lost one of our leaders during the operation. I told them that this is how our jobs are in the military and we must perform no matter what casualties we have because our mission can never fail. The Dorm Chief was a casualty of our training on this day and the flight would experience many more losses during their careers, and they always must keep moving forward in their mission. I then told them I was proud of their improvements because they had cut their dorm set up time from about an hour to under 30 minutes which was better than I expected.

The Dorm Chief would return after two days in the hospital, but she was never the same. She had given up on herself due to the stress and her performance worsened each day. She was eventually recycled for failing inspections and then administratively discharged from the Air Force for failure to adapt to training. I always felt like I may have failed her by piling too much responsibility on her and if she had just been a regular member of the flight I wondered if she would have made it.

I had to realize that her failure could have potentially saved people's lives later because if she would have panic attacks because of dorm drills she would have issues when deployed to Iraq or Afghanistan when the bad guys were shooting mortars into your housing areas 24 hours a day. I had to put the loss out of my mind and move forward because we had done our job to weed out a weak link in the team.

Another failure I faced was a trainee I felt had unlimited potential. I put her in charge of the second hardest position in my flight, Dorm Guard Monitor, and she did a very good job overall. The Dorm Guard Monitor oversaw the Dorm Guard schedule and ensuring all trainees were trained in the proper procedures for the security of the dorm. The Dorm Guards would monitor all traffic in and out of the dorm and conduct safety inspections of outlets or lights during their shifts. The Dorm Guard log was the record we keep of all the inspections and I found it a complete mess one day and proceeded to yell at the Dorm Guard Monitor for her oversight.

The trainee responded under her breath just loud enough that I could hear, "Maybe I should just kill myself…"

I stopped yelling at her instantly and asked her to repeat her words. She refused to say it again and claimed she did not mean the words. Normally, I would test out the trainee's dedication to making a statement like that because 99.9999 percent of them were not serious and were making suicidal ideations only to get out of training. I felt something was different with this trainee as I got a feeling that made my skin tickle and I calmly began my checklist for suicide ideations.

I asked her to remove her shoestrings and canteen belt then assigned her a wingman to ensure her safety. I called the ambulance and had her sent to the hospital for evaluation. I had a bad feeling about her words and though I had many times before pressed other trainees more intensely about their intentions, I knew something was wrong with this situation. I am not sure if it was the way she mentioned killing herself or if it was just an intuition, but I knew she was serious in her words. I was surprised when she returned several days later and the doctors at the hospital cleared her for training. The trainee would graduate with my flight without any further issues and move on through technical training until she reached her first duty station.

I received an email from another member of that flight about a year later with the bad news that my former Dorm Guard Monitor had killed herself. I was devastated because I felt I had let her down. The doctors at the hospital had failed her because she had been identified and their professional opinion was that she was not serious, and this was not the correct diagnosis. I wrestled with the fact that she killed herself and I failed to stop it when I knew she was serious. Her suicide would affect me the remainder of my career and I would not forgive myself about it for many years.

I would get the chance at redemption shortly after I found out about her suicide when another trainee decided he could no longer take the burden of BMT. The trainee had been performing poorly since the day he had arrived at Lackland. He was the slowest member of the flight in every aspect of the training. His attitude was sad and unmotivated resulting in him getting a lot of attention from the instructor team.

One evening an element leader reported to me that a trainee in his element was saying he was going to kill himself if he was not allowed to go home. I instructed the element leader and Dorm Chief to take his shoestrings, canteen belt, and any medications he had then bring him to me. The trainee reported to my office crying that he wanted to go home. I lit him up immediately for his lack of military bearing and assuming his tears would influence me to go easy on him. I called my teamie from his dorm to come to assist me with the trainee and before he knew it there were two instructors giving him a masters class in stress tests.

The trainee continued crying that he just wanted to go home, and I responded "There are only three ways to leave basic training, 1. Cop Car – refusal to train, 2. Ambulance – hurt yourself like you have threatened, 3. Graduation – the fastest way to leave. I am not allowing you to hurt yourself so now you have two choices, what will it be, cop car or graduate?"

My teamie was a little more aggressive and was continually yelling at him for his loss of military bearing and inability to stop his crying. We escorted him down to the main office area in our squadron where the ambulance would come to get him. There was an additional instructor down there that joined in on the yelling at the quitter trainee and before long the trainee was making himself hyperventilate from the stress.

The ambulance arrived just as the trainee was getting the worst butt chewing of his life from three instructors. When they attempted to get his heart rate it was impossible to read it because he was so stressed out from the yelling. About that time, I got a feeling that I needed to change tactics with him, and I asked the other instructors to step back.

The trainee was sitting in a chair, slouched over with tears pouring out of his eyes and snot all over his face. I took a knee in front of him, something many instructors would consider demeaning to their ego, and told him that he was not killing himself, this was not an option, and he had only two more choices as I had explained before. If he refused to return to training I would have no other option but to call the Security Forces to come to pick him up for refusing a lawful order to return to training and he would spend months at Lackland in a similar situation as he was in awaiting his legal outcome for his case.

I explained that the fastest way to leave BMT was to graduate from basic training with his flight and I would make him a deal. If he would stick out the training and give his best effort always, then on graduation day after he had marched down the "bomb run" and had been officially sworn into the Air Force as an official Airman, then he would march up to me and give me one of two answers:

Answer number one: YES – he still could not take the stresses of training and wanted to leave.

Answer number two: NO – he had gained pride in himself and he wanted to remain in the Air Force.

The trainee considered his options and agreed to return to training. I told him I was not going to let him quit and I believed in his ability to make it through the training, but if in the end he still could not do it then I would do anything in my power to get him out of the military. His demeanor changed a slight bit, and he had stopped crying. I told him to go get his calling card and go call his family to tell them he was ok, and he was going to stick it out in training. I assigned a trainee to monitor him to ensure he did not attempt anything stupid when we were not watching him, and he left to make his phone call.

I never had another issue out of the trainee again and I put the deal out of my mind after a few days. He integrated back into the flight with no issues and he performed his duties without any problems for the duration of his training. The flight was set to graduate on 21 February 2003, and I had not thought of the trainee's issues since the night he had his breakdown. That set the stage for one of my most cherished memories of being an instructor.

The graduation parade was on a slightly rainy day in February making it wet and cold. Our flights were chosen to carry the national and state flags for the ceremony. They performed the honor with exact precision and after the parade was concluded we had to take inventory of all the flags then secure them in the storage building located on the parade grounds. I oversaw the detail for securing the flags into the storage building and I was juggling 120 Airmen who were eager to be released to their families whom they had not seen in about eight weeks. We had to account for all the flags first and ensure they were ready for the next week's ceremony prior to being released from our duties. Suddenly, a lady came bursting through the crowds making a direct path towards me and fell at my feet clutching my legs.

The lady was crying and repeatedly saying, "You saved my son's life, you save my son's life".

I had no idea who this lady was or what she was referring to and I attempted to get her to her feet with no luck. That was when the trainee came marching up to me with pride in his eyes and he stopped at attention and said "Sir Airman _____ reports as ordered. NO SIR!"

My mind searched for an answer to what was happening and finally, it registered to me that he was the trainee who had tried to quit in the first week of training. He had completed his training and was upholding his end of our deal by telling me that he was ready to stay in the Air Force. I then knew why his mother was crying at my feet and helped her up. The scene the two had made caused a crowd to form around us and several STAN TEAM members looked on with disdain for the awkward situation that they did not understand.

I told the mother to meet me at my office in the squadron and we could discuss the details of what had occurred. I then proceeded to complete my detail and returned to the squadron for the scheduled open house where I would meet all the new Airmen's families. The mother promptly showed up to the dormitory and I invited them into my office for a private talk about what the situation was about. I felt like I only had a piece of the story and was eager to find out why the family was so emotional about what had occurred. I had trained hundreds of trainees and this was the first time I had ever been accused of saving one's life.

The mother explained that the Airman had lost his father the year before he had enlisted in the Air Force and had fallen into a deep state of depression. He had refused to leave the house or eat food and she feared he would die from his depression. Shortly after, a recruiter had been visiting the young man and convinced him that joining the Air Force was the best thing for his life then signed him up and shipped him off to BMT. This is when he met me and quickly regretted his decision to join the Air Force. He was still suffering from the depression he had felt from his father's death and the stress of the first week of training made him want to quit. My deal with him had given him hope that he could have a positive change in his life and the fact that I had told him I believed in him and would not let him quit was the motivation he needed to move on with his life.

I am not sure why I had changed approaches that night early in training when hundreds of times before I had shipped off trainees like him the psychiatric ward. I remember having a feeling that I needed to not let him quit and that I needed to train him to be successful, so I went with that instinct. I have found that when you are a leader in the trenches with your people you will gain a cognitive advantage to be able to sense changes in your people or the organization if you have spent time preparing yourself through professional development. The more you study the art of leadership, the more you will be in tune with the energy of the teams you are leading, and you will be equipped for the changing dynamics of the situation. I do not believe that I would have used the method I chose with this trainee had I not been enthralled with the study of leadership over the two years prior to this occurring.

My biggest success when I was an MTI was getting my sister to join the Air Force. She had spent the first few years of my career alone in Georgia struggling as a single mother and needed an immediate change before she fell into the life her mother had shown her. She was not afraid to do whatever it took to ensure her daughter had the life that my sister never had, and this led her to fall into the same traps that most poor single moms find impossible to get out.

My sister had attempted to talk to an Air Force recruiter and the NCO had all but thrown her out of her office. The lazy recruiter heard she was a single mom and immediately stopped trying to recruit her because there was a lot more work required to qualify for single mothers due to custody issues with the children. The system was not fair for single mothers and when I heard about the dismissive encounter my sister had with the recruiter, I told her I would deal with them when I was home on leave in a few weeks.

The actions of this NCO recruiter were very common where the leaders would only attempt to do things that were easy and try to imply to other people that what they wanted to do was impossible. I personally experienced this both when I applied to become an MTI and also the final time I applied for Combat Control, and I was told by the personnel laggards that in both cases I was "not eligible to apply" but both times I did it anyway and I was accepted to both programs. My sister needed my tenacity and NCO knowledge to help her change her life and out of all the Airmen, I ever helped she was the most important.

The first day of my leave I reported to the local recruiting office that she had been kicked out of and I showed up intentionally not in uniform, unshaven, and inconspicuous as if I were a walk-in looking for information. I wanted to see how much integrity these recruiters had and when I arrived there was only a SrA in the office who gave me a once over before prejudging me as a candidate or whether he should continue surfing the internet. I was training for Combat Control and leading basic training physical fitness and I was ripped so he immediately started trying to recruit me.

The SrA spent about 30 minutes speaking a bunch of nonsense that he thought would impress a civilian recruit, and his pitch was horrid overall. He showed that he had a good bit of knowledge of what he was supposed to do but he obviously never applied his craft to perfect the sales pitch like the Marines had trained my former stepfather and recruiter. Finally, I stopped him mid-sentence to inform him his "Expeditionary Medal" was backwards on his service dress ribbon rack, and the colored ribbon had a sequence of colors that went in a specific order and should be displayed "red to the right".

The SrA recruiter responded annoyedly, "what are you some kind of drill sergeant or something?"

I answered, "As a matter of fact I am an Air Force NCO and I am an MTI, so to answer your question YES!"

The SrA turned pale and stood up immediately. His entire demeanor changed now that he realized I was not some idiot off the street as he had initially addressed me. I informed him that he was full of crap and I wanted to speak to his supervisor. He looked concerned and called her on her work mobile phone. She informed him she was almost back to the office from her appointments with recruits and I agreed to wait in her office until she arrived.

The TSgt recruiter arrived shortly after and greeted me warmly. She seemed to be squared away and both to the recruiters were highly interested in what it was like to be an MTI. I allowed them to ask me questions for a short while before explaining why I had come to their offices. I told them that my sister had spoken to the TSgt and was all but kicked out because she was a single mom, so I was there to figure out a tangible plan to get her into the service. I explained that unlike my sister I was not leaving until we had a plan that my sister could execute to enter the service.

The recruiters attempted to tell me once again that she was not a valid candidate because she was a single mom. I explained to them that I did not care about the barriers to entry that were too hard for them, I only wanted to know the circumstances that would allow her to be allowed to enlist. The problems most people face when there is a challenge outside the norms of their duties is that if something is difficult, they will lie to themselves and say it is "impossible". I had seen this trend with many NCOs I dealt with and office worker types were the biggest violators of this issue.

The recruiters and I came up with three scenarios that would allow my sister to enlist;

1. She could give up her custody to her daughter's father

2. She could give up custody to a third party

3. She could enter the service if she was married

There was only one true option that my sister would accept, and I told the recruiters I would return to brief her on the situation then we would be back immediately with the plan of action. I left the offices and met with my sister. I knew she would not like the answers I got for her, but we at least had options that she could explore.

We decided that her getting married was the best thing she could do because she would not have to give up custody of her child. The fact the Air Force shuns single moms, an extremely motivated category of people many times, was more proof of the service's inability to see barriers as opportunities. The rules made little sense because the service was filled with single parents due to the chronic divorce crisis the operations tempo created, but if the recruit was a single parent before joining no matter how qualified they were the Air Force recruiters and the service, in general, discriminated against them.

My sister approached her guy friend at the time about the opportunity she had and what she needed in return from him. Luckily, he accepted her impromptu wedding proposal and they were married shortly afterward making her eligible to enter the service. Had this been left to the recruiters they would have continued to discriminate against her out of laziness and this was not emblematic of what the Air Force core values represented. My sister was one of the lucky single mothers because she had a tenacious, NCO, drill instructor brother who called out the bullshit when it was given, and we got her all set for her new life in the military.

I also warned the recruiters against putting her in asinine jobs that would give her little chance at a career after her service like I had received when I joined. My job selection was useless in the civilian world overall, and I told them I wanted her to be placed in a shortlist of jobs that I had researched that I found gave substantial financial bonuses for enlisting and re-enlisting, but also gave her transferable skills in the civilian market. She would be selected to become a computer network programmer and after she completed her enlistment, she would go on to have a successful career with Verizon as a network engineer making well over six-figure salaries and changing her life forever.

Ellis Franks "Always Leave An Airman Behind: A Real Story of Surviving The Crab Leadership Culture

I was proud of my sister for having the courage to enlist in the Air Force because I knew the mindset she had coming into the service because I had mostly lived the same life before I joined as well. She attended basic training in the same squadron I had attended when I was a recruit and I had the pleasure of monitoring her progress from afar while she was in training. I would also pull her out of briefings to spend a little time with her because I knew how it felt to be alone in that cold training environment. She would successfully complete all her training and be assigned to a very nice location in Hawaii for her entire enlistment before separating and beginning her real life. She had learned a lesson that would propel her forward in her life that we in the leadership world called "The Law of the Price Tag". The principle means that in order to achieve the success you must engage in the uncomfortable things in life that create personal growth to be able to enjoy the rewards of true success. My sister was never the type of person who would have joined the military, but she did it for her daughter making the best of her situation to change both of their lives forever.

In my own career, I was distancing myself further from my peers in my awareness of leadership and the more I studied, the more disenchanted I became with the Air Force leadership methods that were in practice.

The service paid hundreds of millions of dollars to train all NCOs in several levels of leadership from the tactical level to strategic leadership for Senior NCOs, but the practice of leadership was different from the courses everyone attended. The trend seemed to be for the NCOs to skate through their mandatory training to gain promotion then throw out the knowledge when they graduated. I could not bring myself to do this and I had a huge thirst for more knowledge that I never could seem to quench.

My efforts were not going unnoticed outside of my unit and one day while waiting to take my flight to eat lunch I was given a "once-over" by a sharp "blue rope" instructor who said he was from the MTI Recruiting Team. He asked me a few questions that I did not think too much about at the time. He commented on how sharp my uniform looked and then thanked me for my time and left. I did not know who he was or why he was talking to me. Most MTIs were not real friendly towards each other and this NCO was extra friendly.

Several days later I was called to my Superintendent's office with my Section Supervisor and informed I had been chosen as one of four MTIs to be featured in the Air Force's new MTI Recruiting video they were planning to shoot. I would be a featured instructor and my testimonies about pushing flights would be used to recruit other NCOs from the Air Force to volunteer to become MTIs. The opportunity was huge and there were a lot of resentful instructors that were not happy that I was chosen. Those opinions did not matter to me as I accepted the chance to be featured as one of the elites of a core of NCOs that represented a fraction of the entire Air Force.

  The video shoots were a new experience and I had to juggle my flight responsibilities with this extra duty. There was no relief as we had no reserve instructors to cover for me and me somehow managed to meet all my obligations. The Air Force film crews filmed the four chosen instructors teaching classes, marching flights and shot a personal interview with each of us before cutting the video to meet their desired time constraints. I made the final cut of the video for my interview where I explained how all the long hours and stress of the job was rewarded by the feeling of accomplishment I received when my Airmen marched down the bomb run and the pride they displayed when showing off their accomplishments to their families. There was no better feeling than changing these young Airmen's lives and I explained it took the entire team of instructors working together towards the same goal to make it happen. The new recruits would learn that the job was going to be the most challenging of their lives and that they would have to create strong bonds with their future teamies in order to survive.

I was by this time fully convinced that professional development was the key to success for all Airmen. It really bothered me that NCOs at all levels across the Air Force refused to implement leadership principles they were taught in their Professional Military Education courses. The leaders I had worked for considered drinking beer at the NCO Club as mentoring their people. Very few people were taking professional development seriously and most thought that their rank signified they were leaders by right.

I had set forth on the path of becoming an MTI looking for like-minded people and never found what I was seeking. I was growing unhappy and I was unsure I would find my place anywhere in the Air Force. Then one day I decided to start training for the job that I had joined the Air Force to do but had failed to qualify. I researched what I needed to do to become a Combat Controller and then created a plan to qualify for the career field.

Facing My Biggest Fears

My quest to find my rightful place in the Air Force led me back to the idea that I should try out for Combat Control one last time. The career field was touted as the best of the Air Force, and every member of the career field could not just join, they were required to volunteer, be selected, tested, and only around 10 percent of all candidates would don to coveted scarlet beret worn by CCT members.

I began training at the Skylark Pool where the Pararescue teams trained and it was also the place I had failed my initial PAST Test while I was in basic training. I was thrilled about the opportunity to be part of the most elite Special Operations units in the world and to be surrounded by high performing team members. I knew I had a lot of work to do to be ready for the challenges that I faced, but I was determined to find my niche in the Air Force to fulfill my desire to be the best. My biggest challenge was the water confidence training because of the mental trauma my mother's drug addict friends had caused me in the pool where they almost drowned us many times.

Growing up with a drug addict parent meant that we spent a lot of time hanging out with low-life people in crazy places. I remember a favorite hangout for my mother's friends was the local Howard Johnson hotel. The low-end hotel had a pool that the kids could play in while the adults got high and drunk in the room or hotel bar. When the adults were done getting high, they would come out to the pool and harass the kids by tossing us from one person to the other without allowing us to catch our breath.

I do not believe they even realized that they were nearly drowning us as they repeated the act with each kid. The experience was so bad that I hated going to the pool or any water for the next few years of my life. The next time I would swim was when I took my first Combat Control PAST Test when I was in basic training. I had to face my fears to be able to qualify for the career field and therefore I began training about four hours per day at the pool.

When I first started my preparation, I could not complete the required 1500-meter finned swim. My technique for swimming was horrid because I had never been trained on how to properly swim. I decided I needed to get a few books read about the proper swimming techniques. I used the books to perfect my swim stroke and improve my efficiency in the water. The anxiety I first felt gradually passed and soon I could move through the water with ease.

A Pararescue trainee approached me about my training and offered to help me with my techniques to which I gladly accepted. The guy was an administrative holdover in his training pipeline because he had broken a team rule and was being evaluated for future training or release from the program. He would later be allowed proceed in training and was featured in the Discovery Channel documentary "Rescue Warriors" episodes about his difficulties with the medical training portion of the pipeline located at Kirtland AFB, New Mexico.

He trained me on underwater confidence tasks and how to maintain my composure while completing tasks or being harassed. I was able to become super-efficient underwater reducing my 25-meter underwaters to three strokes which helped me conserve oxygen and gave me an ability to stay underwater longer. I had overcome the first barrier to my training success, and I would spend about two years preparing for my PAST test to ensure I was completely ready for the training.

One of my peers and former classmates from MTIS decided he wanted to join me in training for the career field. He had failed in his first attempt at Pararescue, just after hell week, when he first entered the military and believed that he was now ready to transition to Special Operations as well. He would join me in my daily training sessions at the pool, gym, and runs as we prepared for the challenges ahead.

SSgt Chad Rosendale was fellow MTI and worked in our section for our squadron. He was assigned to another team of instructors and we were on differing weeks of training the entire time we were assigned to BMT. We had become friends while we were students making our way through the MTIS curriculum and would study together frequently for all our tests. We also hung out in our minimal amount of idle time and would frequent a local hangout called "The Fox & Hound". Chad was an intense instructor and very sharp Airman who had been selected for MTI duty as a Senior Airman. He was one of less than 10 non-NCOs who were instructors when we graduated MTIS. He was strong-willed and not afraid to take on a challenge. He had endured the worst training situation in his final six weeks of MTIS when he was assigned to the previously mentioned SSgt Andrade that I had nearly had a fight over the dining facility procedures.

When we first became friends, I was married, and my wife had left just before I started training for Combat Control. I probably started training because of her leaving with our daughter who I had not seen in about a year at this point. Chad was single at first but would later marry one of his former trainees, and this would cause quite the gossip scandal as people speculated that they had messed around while she was in his flight. I am very certain that she began emailing him once she arrived at her first duty station because he had asked me what I thought about the intent of her emails around that time. Despite the people's gossip nothing was ever done about their marriage and they proved to be a very successful couple that is still together today.

Chad and I began training together for our journey into Air Force Special Tactics and daily we would meet to train for about 3 hours. Chad was not the strongest runner and was strong in the pool because he had already endured Pararescue training he had good insight on what to expect for our long pipeline of training. I used his knowledge of the program to work towards overcoming my shortfalls in training and quickly improved my abilities in the pool. The hardest part was getting past the mental fears that were ingrained in me from my time as a kid when the intoxicated adults used us as a beach ball many times. I was not bad in the water, but it paralyzed me when I attempted underwater confidence drills making it hard to complete simple tasks.

I knew that the water was the make or break training evolution for most Combat Control trainees. I made it my focus to overcome all the mental barriers that I had to complete to excel in the water. I started coming to the pool for extra sessions and was training about four to five hours a day in my water confidence tasks. I started to improve rapidly and before long the dreaded underwaters became second nature to complete.

The underwater event consists of a trainee starting at one end of the 25-meter pool and completing a length underwater to the other wall by touching the bottom crease of the wall then ascending at an angle towards the surface of the water. The trainee then sprints back to the starting point using a freestyle stroke and must arrive before the interval time is exceeded. The starting intervals for training were about one and a half minutes to complete the repetition before the trainee was ordered to start the next repetition. The faster you returned to the starting point the more rest time you earned. The key was to return as fast as possible then spend the remaining time lowering your heart rate for your next length underwater.

Most trainees that failed this evolution were unable to lower their heart rates and burned up all their oxygen while underwater. The initial response the body autonomically had was to create anxiety in the mind to alert you that you were running on low oxygen levels and it would tell you to surface immediately. The fact is that you are not really running out of oxygen when you feel this, and it is a buildup of carbon dioxide that you are feeling in the lungs making it seem like your chest is burning for air. The trick was to blow out some bubbles slowly as you were moving to lower your carbon dioxide levels and reduce the burning effects and anxiety you experienced. I would also sing songs in my head to take my mind off the anxious feelings that built up as I moved underwater.

Completing an underwater lap is all about proper technique. I used the knowledge my Pararescue trainee friend had showed me and Chad monitored my stroke to give me feedback on wasted movements. I was able to reduce my overall body movements to two and a half strokes to complete an entire underwater length across the pool. The reduced movements meant I finished my repetition with the maximum amount of oxygen and a lower heart rate making it easier to complete successive repetitions or travel farther underwater. I peaked in training to be able to complete over 150 meters underwater and then put on my scuba gear before ascending to the surface of the water. All the training had improved my skill level to many times the expected graduation standards for the Combat Control School minimums and I was ready to join my first team in training.

The entire time Chad and I were training we had constant appointments for medical testing to clear us for Special Operations duty. We were required to be certified that we were fit enough to conduct freefall operations from altitudes above 30,000 feet, military scuba operations, and overall fitness levels that were off the charts for the average Air Force member. Combat Controllers represented significantly less than one percent of the total Air Force and the medical professionals were charged with ensuring all candidates met the strictest of health readiness levels making the process tedious.

The process required us to submit a package that evaluated the whole person for mental, physical, and psychological toughness as well as looking at our past performance of our duties to ensure only the best trainees entered training. I ensured my package was the best and solicited several of my former commanders to give me letters of recommendation for Special Operations duty. I received recommendations from three four-star generals that stated I was a top-performing Airman and was an excellent choice for becoming a Combat Controller. These letters were a sore subject for my chain of command who viewed my bold actions requesting the letters from such high-ranking Air Force members negatively, but the career path I was choosing was for the Airman who was not afraid to take the risks required to achieve the highest level of rewards and I was honored to receive the letters. The original copies were lost during one of my permanent change of duty station moves and it saddens me as these letters were from men who will be remembered in history for their efforts throughout the war on terrorism.

The package was completed for all testing aspects and we were required to complete the final physical test to ensure we were fit enough to join Combat Control. The average trainee is required to complete a 500-meter swim, 1.5-mile run, 2 minutes each of pushups, sit-ups, and pullups while meeting a minimum number of "correct" repetitions to qualify. I highlight the word correct because the average Air Force member would not complete a single correct repetition for Special Tactics due to a poor technique of the exercise. Chad had warned me that the cadre who was going to test us would be sticklers for correct form and that we should overemphasize the reps to ensure it gets counted and not waste reps and energy.

We were notified we would take was the Combat Controller annual certification test and it was harder than the basic PAST test. This test included a 1500-meter finned swim, 3-mile run, one 25-meter underwater, and the calisthenics as mentioned. The test was double the distance of the basic one for both the swim and run meaning more energy lost for the last few exercises.

Luckily, we had prepared for the graduation standard, not the entry one or we would have failed epically.

I was very confident in the run and pushups and sit-ups, but the swim and pullups were my weaker areas. I had consistently exceeded standards for my swim times for the past few months, but I had not completed it with the stress of Special Tactics operators evaluating me. I also had the memories of the past two failures when I had not made the minimum times. The difference now was I had spent many months training for the tests. I had been performing at the graduation standards for months at this point. The uncertainty caused a slight degree of anxiety. I made a choice to keep pushing no matter what to make it to the end.

Chad was very confident about all the events except for the run. I promised him if he helped me make the swim, I would not leave him for the run and push him to the end. We made a pact to push each other to succeed. We scheduled our test date because we were ready. It was time to begin officially on our next journey.

The test date came fast, and we met at 6 am at the Skylark pool to start with our swim. When we arrived, we were met by three Combat Control School instructors who briefed us on the day's activities and instructed us to get ready to begin. Once the testing started the entire process was under an overall time limit and if exceeded the test was a failure. We would move from event to event with a minimum amount of time in between to test our overall fitness levels.

We got dressed in our swimming gear and proceeded to the pool to start. We were surprised when we found out the current class of Pararescue trainees would be training in the pool while we tested. The team was in their early stages of the course before hell week and had over 100 trainees in the water at once. The sounds of that many trainees swimming were overwhelming and created a more stressful swimming atmosphere than I was used to in my preparations. Chad and I were given one lane to swim in and this also created more stress as we had to constantly be alert not to hit one another as we completed our laps.

The first few laps Chad was slightly ahead of my pace and the wake of his movements made it more difficult for me to swim and I slowed my pace slightly to let him clear me by a good distance. The Pararescue trainees were completing a task called "under-overs" where they would complete a set of underwaters wearing fins but instead of taking a break in between they would restart again immediately. Some of their team members were messing with Chad and me from the bottom of the pool making faces and gestures to break our concentration. The first 500 meters of the swim was stressful from the noise, the sheer number of bodies in the water, and dodging Chad constantly in the lane. My mind began the routine of making excuses to quit. I fought them back as best I could. I just lost myself in the technique of the motions of finning and before long I was in the zone. My pace was good and well ahead of the minimum standard of 36 minutes maximum time.

Chad finished his swim at about 30 minutes and got to begin his rest period. I would complete my swim at 32 minutes and was relieved. I had overcome the single event that I had failed twice since joining the Air Force. The underwater test was very simple and we both completed it with ease. Next up was Chad's hardest event and I could see he was visibly concerned about passing it. I reassured him I would pace him to make it. We dressed in our running gear then headed to meet the Combat Controllers at the track.

We began our runs and settled into the agreed-upon pace. I kept pushing Chad to keep going each lap and he did a good job keeping pace. Our goal was to maintain no less than a 7:30-minute mile pace to ensure we completed our run time under 23 minutes. The times would not be Combat Controller level good, but it would pass and get us into the training. Chad struggled throughout the run and showed his doubts. I did my best to encourage him to keep pushing. The Combat Controllers called me out for not running at my own pace, but I could not leave Chad behind. Once we completed enough laps at a pace where Chad could not fail, I picked up my pace for the remainder of the run. I completed the time well ahead of the minimum and Chad finished about two minutes behind me.

The next exercises were easy to max out and we passed the pushups and sit-ups with ease. The dreaded pull-ups were the last exercise. Chad and I were both tired but pumped for the last test. The minimum total we had to complete was six. This may seem like a low number if you went straight into a gym and attempted it without worrying about form. We also learned that chin-ups were to be required which was different from how we had trained and more difficult. Chad and I had trained to do pullups with our palms facing us. Now we were instructed that they only would let us do it with palms facing away. The small change completely changed the muscles used to complete each rep. Added to the difficulty the Combat Controllers informed us they expected us to perform the exercises without using any momentum as most people did the exercise. We would lift ourselves up with our chins fully clearing the top of the bar by an inch then they would tell us to lower and that would be a rep. I was nervous that the changes were going to cause me to fail, but I was determined to make it.

Chad completed his chin-ups with ease and did about 12 reps total. I mounted the bar and began my test. The first few reps were easy, but I was spent from all the other exercises making the third rep difficult. I struggled through rep number four and five barely clearing the minimum distance over the bar. I only needed one more rep to pass. I pulled as hard as I could but did not clear it enough for the Combat Controller to count it. I had come this far and used up what felt like my last energy. Failure seemed evident. I pulled as hard as I could. The memory of the first two failures flashed into my mind. I got a burst of adrenaline as I pulled hard to the top of the bar. I struggled to clear it. The Combat Controller shouted at me "not high enough keep going higher". I pulled harder. I tapped into energy I did not realize I had inside me. With my last exertion I cleared the bar. He counted it. I passed for the first time in three attempts.

The journey to this moment had been filled with a lot of detours in my career that were necessary to give me the skills to realize my dream of becoming a Combat Controller. I had learned that preparation was paramount to success along the way and set forth to prepare harder than I had ever done for anything else in my life. I would use these lessons as the basis for success for the rest of my life. Now I was done with all the qualification testing for the job I had joined the Air Force to do and I had to wait for the final approval from the Air Force to begin the training.

If you have ever dealt with a government agency, then you are aware of the sloth-like pace things get accomplished. We submit our packages immediately upon passing the PAST test and our wait began. We had completed all our medical requirements and received our Class III Flying & Special Operations Physical approval and the paperwork was sitting in an office somewhere in the Air Force. The time crept by and months passed without any update. Calls to the program representatives were a waste of time as they referred us back to the online platform that showed our packages as "Pending Review". I was certain our approval would come any day, but time dragged on and we never were notified about the approval for months.

I woke up one morning and went through my normal routine of the day. I checked my online platform and it finally updated, "Approved for Retraining 1C2X1, Combat Control". I was finally going to be a Combat Controller. I was elated and could not wait to begin the first course. I received my school date to start in a few weeks and Chad was still showing as "Pending" online.

We had hoped to start together but now that was not a guarantee. Luckily, Chad received his approval a few days later and was assigned to the same team as me.

Our training kicked up a notch as we made the final preparations for one of the toughest military selection courses in the world. Each day we spent three or four hours in the pool working on our distance swimming and water confidence. When I had first started training in the pool, I was not a very strong swimmer. Two years prior to being selected for training I had decided I was going to give Special Tactics one last try and set about learning all the skills that would be required of me in the training. I was extremely lucky to be stationed at Lackland Air Force Base at the time because both the Pararescue and Combat Control selection course was at the base. I would use the trainees that I interacted with to gain insight on the training as well as learn the techniques required for each water exercise the Special Tactics cadre would use to weed out the weak performers.

I bought a book titled "Breakthrough Swimming" and used it to learn the proper method of swimming. This book was very important in the beginning to help me learn proper techniques because my swimming was not good enough to even qualify for the training when I started. Slowly I gained confidence in the water and my swim times began dropping quickly the more I executed proper form and gained more repetitions in the pool.

My weakest area and area of concern was the underwater confidence training. Growing up I learned to fear being submerged underwater. When I would submerge underwater my mind instantly would generate irrational fear and I would not be able to stay under long due to the anxiety it created.

The training I was set to face would require me to spend long periods underwater without oxygen and all while a Special Tactics instructor would be harassing me. Water confidence harassment had several levels of intensity starting with the student just performing a task underwater and going all the way to full harassment where the instructors splashed, dunked, hit, and otherwise created mental chaos for the trainees being tested. Full harassment was the make or break moment for most Special Tactics trainee's success. The trainees who could mentally withstand the test of nearly drowning would make it to the end and the others would all take the easy route by quitting in training.

Every person has their own breaking points for stress. The training I was getting ready to endure pushed everyone past their comfort zones to a point that the person did not even realize they could achieve. The instructors were experts in getting more effort out of a person than the individual thought possible. If the trainee did not step up to the challenge then their training would be over. While training for my upcoming selection course I made some egregious errors in my preparations that would be painful when we started.

The first lesson I had to take on the chin was that there should never be a set number of repetitions that you do in for exercises. The Special Tactics instructors would make you do endless repetitions that far exceeded the number of reps the normal athlete. I thought I had trained hard for each one of the standard exercises that were common for the selection course but found out my mentality was wrong. Flutter kicks was an exercise I thought I was very strong, but I had trained to be able to complete about 100 four-count repetitions. The first time one of our instructors dropped us to do them we spent about an hour on this one exercise. Every one of my teammates was smoked by this workout and to make matters worse the instructor was doing the exercise the entire time without hardly breaking a sweat.

He made us all look bad and as he was calling the repetitions, he began taunting us. He began making statements in cadence with the exercise like "One, Two, Three,…why, are, you, whining" or "One, two three,

...crying, like, a baby..." and our favorite "one, two, three,...bunch, of, fucking, pussies..." There were many clever ways they would try to mentally mess with us and show us up.

No one who came to the course was prepared for the full wrath of the instructors. Their team was all seasoned veterans fresh from the battlefields in Afghanistan or Iraq. They were being given some downtime due to their top-level performance. Our primary instructor had been in the battle on Roberts Ridge where the Air Force lost two heroes, TSgt John Chapman (Medal of Honor) and SrA Jason Cunningham (Air Force Cross). Both heroes sacrificed their lives to ensure the Navy SEALs and Army Rangers they supported survived. Our instructors knew what it really took to be a Special Tactics operator. They were dedicated to ensuring no one passed that they thought did not meet these standards.

Our team started out with about 35 trainees which included our team leader Captain Lungren, assistant team leader Lieutenant Connelly, Staff Sergeant Rosendale, and I served as the team first sergeant. We mostly had new Airmen who had just graduated basic training and thought this job was cool. Most of the trainees who started with us were gone before the third day due to them not being able to handle the stress of the physical and mental events we endured.

The first day of training we spent a good part of the morning getting dorm rooms and being issued gear. Our team was required to attend an orientation class or two after we settled into our training routines. The first day required us to take another PAST test to enter training. The test was easy for me, but we lost several team members who failed at least one of the events cutting our team numbers to the twenties. This day was easy but was not representative of what was to come.

The second day of training was the real start to our course. We began the day with a pool training session followed by a couple of classes on the skills we would be required to learn for qualification. Then all hell broke loose in the late morning. The Special Tactics cadre gave orders for our team leader to assemble us in an open field near the training center. Our team quickly formed up for the unknown evolution we were about to do. The team stood nervously in our formation as the cadre slowly walked out of the building with their megaphones in hand. Nothing good ever came from a Special Forces operator conducting training using a megaphone, and today was going to be no different.

The Air Force Special Tactics pipeline is extremely long and multiple teams were on-site in between training to stay in shape as well as assist the cadre in training the lower level teams. There was no team lower than us on this day and we were about to receive the first test of our heart and will to become Combat Controllers. While we were watching the cadre, the other teams had pulled out water hoses to the field and began spraying us all down with water, soaking our battle dress uniforms completely and making every movement we made cumbersome through the weight of the water the uniform retained.

The cadre started out slowly with us by starting the evolution off with some grass drills which consisted of a multitude of calisthenic exercises designed to get your muscles burning past failure. The exercises all required us to hit the deck, roll over, jump to our feet, squat, fall, roll, and any other variation you can imagine. We did bear crawls, crab crawls, log rolls, buddy carries, reverse crab crawls, reverse bear crawls, and other creative exercises that simulated us dragging our teammates out of the line of fire. The only difference was there was no one shooting at us with guns, instead, they used water hoses on full blast shooting water into your eyes, ears, nose, and mouth. The cadre would intentionally ask you a question and as you answered the water would blast down your throat. This made it impossible to talk. The more you could not answer the more, they applied the water to stress you out.

The field became a muddy mess and soon we were ordered to move to a new location for a new test. This new "mission" was for the team to infiltrate the swim training facility without using the entrance. The bonus of not being allowed to walk on the ground. We were about 100 yards away from the pool. The field was sometimes used as a softball field so there were a backstop and a fence that ran along the perimeter. The team leader decided that this was our entry method into the pool. The entire team would have to make it inside without anyone touching the ground or we all started over at the beginning.

This sounds very straight forward. It should have been simple, except for the fact that the entire team was completely soaking wet and all our muscles were already at failure. We found it very tough to get a grip on the fencing. Some weaker team members were making life harder than it needed to be by constantly falling off the fence. This forced us all back to the start. Every trainee was carrying their rucksack full of our personal gear and the water hoses never relented to add to our difficult task. The restarts happened a half dozen times before the entire team successfully made it into the pool training area. Once inside the pool training area the

Special Tactics Commandant was waiting for us and instructed immediately "Prepare to enter the water!"

The command was familiar as it was the command given to each team prior to a long pool training session. The difference this time was that the entire team was in full battle dress uniform including our boots. The look of despair immediately took over the weak swimmers' faces as they realized they were about to start pool training in full gear. Many of the weaker swimmers struggled in the minimal swim attire we wore that consisted of skimpy shorts and a t-shirt, now they were going to do a full-blown swim evolution in their uniforms.

The team quickly stowed our rucksacks and took our places on the gunnel of the pool and waited for instructions. The Commandant instructed us that we were to complete a timed 1500-meter freestyle swim in full battle dress uniform and that the swim was timed and graded.

He gave the order. "Enter the water".

The team sounded off in unison "Entering the water Sergeant", then rolled into the pool over our right shoulder simulating an entry into the water wearing scuba tanks. Each team member surfaced and gave the "Ok Sergeant" hand signals and we backed up to the pool wall for further instructions.

The pool erupted in a frenzy on the command "Go" as each trainee fought for pool space. The sound of nearly 30 people thrashing about in the water is a sound that not many people understand. The sounds are nothing like training in a calm pool at your local gym and the chaos could overwhelm you if you did not calm your mind to focus on the task at hand. My theory was being out front was the less crazy position. I pushed harder than I ever had to get some distance from the struggling team members who could be a potential danger if they freaked out.

I quickly took a big lead on the team by a full length and got into my groove as best I could. The difference of swimming in swim gear and full uniform is there is added weight each stroke from the excess water retained by the uniform. Uniforms fit a certain way when you wear them and when you add water plus motion to them it makes it almost impossible to move. Some strokes I nearly swam out of my battle dress top as air continued to get into it making a huge air bubble of the wet uniform where my normal breathing space once was located. I just stuck to my training and went through the technique of each stroke to calm my mind and ensure I was not losing technique because of the chaos.

REACH – PULL DEEP – TOUCH HIP – REACH WITH OPPOSITE ARM AS FAR AS POSSIBLE – REPEAT

The swim seemed to be in slow motion as team members began to panic in the water after a few laps. I was in a very controlled groove with my technique when I reached out with a stroke only to slam my hand against something hard and sharp.

The Commandant had conducted impromptu rucksack inspections and found several rucks not having all the mandatory items required to reduce the weight they were carrying. The hard, sharp object I hit my hand on was someone's rucksack floating in my lane where it had been thrown by a now angry Commandant. I took a second to look around to access the situation and found a mess in the pool.

The Commandant poured the contents of nearly 30 rucksacks into the pool and items floated all over or sank to the bottom. The scene was sensory overload as a few hundred items bobbed, floated, or slowly sank to the bottom of the pool. I could see boots, clothing items, food items, water bottles, extra socks, scuba gear, and a bunch more items littering every inch of the pool. I concentrated on my stroke and now had to pay attention to floating debris that could injure me as I continued knocking out the laps.

I found out the hard way that finishing first was not always the best as I completed my final length, I heard the cadre say "Good overachiever, now let's see how long it takes you to drown…"

I was ordered to swim back to the deep end of the pool and tread water until the remainder of the team completed all their laps. Some trainees were not even half-finished with their swims as they concentrated more on how much it all sucked than just knocking out the reps. Trainees were trying to leave the pool without finishing and were met with a boot to their back, head, hands, or whatever body parts they stuck out of the pool water to escape. The lesson was to never quit until your mission is done and the reality of drowning for a few weak team members was getting higher by the minute.

I tread water for what seemed like another hour when the cadre collected the team in the deep end for a team water-treading exercise for another extended time. I had already been treading water for a long time. I had gone through cycles of cramping a few times. I was more tired than I had ever been. I was struggling to keep two trainees above water because they could no longer tread water. I would tread under the water bobbing up periodically to take my own breath.

My survival instinct was to let them go and worry about myself, but the leadership instinct inside me never let them go. While I kept the group together the team leader had a few stronger swimmers collecting all the gear that had sunk to the bottom of the pool. The Commandant told us we would tread water until every rucksack met the minimum standards we were always instructed to carry. He scolded us about how we were failures because we had "deployed" without our required gear and we were combat ineffective. The leaders got the brunt of the harassment as we were charged with ensuring all our people were meeting standards.

My punishment was realistically a break from the real challenge of treading water since I was the first finished with the swimming, I had been treading water for over an hour. The Staff Sergeant cadre called me up onto the side of the pool and instructed me that I was to do flutter kicks with my fins on while singing the Air Force song. What he omitted was he was going to fill my scuba mask up with water and place the running hose in my mouth on full blast.

I took a deep breath and laughed inside. I had trained for this moment. My mind wandered back to a memory of something crazy I had done while preparing for training.

One morning at 0200, I could not sleep. The stress of working as a basic training instructor was very high and my physical training regime was also intense. This was compounded by the large amounts of caffeine that I, and most instructors, lived off during training. Now I could not get to sleep and decided to take a run. My run training was strong, and I always attempted to do things to make it harder. I sat on the steps putting on my running shoes thinking about what I could do to make the run challenging. I had a big idea – gas mask run, with water flooded mask. I linked up to my two Siberian huskies, grabbed my gas mask and took off to the running trail.

Running at 0200 is very peaceful. There is no stress on the running trail for a normal run. The late-night runs gave me a chance to clear my mind and focus on figuring out the things that I needed to do to test myself. It was just me and my dogs out on the entire military base as I warmed up with a few miles. Then the time for the test came. I donned the gas mask, filled it with as much water as it would hold and ran.

Running with a gas mask on is already challenging. Doing it with it full of water at 2 am was insane as I could barely see or breath. I looked around and still, no one was out. It was just me. No one would see what I did if I looked stupid. If I broke my leg, I was alone. I told myself this was the crazy stuff they would do to me in training. I needed to be crazier to survive the dreaded 10 percent graduation rate I faced.

Now here I was on the side of the pool, mask flooded, water hose in my mouth and I laughed a little as the memory of all the 2 am training sessions I had done flashed through my head. I sang a few lines of the Air Force song. The cadre realized I was on a break and he kicked me into the pool again. I was told to remove the fins and get back to treading water. Now I just had these giant scuba fins I had to keep ahold of while I did it.

The team leader got all the rucks squared away after what seemed like forever. We were ordered out of the pool. We gathered our gear and formed up as required. A younger cadre then screamed "Follow me…" then took off on a sprint through the fields. We ran for a few miles before he stopped us and gave us a new mission.

The cadre pointed to the ground and there was a manhole cover. He told us there was only one correct exit and we were ordered to go underground and find our way to our next waypoint for this training evolution. The entire team climbed down into the manhole into a very cramped, dark space. If they were testing our team on fearing tight spaces and the dark this was the perfect mission. We could not see anything we just communicated and moved forward towards where the team leader instructed us to go. I am not sure how long it took us to find the exit, but I was last coming out of what seemed to be a sewer drain that dropped into a mostly hidden ditch.

I could see the team low crawling across a field in this covered ditch as the cadre sprayed them with more water from their infinitely long water hoses that they had in every area we trained. The ditch filled with water up to our mouths and noses turning every team member this odd, brown sludge color, as the mud stuck to us like sticky honey. The Staff Sergeant cadre that had attempted to "punish" me in the pool was on me as soon as I popped out of the sewer drain. He was spraying me with the water hose and ridiculing me about being a basic training instructor.

He kept saying "You do not have to be here sergeant, you can quit and go back to wearing that funny looking hat..." referring to the campaign hats that basic training instructors wear.

I sounded off each time he made comments, "HOOYAH SERGEANT!"

The team formed up briefly at the edge of the woods before a fresh cadre yelled "FOLLOW ME...." Then took off into the forest at a sprint.

The team was full of excellent runners. I was a strong runner but out of 35 trainees that started our team, I finished 9th overall in run time in the first evaluation. While I was on the team, I was always last in runs to collect people who fell out and assist as needed to keep the team on track. Immediately, guys started falling back. I had to spend all my extra energy motivating them to get moving. The job of surviving Air Force Special Tactics indoctrination is already tough if you only have yourself to worry about. Now I was pulling, dragging, yelling, and attempting to motivate the guys who were falling behind.

The cadre had a brilliant idea to punish us for a lackluster run. They ordered the team to "damn up the creek…only using our bodies…"

The task was harder than it sounds. I guess impossible in the end. The team had to lay down one at a time to inter-link our bodies together until the water ceased to flow past us. The first few guys end up being underwater while guys laid on top of them trying to stop the water flow. The whole time the cadre are yelling in their megaphones telling us how we are the worst class they have ever trained.

I learned to turn off the insults and stop listening to the words the cadre said at us. The only words that mattered were the orders from the team leader after he got our official instructions from the cadre. Some of the guys took the words to heart. They began getting that distant look people to get before they check out mentally and before they quit shortly after it.

If I attempted to tell you how tired I was there are no words that I can use to explain the pain I felt. I have been asked a million times what training was like and I can never quite represent the fatigue, stress, coldness, heat, and doubt that every man faces when in Special Tactics training. Exercises that most people do for three of four sets of 10 to 50 reps we would do for over an hour without a break. Flutter kicks were in the thousands. Eight-count bodybuilders were in the several thousand. Simple tasks like carrying a rucksack were taken to the extreme of simulated straps breaking making the trainee carry the rucksack and all its contents over your head for hours at a time.

      The fatigue you see on people's face at the gym after a set and five minutes of chit-chatting in between each was all fake. I had left that level of pain in the first few minutes of this torture run and experienced many levels of pain along the way. The weird thing is that while you are doing a crazy evolution your physical limitations are easily overcome. If you take off running, you can go. If you are told to do laps in the pool, you can go. Physically, humans use a small percent of their body's capability.

      The challenge is the mental war that goes on inside your head. The first time a cadre wrote 7587 eight-count bodybuilders on the whiteboard for punishment I laughed thinking he was joking. Then the team spent an entire workday doing the reps, breaking them up into 10-20 rep chunks, and knocking them out slowly over time. That changed my perception on ability because I thought my workouts were crazy when I did a few hundred reps. Now I found myself doing thousands of reps.

Each set your mind had to be checked. The thoughts were always the same "what are you doing here…why are you doing this…. you can just leave and there are no consequences…."

No one in Special Tactics training is required to stay in training. Everyone is a volunteer and can leave on request at any moment. The guys who make it through are not the strongest physically. They are mentally strong. They break every evolution up into chunks, not thinking about the next training evolution or the next day. The thing that is ever-present is that little voice telling you "it's ok to quit, you have nothing to prove".

The team leader's orders snapped my mind back to reality. We were formed upon the bank of the creek we previously had attempted to dam up, but now the creek was about 20 feet deep and 30 yards wide. The cadre wanted to play a game with us where we raced across the creek as a team, up a hill 25 yards on a steep incline, and back across in under a minute.

The order to go was given and it was a melee with guys running for their lives to make the time. That energy was quickly gone when the weak swimmers began nearly drowning again in the center of the creek. I was assisting everyone across while keeping several of the weak swimmers from going underwater when a team member panicked and pushed my head underwater just as I was yelling an order.

I gasped for air as I was completely not expecting to be dunked at that very moment. I swallowed a large amount of very dirty creek water when I went under. When I surfaced I smacked the kid who grabbed me and pushed him towards the shore before someone grabbed him. I did not think about swallowing the water at that time as we had a mission to complete. The team all made it back across in 55 seconds, and the team leader made the mistake of saying "I told you we could have done it in 45 seconds…"

The words, "good, let's see it…" came from behind us and the Commandant said, "GO!"

The team would fall a little short on this attempt making it back in 47 seconds. We received a good "smoke session" for failing. We were given more bodybuilders, flutter kicks, and pushups before someone said, "Follow me" and taking off on another sprint.

The cadre always rotated out on us making them 100 percent fresh each time we took off on a run. The time had ceased to exist at this point. We had been on the go for several hours straight doing exercises, running, swimming, and other obstacle course things we came across randomly in the woods. The woods were like a scene from an 80's scary movie, but the bad guys were not super-villains they were exercises and obstacles that were unknowingly built and hidden in the woods. Everyone was smoked and wondering how long this day could last, but it kept going forever. When we thought it was over because we came out of the woods, we found out the worst was yet to come.

The team let out a collective sigh of relief when we crossed back over the creek near a bridge that was near the training facility. The thought seemed to be that we were on the downhill stretch. The truth was we were about half complete at this point.

The cadre lined us up on the goal line of an old football field. They told us we were now doing graded races with the calisthenic of their choice each time. My brain was smoked. My body was smoked. I just learned the home stretch was just another mental trick to test our mental toughness. In the distance, we could see the other higher-level teams not assigned as training assistants going through the motions at the main training building. They were enjoying a peaceful training day. We were going through a hell of a training evolution. This was a tease to test us. Many guys were ready to quit.

The first race we did was called "leaping lizards". This consisted of the team lining up at the goal line of the football field and racing to the opposite goal line. The exercise was a tough one, especially after the number of physical activities we had already endured. Each trainee would squat down to touch their heels then spring forward as far as possible before standing up and repeating it. Trainees were sent back to the start line if they did not fully squat down or if they did not jump far enough forward.

The cadre labeled this "Skerving", meaning the trainee was attempting to half-ass do something and anyone labeled a skerve would feel serious pain from the cadre.

The races were brutal. The lactic acid build-up from squatting and jumping was almost unbearable. The cadre constantly restarted trainees they wanted to test. They focused on the ones they saw as weak links to make them quit. The first team attempt the cadre allowed us to make it almost 60 percent of the way to the finish before sending us all back to the start because they said we were an embarrassment to the Air Force for our poor efforts.

    Normal counseling sessions in the Air Force would have the Sergeant in charge talk to the offending troops. There could also be some yelling about the expected corrective actions to be taken. This counseling session was not a normal Air Force one. The cadre made the entire team flip upside down with our feet resting on a fence as they blasted their discontent through the bull horns. They also made us do these inverted pushups from that position. They would not let us recover until the entire team finished 100 repetitions without falling. This was nearly an impossible request as most of the team was running on fumes at this point. Weaker trainees would fall taking out several of their teammates. The punishment continued for a very long time. My arms were shaking uncontrollably by the time the cadre ordered us to recover. They ordered us to return to the leaping lizards starting line.

    The punishment seemed to have worked as the efforts from the entire team was much improved overall.

My legs were tired to the point where I was becoming nauseous as the lactic acid built up with each rep. The more it hurt the harder I pushed and with each leap I was several feet closer to the end. I finally made it to the end and collapsed to the ground in triumph. Since I was near the front of the team, I earned a small, much-needed rest which was quickly turned into being ordered into the front leaning rest position. It was better than the burn from the leaping lizards. By this point I was nearly immune to the pain of pushups from doing countless reps as punishment for team infractions.

The final team member made it to the finish line with several cadres in his ear about how he did not belong in this job. They repeatedly told him "weak links are what gets teams killed" and offered to ease his pain through quitting. The trainee struggled but pushed forward in what must have been a black moment, but the team rallied him on to the end.

Once the final trainee crossed the line the team was ordered to get on the starting line facing the way we just had come. The direction was now away from the home base we saw as our finish line. The morale dropped immediately for the entire team. We would find out that the leaping lizards were the first of about two dozen races we were going to be doing this day. The list of hellacious exercises included long log rolls, front shoulder rolls, crab crawls, bear crawls, reverse crab crawls, reverse bear crawls, fireman's carry races, buddy drags, low crawl races, and a host of other evil exercises that burned and made trainees puke all over the field.

The team was so disoriented that we did not even realize we had inched our way right to the finish line at the Combat Control training facility. The final race was a buddy carry race across very uneven terrain. The team moved with added energy as we believed our torment was finally ending. When the last trainee crossed the finish line there was a sigh of relief as we stood on the training pad exhausted. There was a feeling of pride that the entire team had made it without a single quitter.

Our fortunes quickly changed when the Commandant came up to us and ordered us to "Prepare to mount the rail". The rail he was talking about was a 66-foot-long railway rail painted in the Combat Control colors and logos. The weight of this rail was approximately 2,800 pounds. We mounted the rail by alternating on each side of it. When ordered we squat down to lift it up to our shoulders. The cadre would command us to lift it and lower it on the opposite shoulders for countless reps. We were told from then on when we left the training area the rail was always to be in our possession and guarded unless otherwise instructed.

The big difference in the logs used in other special operations training and the rail was, logs were rigid, and the smaller trainees did not bear much of the weight when carrying them. The rail would bend down to each man. It ensured everyone carried their fair share of the load. There was no escaping the rail's pain no matter the height of the trainee.

The team was tortured with the rail for what seemed like forever before the commandant ordered us to take the rail to chow. The dining facility was about a 1.5-mile hike over rocky, uphill terrain. The team leader called commands to ensure we marched together as a team, ensuring we made it there safely. The journey took us much longer than our usual formation jogs to eat. By the time the team leader commanded us to dismount the rail all our upper bodies were on fire.

I volunteered to guard the rail first to allow the younger team members to eat first before relieving me. I felt this was the most appropriate thing to do as the highest-ranking NCO and most seasoned Airman on the team. I took the opportunity to lie down to let my entire body rest. I remembered that the Confederate general Stonewall Jackson had always made his men lie down when not marching to ensure their bodies could fully rest and this stuck in my head at this moment.

When your body is being punished by excessive amounts of physical activities the only way to make it through is never to stop moving. Once you stop moving your body has trouble getting started again and your mind will begin to make excuses for why you should not continue. I never had those voices in my head during a tough evolution but found it was those short minutes in between exercises where your brain asks you what the hell you are doing. Laying there on the ground my body and brain were busy rationalizing the "whys" of enduring such an ass-kicking. I was exhausted, hungry, and unknowingly in the early stages of being sick from that creek water, I drank earlier in the day.

The first Airman ran out to relieve me after about 20 minutes and I headed into the dining facility to eat something after a long day's work. I wish there was the technology there is today like Fitbit to know how many calories I burned during a workout like I had just completed but those were several years from being created. If I had to guess I think we probably burned about 7,000-10,000 calories. The weird thing for me was I was not hungry and could not eat very much at this meal.

I struggled through it and ate what I could to at least replace a few hundred calories of what I had lost. I did not think about it at the time as being significant but looking back I was starting a cycle that would end my Combat Control career by working out hard and not replacing calories as needed. I was unaware that there was a hidden enemy inside me that was going to wreak havoc on my insides and destroy my physical ability to perform.

The team finished the meal, mounted rail, and marched back to our training facility. We were all feeling very good about surviving one of the hardest days in training to this point. When we arrived the SSgt cadre was there and gave us our evening orders. He also told us our report time for the next day of training then dismissed us to the team leader for the day. We had survived a hard day. Now it was time to clean up and go to sleep.

When you are on a team, what we called being in training, training time seems to move very slowly, and the days are extremely long. The nights are not as drawn out because you are exhausted to a point where your body shuts off the second you hit the pillow. You wake up in what seems like minutes to begin the next evolution and the uncertainty of what the day brings. The cadre love to play mind games and keeping the schedules secret is their favorite game because it leaves a cloud of uncertainty that creates anxiety in each member of the team. No matter how hard you try to tame your thoughts you cannot help to wonder what fun activities the cadre will have in store for you the next day.

    I woke up feeling off. My stomach was a mess and after a few trips to the bathroom, I knew I needed to get something to settle it as soon as possible. I tried some over-the-counter medicines and got no results. I decided I had to let the cadre know I was not feeling right. I had to let them know I needed to get something stronger from the flight medicine doctors. I also knew that saying I was not feeling well would be viewed negatively with the cadre who would make me pay for it later.

    I spoke with the commandant about how I was feeling. I explained I had swallowed a large amount of creek water and had not felt right since. He questioned me about being weak and using the "break" to escape from training for a small time. I defended how I felt the need to get something strong to settle my stomach issues. I would return to the training immediately after I was done with the doctor's appointment. He then told me to catch a bus and head over to be seen.

I rode the bus over to the main training side of Lackland Air Force Base where the flight medicine clinic was located. The doctor's office was filled with trainees from Air Force basic training that were all hanging out getting physicals for acceptance into the various Air Force Battlefield Airmen career fields such as Combat Control, Pararescue, Tactical Air Control Party (TACP), Special Operations Weathermen, and Survival Evasion Recovery Escape (SERE). The wait was long. I was missing important training evolutions every minute I was gone. This created more anxiety as I sat there listening to all the new wannabes running their mouths about their one to four-week-old military careers.

I had been in the military nearly half these young men's lives at this point. I had more real-world time in the Middle East than they group had combined time in the service. I found their stories about the nonsense of their training humorous. They complained about their instructors, food, their schedules, and other meaningless things. I remembered when I was a new graduate of my technical training how a few Army guys had laughed at me for telling those very same stories. I did not understand why they laughed at me at the time. Now listening to these young trainees complain about things that did not really matter in the big picture of the military made me smile.

The lessons you learn through serving can be easily overlooked if you focus on the negativity that surrounds you daily. The military can be a tough place because 99 percent of the time you are training for war and can lose sight of the big picture. The training seems like an inconvenience until you are on the ground in a foreign country. This is when the skills you trained a few thousand times in simulations, during exercises, or other training evolutions make sense. I knew in a short few years these young men would have real stories to tell others. Many would have a sadness inside them as they remember the losses they would face. Right now, they were unaware of the true nature of the business they had volunteered to do. They were just chasing titles that they did not understand.

The receptionist snapped me from my thoughts. She called me to the back to wait for the doctor. The military has a concept that always annoyed me. Doctors were the masters of the art. The concept was called "Hurry Up and Wait". This is where they demanded you be fifteen minutes early then they would make you wait an hour for your scheduled appointment time. The doctors were the least efficient people in the military because they were not trained like to the same level as everyone else. Because of their specialized skills the military gave concessions on their level of military training. They were mostly given some uniforms and sent to a facility to get to work.

The doctor's offices had several levels of waiting. First, you had to be there early to wait in the waiting area for a long time. Then after being called to the back they would hold you hostage in a room for another hour while the doctors did whatever they felt like. You were required to value the doctor's time, but this was not reciprocated to your own. The room they left me in was like any of the other ones I had sat hours in around the world, mostly empty minus a few medical items and very cold.

The doctor came in after what seemed like hours and went through his routine checking my vitals and entering the data into his computer. He ordered me to take more tests at other sections of the hospital. This meant I was given a half dozen appointments where I would repeat the "hurry up and wait" process for the entire day. This made me very anxious because my team was in training and I was wasting time sitting in waiting rooms while they were suffering together.

The suffering a special operations team endures together is the foundational bonds that will last a lifetime. The respect that each member earns in the mud, water, sand, or other clever and uncomfortable location builds into the bond that will carry over into their operational side. Each member who makes it knows they can count on everyone around them in all things they face. I was absent. This was viewed as a weakness by the cadre and they would let the team know.

I completed all the appointments I was given and returned to my doctor sitting in the waiting area for another hour before being called to the back. The doctor returned after another long wait. He informed me that I tested positive for something called "H. Pylori". He gave me a prescription for a Z-Pack, a strong short-term antibiotic that he said would take care of it. Sitting here today I know that his treatment was not the correct one. He possibly caused my death as I am currently dealing with internal bleeding issues due to the H. Pylori not being treated correctly, and the Department of Veterans Affairs blowing off my treatments as they have done to thousands of other veterans. So this part of the story is to be continued.

The doctor issued me an order to be placed on quarters for 24-hours to gain some of the strength I had lost while being sick for the past two days. The quarter's order was not good. I knew the cadre would think this was another weakness. They would use it against me.

340

Looking back I know I should have taken the medicines and trashed the paperwork. But I turned it over as ordered when I returned.

The cadre team took my paperwork as soon as I returned and read the quarters orders. They then took turns trashing me about being weak and wasting their time with this "made up sickness". Then finally they told me to go to "nappy time" in our barracks while the team "pays" for my "weakness". I knew nothing good was coming from this result and left as I was ordered.

I stayed in my dorm room as ordered until the team returned late in the afternoon. The entire team was trashed and not happy with me. I talked to SSgt Rosendale and he told me that since I was gone, they decided to do grass drills for hours, all the while the cadre had their bull horns blasting out that anyone could "quit for nappy time with SSgt Franks". The entire team had crawled on their hands so much that no one had skin left on their palms. The bear crawls, crab crawls, and other heinous activities had ripped their skin off completely as the cadre tortured them in my honor.

The team all showered and crashed out for the night after a tormenting training day. I laid awake in the bed knowing I was in for an ass-kicking the following day. The entire cadre team was now pissed at me for being weak and I would need to be at the top of my game to survive. I had many thoughts running through my mind, and I am not sure when I even fell asleep. Before long the alarm sounded for another day of training to begin.

I continued to battle feeling ill for the next few weeks of training. The cadre's daily array of workouts was ever-increasing in difficulty and the more I worked out the worse I felt. I survived the evolutions by putting my head down and sucking it up even though I felt like I was always a step behind my normal energy level. I endured endless grass drills, confidence courses, long pool sessions, intro to rappelling classes, and other mission-critical tasks like weapons training. I did my best to keep up despite the lack of energy that was getting worse daily.

The days of training finally culminated in the final training evolution of the indoctrination part of our training. The cadre drove us up to the Texas highlands in the middle of nowhere and marched us out through very rough terrain north of the San Antonio metro area. The area was covered in moderate-sized hills, creeks, and isolated landscapes that were hardened by the climate's lack of rain in the area. When we climbed off the bus the cadre stated, "Welcome to Enchanted Rock" and proceeded to march us through the wilderness at a fast pace.

We all carried climbing gear, medical gear, and an abundance of water adding an additional 50 to 100 pounds to our already heavy rucksack loads. The march out seemed to take about two hours, and we reached our destination in the later morning hours. The location was a pre-identified climbing point that some cadre had discovered maybe decades before. The location was used by Combat Controllers and Pararescuemen to hone their climbing and rappelling skills. I was sure thousands of wannabes had maneuvered up and down these same hills over the decades of Air Force Special Tactics training. Now it was our day to enjoy the cliffs.

The cadre took the lead and easily ascended to the top of the hills to secure the rappelling lanes. They created a climbing lane that we each took turns ascending to the top. Then we were assigned one of five rappelling lanes that each presented its own challenges to the novice rappelling students. I had learned on the training towers that I was not afraid of the commonly used rappelling techniques where you descend facing the surface of the mountain. This method felt safe. The safety equipment made me feel secure.

The scary rappelling technique was called "Australian Rappelling" or "Aussie Rappel". This required us to run down the surfaces face first. The method is very important to learn to be able to infiltrate buildings with access to your weapons as your shooting hand is free. It is a very fast method for rappelling to the ground. The equipment set up is very safe, but you cannot visually see the lines securing you. Your mind plays games with you about the overall safety. My first time doing it on the rappelling tower the SSgt Cadre had kicked me off the side when I hesitated. He chewed me out for being a "pussy". I could not control that initial reaction as my mind stopped my feet from moving because of all you see it the ground 100 feet below you. You cannot see the safety lines.

I was determined to face this fear head-on and decided to only use the Aussie technique for the day. I started out on an easy descent point and the rappel was fast and easy. I felt mild anxiety at first and it subsided quickly. I made my climb back to the top and completed the harder descents in progression. The final rappel point was a big challenge that required me to rappel quickly to a ledge then jump across a 12-foot crevasse to another descent point. The jump looked like something a Jedi might do with ease. Not having the powers of the force to aid me I felt somewhat intimidated but jumped with all my might. I made it with ease before descending to the ground for the final time.

Ellis Franks "Always Leave An Airman Behind: A Real Story of Surviving The Crab Leadership Culture

Our team leader would not have the same luck as I did. The captain rappelled to the ledge before the jump. His lines were not in the correct position for him to make the jump. Our experienced cadre, a retired Senior NCO with three decades of combat experience, ordered him to stop. The team leader vetoed this order and said, "I got it", then jumped against the cadre's orders.

I was on belay, the position in rappelling that controls the slack in the climbing ropes at the bottom of the cliffs, on the lane adjacent to the team leader's position. I was the only person that could see his movements fully. I watched as he jumped into the air. The ropes tensed stopping his momentum. The ropes then caused the team leader to stop abruptly in the air. He crashed mouth first into the cliff. I instantly saw blood splatter on the rocks as his mouth met them with a giant thug sound.

The cadre that had ordered him to stop let loose on him with a tirade fit for a first-day basic trainee. He told him he was lucky he did not kill himself because he made a stupid decision. He also said he hoped that it was not a testament to his true leadership capabilities because if it was then he would get his teams killed in combat. The captain did not need those words to know he messed up. His blood all over the rocks in front of him was proof enough. He struggled to climb onto the ledge he had attempted to jump to before finishing the descent with little effort after his failure.

In the regular Air Force, mistakes can be bad and cause damage to equipment or injure personnel though most jobs in the regular force are mostly safe overall. Combat Control is a whole different beast as every job we were being trained to do was very dangerous and could cause the death of personnel. If you make a single bad decision the lives of thousands of innocent people could be at stake needlessly and the captain's decision to override the experienced operator's judgment was a good lesson for the entire team. In the special operations world there is no rank that overrides experience and for me, the vision of the captain's blood splattered all over those rocks is a very good reminder of that lesson.

The team continued to practice the climbing and rappelling techniques for a few hours before being ordered to prepare to move. The intensity in the cadre's faces changed from one where they were concerned with our safety to a look of an evil scientist about to deploy their latest evil creation. We soon found out what that meant when the bull horns came out and the games began.

The cadre had created an exfiltration exercise over the decades punishing trainees at Enchanted Rock. The march out seemed to be a very roundabout way designed to tire us out. The path back was more direct, yet very intense due to the calisthenics added to the march. The team would mostly bear crawl or some other equivalent exercise the entire way back for what was at least two full hours of physically demanding training. Every exercise seemed to be underwater, in wet sand, or some other challenging position.

I was taxed already when the training started and now, I felt out of gas. My mind was ready to quit at this point because I was not 100 percent. The average person will give up at this point and retreat to the safety of mediocrity. I was ready to say those words as my mind tricked me with every thought.

"You cannot make it through this…" my mind repeated.

"You're sick, idiot, what the hell are you doing here…" the negativity built up.

Then my mouth said the words my mind was repeating to my wingman, who luckily was the lieutenant and he snapped me back to reality with positive, encouraging words that I needed to find my second gas tank.

The second gas tank is the term used to describe the energy that a person or leader can tap into when they have been giving a lot of effort and they feel like they have no more energy to proceed. The second gas tank is more than just a second wind that lasts for a short period, it is more like an entire energy source on-demand that comes from a mental place and not a physical one. The lieutenant snapped me out of my "quitter's mind" and into my second gas tank at the precise moment, I felt like I could not go on any further.

I was in the middle of wheel barrel races; all being done with full rucksacks and additional climbing or medical gear. The lieutenant had my feet in the air, and I was walking on my weakened arms in six inches of wet sands in a creek bed when my rucksack waistband snapped with the entirety of the weight flying forward to pin my face and upper torso underwater. I was too weakened to get up and I was ready to quit when the lieutenant all but slapped my face back to reality. He told me "you got this, you are the strongest one of us physically and I am not letting you quit…"

The rush of energy was like how Star Wars describes a padawan fully opening to the force for the first time and I felt like I had 1000 times the energy I ever had. My pace in every evolution grew as I gained strength from my second gas tank and time seemed to slow down completely. I cannot fully even remember every exercise I completed as I vaguely remember doing flutter kicks with only my head above water and low crawling through rock crevasses that had hard flowing water also flowing through it and buddy carrying a team member plus both over gear in chest-high water for at least a mile.

Then like it had just started a few minutes before I collapsed on the shore of the creek at the end. I had survived it all. Now we had finished the physical training part of the Combat Control pipeline. The feeling was amazing because I remember the many times I had tried out but failed to even qualify to be part of this amazing community. Now I had finished as one of about 15 out of the 36 Airman who started to graduate from our "selection" training. The final test was the PAST test the next day which was a formality. I easily completed each exercise at the highest level even though I was still declining in energy from whatever was going on inside me.

The next day we all woke up early and readied our minds for the PAST test. Then promptly completed all circuits with ease. I had an amazing swim where I finished well ahead of all my teammates completing the timed 1500-meter finned swim in about 23 minutes. The 3-mile run was a cruise around the track at a personal best 18 minutes. I also made personal bests on push-ups, sit-ups, and did 25 proper pull-ups which were four times the amount I had done in my original test to qualify.

My performance overall was rewarded by being selected as one of three from my team to attend Airborne School at Fort Benning, Georgia. I was personally selected by the cadre and my team leaders. The SSgt cadre delivered my orders and told me I did well despite getting sick and that my team leadership had said I was "the person they would like most to take into combat…" which is an honor I cherish to this day.

My body was beaten up and I was declining in health rapidly at the end of training. I was looking forward to a few weeks of much-needed recovery time. The mental toughness required to overcome the training that I had completed would be a tool I would use for the rest of my life. I always compared any situations to what I had endured. If there was no water hose in my mouth or no creek to cross with full gear or no wet sand in every part of my body then the challenge was not that hard. I have tried to explain this lesson to people who have never completed anything close to this level of intense training and people look at you with glassy eyes and never understand.

The intensity of Air Force Special Tactics training is like participating in an Iron Man plus "Tough Mudder" race every day for weeks at a time. Except instead of having people cheering you on you have ones who do not want you there and want you to fail or prove you belong but the only encouragement you get is from your team and your own mind. The experience is an internal awakening where you begin to not see challenges or barriers any longer and opportunities become more apparent and abundant.

Fear also becomes something that you no longer create inside your mind because fear is an illusion, created in our minds to explain the things we have never challenged ourselves against. When you volunteer to become a person who runs towards the gunfire that others run away from, in a service full of mediocre people who shuck any responsibility at all costs, you begin to really stand out from the average service member. The way you walk and carry yourself changes. Most people misidentify this change as arrogance. It is really humility learned from being tested in the mud, sand, and facing the fears that each person carries within them. I would spend the rest of my career battling this misconception applied to me by the mediocre class of the Air Force. I had been part of something that less than a percentage of one percent of the service could even qualify for what I had completed, much less understand it.

The next few weeks would be spent training with the Army learning the doctrine of the paratrooper and seeing my health decline daily as my illness worsened. When I graduated from Airborne School, I not only had the stomach issues, but I had added a severe sinus infection to my list of obstacles. Feeling like a dead man walking I was informed that one of my Combat Controllers had gotten in trouble for some uniform infraction by the Airborne cadre. They were threatening to recycle him to a class starting two weeks later. Feeling like trash I tapped my second gas tank and personally went to the Sergeant Major's office to get my troop and leave.

The Sergeant Major was a big, loud-mouthed, old school Army Senior NCO who I already had a run-in with at the start of Airborne School. I had arrived earlier than my teammates and they were not present when I was inprocessing. I was the ranking member, as I was promoted to Technical Sergeant on the way to Georgia.

Ellis Franks "Always Leave An Airman Behind: A Real Story of Surviving The Crab Leadership Culture

I was trying to locate the team who had not shown up and I was calling our home base to see if they arrived. The Sergeant Major took the opportunity to try to "embarrass" the visiting Air Force NCO by publicly by screaming loudly the Army policy for cell phone usage by Airborne trainees. I respectfully adhered to his banter and got off the phone. I apologized and informed him I was trying to locate my Combat Controllers who had not shown for inprocessing. The old Sergeant Major was a big jerk. He made a big scene for no reason. This was a common trait of Senior NCOs who had spent too much time around the training environment making them lose any sense of empathy.

Knowing the Sergeant Major from my own experience I knew the troubled Combat Controller was in for a bad experience and needed me to top cover for him. I reported to the Sergeant Major's office professionally and officially reported as if I were on the carpet personally to maximize the effect. I explained to him he had pulled one of my Combat Controllers from training and was threatening to recycle him several weeks in training which I could not allow due to his requirement to report to a new training location in the next few days.

I told the Sergeant Major that I was responsible for this Airman and that he could "smoke" us both for the entirety of the day. But I was pulling out of the Army post at the end of it with my Airman with me because he could not miss his report date. The look on the other support NCOs' faces in the Sergeant Major's office was shocking that a lower-ranking NCO, much less an Air Force NCO, would tell the Sergeant Major how things were going to be. They braced themselves for the wrath they knew I was about to get.

The Sergeant Major crinkled his brow and stared at me for a long period of time before turning to his First Sergeant and stating, "You see that First Sergeant, that is what an NCO is supposed to do right there, take accountability for his people and stand up for them when they need it…" then he laughed heartily at the scene unfolding in front of him.

He said "Air Force, I like you, and you seem to have your act together so I will release your Airman to you to deal with for his discipline issue, thank you for epitomizing what an NCO is supposed to be…" and then said to get out of his office.

Facing that man for a second time was a challenge because the first experience was very uncomfortable and embarrassing. The leadership lesson I learned was that a leader must stand up for the right things no matter the personal sacrifice that may occur. The Sergeant Major could have taken me up on my offer to "smoke us" for the next few hours. If he had ordered us to do it I was prepared to pay the price right next to my Combat Controller, even though I had nothing to do with why he was in trouble.

I believed that even though I was not even assigned to his platoon or squad throughout the training I was still accountable for all the Airmen assigned as the ranking representative from our service. Leaders cannot pass accountability just because they were not present and must be willing to personally sacrifice for their people if it is the right thing to do. The experience I had as an Airman coming up was the opposite of this belief.

Throughout my career I witnessed nearly every NCO I encountered, minus a select few at my first duty station, throw Airmen under the bus to make themselves look good. I was personally the victim of retribution by weak NCOs who did not lead their troops. They instead, they pulled rank and made Airmen do tasks that were asinine to punish them for menial infractions of rules. I was lucky that I had two good NCOs early in my career take a personal stake in my well-being. They stood by me when I made mistakes and when it was my turn to make the same decision it was the only choice for me. I explained this to my Combat Controller after they released him to me. To be safe, I told him to pack his gear and get the hell out of their facilities as soon as possible.

This would be the last real leadership decision I would make as a Combat Controller. I proceeded to my next training, after a slight delay from a hurricane that held me up for a week. I was getting sicker by the minute when I pulled up to the gates. When I signed into my new unit I was the walking dead. My bad experience was about to get worse as my phone rang with bad news from back home. My grandmother had passed away. It was my birthday, and this was not the gift I would have chosen. They wanted me to come for the services.

When you are sick you make bad decisions.

When you have life-altering things like divorce or death you make bad decisions.

If you have a perfect storm of sickness, divorce, and death your mental state is nowhere near-optimal performance. I was now dealing with all three at once. My wife at the time had left me a long time before I had started my training but refused to sign our divorce papers because when I graduated from training I was set to receive a huge reenlistment bonus. She wanted to take half of it making our divorce a long, drawn-out affair. From the stress of divorce I had immersed myself into my training to just not deal with it and this had worked thus far.

The death of another grandparent, my grandfather had died when I was awaiting orders for training, was the second major death I had since starting my journey. I had done well to overcome the first one because I knew he always wanted me to achieve the highest levels for myself. This gave me strength to push every day.

I was so sick at this point I could hardly breathe. I was at the medical facility awaiting care when the call came that my grandmother had died. I am not usually an emotional person but the stress of everything came crashing down on top of me at that moment. I broke down. I called the new commandant at my new training location distraught with the news of the death. I explained I was at the hospital already getting treated for an illness.

He ordered me to report to the offices in the morning. They would do the paperwork for me to leave the training due to her death. I would be granted the ability to return when I dealt with my personal issues since my departure was not a failure in training. My team was notified I was leaving, and team First Sergeant duties were passed to SSgt Rosendale. I was now also missing the only support I had during the past year of training as I was leaving the team I had bonded with behind and this compounded my overall issues.

     I also saw how it impacted the team as I watched several teammates return from their morning training in defeat as they took the shift in team dynamics as an opportunity to quit their own battles. Any time a team changes leadership there will be a resetting of the overall level of performance. My departure was the final excuse about six team members needed to quit their journeys. I maybe could not have saved them from quitting. Still I carried that burden. If I had been stronger and not decided to leave my team for personal reasons, then the lesson to others could have resonated that the team was more important to me and should be to them than any outside issues.

     These were men who would deploy into enemy territories as a team but otherwise alone behind enemy lines, before the main forces would arrive, and would require ultimate dedication to each other to survive. I failed at fulfilling this pact with my brothers. For the rest of my life, I would never have another group of men that I cared about as much as I did that team.

This failure as a leader was also the beginning of the end of my career as I would never feel at home in any other position I held. Little did I know I would serve only one more enlistment before separating abruptly at 13 years, 352 days in the service.

What Do We Do With The Washout?

My Combat Control career did not immediately end when I left my team behind in training. The death of this dream slowly withered on the vine as I was now alone and reassigned to a team behind me in training, but one that I had not suffered within the mud. There was no connection with the new team, and I was viewed as an outsider to their core group. My mental state deteriorated to the point where I could not think clearly, and I scheduled an appointment with my official unit's First Sergeant to discuss my overall disposition.

I was supposed to be a tough special operations trainee who was not afraid of anything, but inside I was full of doubt for no reason. I had lived in high stress for too long after the turmoil of being a basic training instructor and being treated like a criminal often enough because of fake trainee critiques that were never founded in truth, a long divorce and loss of my daughter from my life, the loss of several grandparents, and being sick for an extended period of time. I was seeking someone to tell me I could get through it all and remind me of what made me desire to be the best again. Instead, I got what most Air Force members get when they are vulnerable which was a crab-minded Senior NCO who gave me bad advice because they could not understand what motivated me and instead pulled me down to their mediocrity.

I was seeking affirmation and instead got the crab mentality that dominates society today and is very abundant in the socialist military structure where mediocrity is celebrated. The First Sergeant told me that he did not understand why someone at my rank would attempt to try to be a Combat Controller and that I should just "stop trying to be 'gung-ho' and just do what other TSgt do…" If I had been in any other state of mind everything inside of me would have rejected that mediocrity, but I was sick, alone, and defeated at this point and I believed the words I heard to be the best for me. I returned to my old unit and wrote my official letter of termination of my training and then watched my lifelong dream die with the signing of my name.

I was now no longer part of the elite. I was back to the mediocre and the crab-minded peer group that I had sought to leave forever. I had absolutely nothing to look forward to in my career. I felt like a failure and a quitter because that is exactly what I was. The First Sergeant had not twisted my arm. He just said out loud the words I felt inside myself. I jumped on the grenade that represented my career. I had nothing left to train towards, no mission left, and the peers back in my old basic training unit who had been jealous of me joining the elite took no mercy on me.

When I walked the hallways of the US Air Force Basic Military Training Warrior Week site, the crabs I worked with did not call me by my name they referred to me as "the washout" and this angered me. I was very upset about it because these were people who could not even qualify to do what I had successfully completed had the audacity to call me a washout. Fat NCOs that had their friends cheat on their annual physical assessments and should have been kicked out of the service for lacking physical readiness had the nerve to trash me for attempting something that would have killed them just on the qualification attempt. I would endure months of being treated like an outcast and had no mission until a member of the Air Force Sergeants Association contacted me about needing a point of contact for the recent Hurricane Katrina relief efforts.

Leaving Biloxi, Mississippi turned out to be a blessing in disguise as a few weeks after I had left the worst natural disaster in recent history occurred across the US Gulf Coast. Hurricane Katrina was one of three hurricanes that hit the gulf from Alabama to Texas that year and it was one of the worst in history. My old team was in Biloxi still and endured the storm as it tore apart the coast in the area, trapping them at the base for weeks.

I had left and was back in San Antonio when the storm hit. I was lucky that I missed what would have been a fourth major life challenge of living through a natural disaster. I was dealing with too much already at the time to add that to my stresses. My team was not as lucky as they rode out the storm as it destroyed Biloxi's coast.

The devastation of these storms caused thousands of people to be evacuated to Texas cities and Lackland Air Force Base became a major hub for evacuees. The amount of support required was enormous and every nonprofit in the area was scrambling to figure out what they could do to assist. The Air Force Sergeants Association (AFSA) was one of these organizations that were tasked with providing support and I had been a member since my first week at my first base making the opportunity available for me to take part in the efforts.

The initial request for someone to manage the relief efforts seemed like an easy task of just managing the volunteers and I desperately needed a mission to get my mindset back on track. I volunteered promptly and was accepted as the project manager for the relief effort. I quickly realized that there was a much bigger need to reorganize and consolidate a lot of smaller nonprofits under a larger organization's umbrella.

I quickly organized a meeting with all the people who were sending mass emails out asking for assistance and met with them about falling under the AFSA effort. Most people were relieved as the amount of support required was overwhelming as people and animals began making their way to Lackland until the government figured out what to do with them. Where others saw obstacles, I was able to see opportunity and I seized each chance to bring in more people and expand our efforts. I successfully coordinated the consolidation of several dozen small nonprofits, from multiple civilian and military locations into one effort that consisted of over 1500 volunteers that provided 24-hour support to the military efforts for the next six months. We partnered with local university student organizations for more volunteers and civilian organizations such as the San Antonio Humane Society which was needing 24-hour support for thousands of displaced pets from the hurricanes.

Our efforts resulted in 10,000s of volunteer hours occurring 24/7, 7 days a week, and raised $10,000s of donations that we created a logistical system from scratch to deliver to families in need. We also provided round the clock care for the displaced pets that were traumatized and missing from their owners who left them behind in the storms. The efforts of all the volunteers were amazing as the entire San Antonio military and civilian communities came together to give as much as possible to the evacuees and their pets.

I was extremely proud of the efforts our people gave. The mission was exactly what I needed to clear my head from the failures and despair I had been feeling from the recent epic failure seeking my lifelong goal of being a Combat Controller. I immersed myself into my work and through it, I healed my mind and was ready to leave Lackland after 4 long years of sacrificing for the betterment of the Air Force. I was ready for a change, even if the change was taking ten steps backward in my career. Now I was set to return to my old career field in Fuels Management.

I had left the career field with no intentions of ever returning and now I faced the reality that I would be placed back in the land of mediocrity and discrimination based on who you drank beer with after work. I had spent the last few years seeking something better and did not find it, in one case only finding failure for a third time even though I was one of the more capable candidates. The reality of re-entering a world I had thought I was done with forever was saddening, but it was also a needed change after the stressful years I spent away chasing the enigma of success that was very elusive in the Air Force.

I was an outcast in every aspect of my career. I had spent time with some of the most capable members of the armed forces and now I was headed back to the most mediocre of them all. I knew I had a huge challenge ahead of me to fit into the "good ole boy" culture. I had grown as a person and leader over the past few years, but I knew that would not matter in the culture of POL where off-duty relationships were the real chain of command. I also knew that the other NCOs would resent me for doing my duties as a Military Training Instructor, if only for their personal biases from their time in basic training. This was the price of failure and my new reality.

The final few months at Lackland Air Force Base was filled with the mundane duties of basic training. The coldness I felt from the rest of the instructors was apparent daily and the fact they stopped calling me by my name and rank, deciding instead it to be more appropriate to refer to me simply as "the washout" was more reasons I knew my welcome was long past worn out. I had made a lot of enemies by excelling and being promoted over most laggards that did not take the appropriate time to study for their own promotions. My new peers in my current rank were even worse as they all had been in the service for a decade longer than me but were too lazy to do the work to get promoted, though they blamed everything except their effort for not meeting the cutoffs each year.

I was relieved when the unit I was reporting to submit a formal request for me to be reassigned to the Lackland Fuels Management Flight to re-do my "7-Level Certifications" that I had completed before leaving Moody Air Force Base, but the flight leadership did not submit my training as required. This was just another slight I suffered for our leadership disagreements at Moody when I was leaving that included not being submitted for NCO of the Year or my Commendation Medal. Now I was returning to that life, and I forever left the training world behind me when I reported to my temporary unit for the remainder of my time at Lackland.

The basic training experience had been the hardest and most rewarding experience of my life. I had directly trained around 2,500 Airmen on the "streets" as an MTI and another nearly 100,000 Airmen as a field training instructor. I had amassed over 5,000 platform teaching hours for a variety of subjects, receiving certifications as a Combat First Aid Instructor and Anti-Terrorism Officer. I received daily emails from former Airmen I had trained that thanked me for changing their lives, and this would be something that would continue for the remainder of my career.

I know I touched a lot of lives and helped set a select number of them on life paths that they could have never imagined when they were know-it-all civilians who joined the Air Force because I received many letters over the next few years of my career. Most of the letters explained the amazing careers the Airmen were having, told me about the awards they had earned, and thanked me for making their Air Force experience easier through the leadership training they had received.

The truth is that the Air Force can be an easy path if you do not care and you just show up to punch the clock every day. These mediocre Airmen and NCOs always lasted the longest in every unit I was assigned. The culture did not approve of people like me who cared about the Air Force and tried to uphold the values that the service instilled within me. These were the same values that saved my life from the mediocrity that I was taught growing up.

The common thing most NCOs did when new Airman or someone who completed leadership training returned to their unit was for the NCOs to counsel them to "forget all that nonsense you learned…we will teach you the way we really do business around here…" Then they would set forth to undo all the training the Airmen had learned and reconstructed the value systems with made-up logic simply to keep the standard as low as possible. If any Airman showed signs of being an overachiever their unit NCOs would set forth to break them down, discriminate against them, or show favoritism to others that they "liked more" instead of basing their opinions on the performance and core values of everyone as the Air Force mandated.

This was the world I was returning to and I knew my road was going to be difficult. I had been freed from "Plato's Cave" and now I was voluntarily being shackled back to the floor, with the fakes images on the wall that I knew were not real but the people around me believing wholeheartedly that it was all the true reality. I got a sample of how hard it would be in the first conversation I had with my new Chief Master Sergeant at my new flight.

I joined the Air Force in 1995 with ambitions to see the world. My dream was not initially rewarded when I was assigned to a base in the middle of nowhere New Mexico. I begged to be sent anywhere overseas and was sent to South Korea where the worldly experience was limited, mostly due to a bad chain of command that kept us in wartime scenarios for most of my time there. Now I was being assigned to Royal Air Force Base Lakenheath, a notoriously tough assignment due to the mission of the F-15E models that were located there.

I arrived in England in the first week of January 2006. The weather was the opposite of what I had left behind in San Antonio, Texas, with very cold temperatures and a constant cold drizzle always. The days were very short with sunrise occurring around 10 am and sunset before 3 pm daily. This was a foreshadowing of how my time at this base would end up being.

I flew into Heathrow International Airport and after a few hours standing in a customs line and searching for my misplaced bags I made my way to the military chartered buses that ran from the airport to the bases in-country. I checked in and found I had about 2 hours before we departed for the base and I left to find something to eat in the airport. The British foods were intriguing at all the stores, and I decided on checking out the "Marks & Spencer" because it had a variety of fresh sandwiches and exotic drinks. I chose a "hoisin duck wrap" and a weird drink I have seen. The selection of British sandwiches was very different than the mass-produced, always frozen solid, and mostly inedible turkey or ham sandwiches at US convenience stores. The first taste of British food was surprisingly good, and

I hoped this was a sign of the new life I would be creating in the United Kingdom.

    I boarded the bus a few minutes before departure and settled in for the four-hour drive to the base. I remember the smells of the country being very strange, a mix of sweet and pungent and unknown, and to this day I can remember them all vividly in my mind. I watched out the window as we traveled through the city and it disappeared behind us and we entered a more rural area in England.

    The freeway drive in England was very different compared to the US where exits were abundant, and the signs of commercialized areas were every few miles. The English countryside was mostly unoccupied lands with the occasional farm life being seen every now and again. There were not many exits on the "motorways", as they are called in the UK, save the occasional "Welcome Break", a British version of a truck stop. The villages were spaced out every 20-30 minutes. The drive reminded me of driving through Alabama or some other rural state that lacked any signs of life.

    I arrived at Lakenheath in the late evening after traveling for over 24 hours. My sponsor met me at the bus stop and gave me the information and keys for my billeting room before helping me settle my gear into it. He gave me the schedule for the week ahead with a lot of inprocessing appointments already set up for me. I was very happy with my room as it was a full-sized apartment with full kitchen and bedroom. This was a good start to my new assignment, and I looked forward to settling in as soon as possible.

I did not sleep too well the first night in the UK because of jet lag and the anticipation of all the long appointments I would be attending for the next few weeks. When you arrived at a new duty station the first month is all wasted time with appointments set up to get you registered in the base systems and giving you time to find housing and move into it. I was also forced to attend cultural appointments that filled you in on the local customs and our military agreements about living in the United Kingdom.

The worst of the appointments was with the housing office as the representatives were very unprofessional and made blatant threats to military members about finding housing fast or they would "kick you out of your billeting". The culture of this office was apparently misguided by the desire to save as much money for allowances paid to military members and I am very sure many awards were won through their frugality and unprofessional methods.

The hardest part about being in England and needing to find housing was that I had no car to drive around and I did not have any friends that I knew of at the base to help me. I had a ticking clock and angry housing official threatening to make me homeless and no way to get around to find a good house. This left me having to take the first place I could find that was not falling apart, or at least it seemed like it was not from a distance.

I ended up living in a very small village in the Norfolk countryside, called Feltwell. My new village had two pubs, which were also two of three places to eat in the area, and a single "cooperative store" that had very limited amounts of food, and nothing else. The area was in the middle of the agricultural center of the area where farmers grew mostly a product called "sugar beets". There was nothing exciting about the area, but I was in a house and could get my household good delivered to settle into my routine.

The next few weeks were all spent in classrooms being drilled with information and filling out the same paperwork a few dozen times. I was completely burned out on inprocessing and looked forward to getting to work and receiving my assignment in my unit. I had been out of the career field for over four years and looked forward to just getting into a routine.

I arrived for my first day at my new unit after being in England for about three weeks. I had not been contacted by anyone other than a few calls from my sponsor during that time and I had no idea who was in my unit or if I would know anyone. The chances that I had former basic trainees at the base was very high since I had trained a large amount and I thought it would be nice to see faces I knew, either old or new.

My suspicions were correct when I arrived and found I had one former trainee in the flight, and he entertained our flight members with stories of his experiences being trained by me. This would turn out to be a negative thing as the leadership in the flight would use him as a basis for judging the NCO they thought I was, and I never would have a fair chance to just make my own place in the group.

The Chief was the first person who addressed my "history" as a drill instructor when he called me into his office this was the first thing he discussed. He began by talking down my experience as a drill instructor and telling me that I was no longer in basic training and he expected me to be mellow in my actions. This was in response to the stories he had gained from my former trainee and his lack of context for anything he was told vastly influenced his bias against me.

Next he asked me about myself and I told him about my background and when he asked what I thought my biggest accomplishment was thus far in my career I answered, "everything I learned in Combat Control working with the best Airmen I have ever had the privilege of serving with and that I cherished being a Paratrooper most of all because I overcame my own fears to accomplish that goal…"

The Chief responded, "Yeah that is all nice and all but you need to stop trying to be all 'gung ho' and accept your place here as a worker in my flight…I expect you to fall in line and leave all that nonsense behind you…"

I was taught at a young stage in my career there are two types of Senior NCOs, the ones who were true leaders and the ones who were not. My old mentors had said that the ones who were not leaders were not Chiefs or Seniors but rather E8s and E9s referring to their pay grades instead of their customary titles we used for each. The Chief was not quite a non-leader but his comments about the most important achievements of my life, where he chose to downplay their importance and chastise me for leaving the career field made him a borderline non-leader in my eyes, or at least in my first impression.

He gave me a rundown of his expectations and he assigned me a few extra duties he wanted me to head up as to use my basic training experiences to his advantage. I found it self-defeating in principle that he would tell me to forget all the drill instructor stuff I learned and then tell me he was going to use it for something he needed. The conversation created a slight role ambiguity for me. I set forth to just find my own path forward in the unit.

My next meeting was with the Senior Master Sergeant and I quickly discovered a huge powerplay within this unit was afoot. The "Senior" probed me on my conversation with the Chief and then he set forth to recruit me to his political camp in lieu of the Chief's agenda. I did not say anything that would give my allegiance in any direction and this would turn out to be the same as choosing the Chief over him. I would not recover in the Senior's opinion of me for the rest of his tour and to make matters worse he would become the Flight Chief very shortly when the Chief was moved to the Squadron to be the Senior Enlisted Advisor to our commander.

Situations like this were not uncommon in POL where they valued personal relationships and cliques were the true chain of command. I seemed to have stepped into the middle of a power struggle that I was unaware existed, and I took note of this by taking notes of who followed who to further understand what I was getting into in this unit. I gradually met the rest of the people in the flight over the course of my first week and most "already knew about me", which meant they had formed some biases based on basic training stories they had heard. I did not pay much attention to it all and focused on getting all my certifications completed so I could receive my assignment in the unit.

The Chief ended up moving a few weeks after I arrived leaving the Senior in charge. I was summoned to the Senior's office one day and informed that he was placing me in charge of our Fleet Maintenance section. This news was not good at first as this was the place that lazy NCOs were assigned, and it was usually the path to nowhere in your career. However, the dynamics of the job had changed over the last few years and the Air Force had initiated a career field merger that was very new and the responsibilities of the new section had not even been fully spelled out, in fact, there were no rules in place when I assumed the position.

I took the initiative and went to my newly assigned section to see what condition it was in and begin to formulate my plan of action to get it performing at the highest level. The sight I found when I arrived was appalling and I knew immediately I was put there to fix a big problem area that no one else wanted to deal with or cared about. The inside of the maintenance shop was dirty and disorganized. Every inch of the building was covered in dirt and grease, and the team assigned were oblivious to how disgusting the place looked. Parts and tools were scattered everywhere, and there was no sign of any processes for anything.

I asked questions to the team and the first issue I found was that we had a high ranking British civilian employee who they told me "would not accept me changing anything" in the section and that I should just adapt to their standards.

I made a big mistake at that moment and stated out loud, "...maybe it is time we replace that guy with a military member we can control..."

This statement was relayed to the deviant British employee and he set forth to create as much chaos with the merger and my assumption of leadership in the section as possible. He was the technical expert and the team looked up to him because he did not hold anyone or anything accountable if the fleet maintenance was done. He was a rank in the British civilian system that placed him in the top percent of technicians on the base, and he had stagnated there because he refused to take a management position because he "detested managers" and he considered himself a better technician than a leader.

My first mission was very evident. I needed to either bend the British tech to my leadership plan or fire him to get a military member that had to adhere to my rank. The easy path would have been to get new tech and train them to the new standard as the British tech was a laggard and fought any change for the sake of not changing, regardless if it made sense. I set forth to bend the British tech to my leadership and this was the hard road as I found out

My first days in my new role I spent getting to know what I was responsible for and what assets we were charged with safeguarding. This should have been a simple task and it proved to be impossible as there was not a single report that showed assets, minus a generic report in the Fuels Management System (FMS) that was very inaccurate and never updated properly. I questioned the NCOs assigned to me and was met with major resistance as they withheld information and attempted to convince me they knew best about what they were doing.

The overall condition of the section was unsatisfactory and if we had been inspected by our Major Command (MAJCOM) we would have been laughed out of the Air Force. The merger that was supposed to have already been completed was ignored completely by the team and they justified this with the complaint they were "too busy" to do the tasks the Air Force ordered them to do over a year earlier.

The two NCOs I was given were not POL troops originally and were re-classed from the Transportation Squadron and they were not happy with the reassignment. The culture of their old unit was nothing like the standards the POL expected with them clinging to their old unit's customs like a child who could not let go of their "binky blanket". They had the potential to be very solid NCOs but had been trained improperly by other NCOs that practiced the "crab culture" and believed if the trucks ran nothing else mattered.

The ranking Staff Sergeant had been the longtime NCO in charge of the section, and he resented me being placed in charge because I was not even trained in the technical skills required to do the job yet. He also had been in the service a lot longer than me but was unable to get promoted via the normal promotion programs due to his lack of dedication to studying for the tests. He was a talented technician with a lot of experience but did not apply himself to the level required to make the rank he should have already obtained at this point in his career.

His lack of leadership skills was also easily recognizable due to the state of the section and the overall attitudes the troops he had been supervising displayed. He believed that leadership was being one of the guys and when needed standing up for your people if got in trouble. These are admirable qualities but are not the traits that make you an effective leader as the lack of accountability he discarded as unimportant led to the section's decline.

The younger Staff Sergeant was also an experienced NCO who was not quite as far behind in promotions as the senior one but still was on the same path. He was well-liked by the troops and he also had the exact same leadership philosophies as the ranking SSgt. The difference was the younger one was a lot more cunning than the ranking one and was closer to a late adopter or laggard mentality making him more difficult to manage. If I gave him a game plan for implementing the required MAJCOM changes for the mandatory merger, he would tell me "sorry that is impossible" and disregard them completely.

Around this time, the Air Force made it harder to identify sharp Airmen when they decided to change the uniform standards and introduced a wash-and-wear uniform and non-shine boots as our standard uniform. The uniform changes fit perfectly into the status quo minded philosophy of the service and now every Air Force member looked dumpy and the same. The old uniforms required pressing and the boots had to be shined. The standards for doing this had the minimal levels that most people did and then the overachievers could separate themselves from everyone else. Now everyone was average looking, and it was easier for higher ranking people to push the Airmen who had just recently looked like slobs as their top people.

I found I was facing a team of people dedicated to the status quo and guys who felt they knew better than the Air Force for what they needed to do to be compliant with the merger standards. They were all controlled completely by the British tech who was very negative in his approach to doing his job and this was where my first challenge rested. I called the British tech into my office a few weeks into my new role and sat him down for a talk about what we needed to do to be compliant with the Air Force.

He was not receptive at all to any words I said and spent the time interrupting and saying "that is not going to happen" to anything I explained was being implemented. The hour-long meeting was a complete waste of time and in the end, I offered to trade him out for a military tech and send him back to his Transportation Squadron. This statement was not taken well, and he stormed out of the office to go see "his Chief…"

A few hours later, I was called by my Senior and ordered to report to his office. When I arrived the NCOs under me were already there and it was clear I was entering a hostile environment and the middle of whatever conversation had been taking place. The Senior instructed me to sit down and then began lighting me up in front of the NCOs that worked for me about how I need to "stop acting like a drill instructor" and a few more complaints they had raised.

I stood my ground and explained that he had placed me in charge of a section that was extremely out of compliance and now he was cutting my legs off by not supporting me implementing the merger changes that were required by MAJCOM. I sarcastically stated, "just say the word boss and we will stop following all Air

Force instructions and just hope the section meets the minimum standards…"

This was a very wrong approach and was met with a stern correcting tirade by the Senior where he told me, yes you are "accountable" for that section but "Staff Sergeant (senior one) is the technical expert and that makes you equal…"

I stood my ground again and stated, "the Air Force disagrees with you on that and has created ranks for a reason….either I am in charge 100 percent or I am not…move me to another section and keep the mediocrity he had before me…or let me do what I do to fix it, but there is no 'equal' involved in that…"

I agreed that the Staff Sergeant was an important asset, but he chose to not get promoted by taking for granted his opportunities each year when the test came around. I explained he had been given more opportunities than me to get promoted to an equal rank and chose to not properly study. Additionally, if he was as good as the Senior was portraying him, the equal to me statement, then the shop would already be in order and I would not be needed to fix the three years of degradation that he had allowed.

Unfortunately, I was outnumbered 3 to 1 and the Senior did not like my attitude, possibly also me personally, and he held firm to his "equal" concept. I changed tactics and just accepted his made-up rank structure and set forth to change the ranking Staff Sergeant. The Senior also took his opportunity to make it more official and submit the laggard NCO for a program called "Stripes For Exceptional Performers", a program that was created to promote deserving NCOs early if they showed higher levels of performance. The program was instead commonly used to promote lazy, popular NCOs ahead of others. The Staff Sergeant was notified a few months later of his promotion to Technical Sergeant thanks to the role ambiguity issues we faced, and the Senior's push to get him officially on my level.

I never did agree with the Air Force's policy for granting STEP promotions because they never considered "exceptional" performers despite the name. The program was always used to promote lagging NCOs who never fulfilled their responsibilities to learn the knowledge required for each rank and never scored high enough to get promoted. The program was a method for the "good ole boy" system to push their favorites without those NCOs having the knowledge to meet the requirements of the next rank.

The misuse of the program compounded the issue of the overall promotion system where no one received accurate performance reports, and everyone was rated as "Exceptional" in their performance and then time in grade was the biggest rated factor for gaining points each year. The problem was Air Force-wide and flooded the ranks with NCOs who were incompetent and detested anyone stepping outside the status quo.

I fought daily with the role ambiguity issues that were forced on me. If I implemented an Air Force policy the NCOs would run to the Senior to complain and he would remit anything I did. I had to change my tactics if I was going to survive the "crab leadership" politics that this unit was dedicated to upholding, and I decided to begin with personnel shake-ups. I requested the NCOs I was assigned be moved to other sections for them to gain more technical knowledge in the whole career field as they had spent 10-15 years as mechanics without doing any other POL related jobs.

I also requested a Senior Airman (SrA) technician that had been re-classed to POL but was assigned to fuel truck driver duties because he was not as high ranking as the NCOs. This would leave me with the British tech to overcome instead of three laggards that were hell-bent on not changing anything. I was rewarded with the NCOs being moved and the SrA being assigned to me, which was a blessing because he was a very innovative and seasoned technician making him the opposite of the guys that left.

I was also given an SSgt that the Senior hated and the other NCOs trashed behind his back all the time because he was a very unmotivated performer with a career field-wide reputation for mediocrity. He was added to my requested trades as a kind of punishment for not toeing the crab leadership lines and I was told to fix him, or my performance reports would reflect his performance as well.

This was a common threat for high-level performers who the senior leadership feared would promote quickly and not adhere to the common practices they believed were the cornerstone of their small empires. If an NCO was feared to be uncontrollable the senior leadership would just mark them down on their performance reports to prevent them from being promoted past Master Sergeant. This was all although nearly 99 percent of the Air Force received what they called "firewall 5's" meaning they were rated "exceptional" in every category despite their mediocre true performance.

Overachievers were held to a different standard for performance reports and the ambitions of the high performers were used as a method of control. If the achiever did not fall in line the unethical NCOs would punish them with markdowns in categories on the report or bad ratings compared to their peers that they clearly outperformed. This was the punishment I received for the group dynamics issues I inherited at Lakenheath.

The Senior punished me by marking me down in the leadership category on my performance report. The rating would punish me for about seven years as I would not even be considered for Senior Master Sergeant until after that report was off my record. He told me to my face that he intended to "slow me down" because he felt I was promoting too fast for his liking and unethically took actions to make it happen.

The Senior's actions to slow me down was contrary to the previous issues he had taken with me rating the younger SSgt assigned to me as only an "above average performer". The Senior had taken issue with my rating even though the SSgt had numerous documented issues that clearly showed he was not "exceptional", to include being moderately overweight and failing several physical training assessments in that rating period. The Senior liked the SSgt and protected him by overriding my rating to change it back to "exceptional", but in my case, he gave me the lesser ratings with no real justification.

The decision was outside of my circle of control and I put my head down to focus on the task at hand of instituting the career field merger that the "exceptional performers" had blown off now for more than two years. I could not worry about promotions that would be about four years down the road at this point and had to just do what I could get my duty section up to standards. I had won a moral victory getting a new team and I now needed to change their mindset on what was possible if they all gave the full abilities to the merger.

I had to reach into my leadership toolbox and use all the methods I had learned in order to beat this backward system. I decided to start with mentoring my new team using the 17 Laws of Teamwork training program. I personally purchased each one of my people the books and training workbooks and then dedicated a few hours per week for us to study and discuss the chapters. The implementation of the mentorship was met with the expected resistance because no one in the career field had done anything like it and therefore the team fought it at first.

I also found a method to gain the support of the British tech when I learned about quarterly bonus competitions the British civilian program hosted. The program allowed supervisors to submit their exceptional performers for awards that earned cash prizes of significant amounts. The day I found out about the competitions I solicited winning packages from people I knew on the base in order to gain an understanding of what performance was winning and set forth to write the best package that I could for my employee. The tech refused to give me any information about anything he was working on and I was forced to give him 100 percent credit for everything I was implementing in the section for the merger.

It takes a lot to suck up your pride and hand over all the credit for things that you have worked hard to create but I had only one choice for success and this was it. I detailed all the merger tasks that I had found and corrected and gave him the credit. I also gave him the credit for all the inventories and processes we had implemented over the past year and built him up as the best employee that had ever lived. The package was written about me, but to gain the needed support of the tech I had to use all my performance capital to make him the best on the base.

I worked well into the late evening until I was confident that the package was a winner and submit it well after midnight. All I could do was hope that I had done enough to earn the tech a victory and gain his trust in the process. Two weeks later the Flight Chief called us all to the main building for an impromptu meeting. When we showed up there was a group of high-ranking officers and a few British leadership officials that I had never met.

The Flight Chief took the floor and announced the highest-ranking commander who in turn came forth to explain why he was there. He called the British tech to the center of the floor and explained that he had been chosen for one of the awards for that quarter and read off a few of his accomplishments to the group. He explained that it was his pleasure to present him with the plague and that he had also earned the highest bonus available for any British employee due to his performance.

I could see the look of shock on the British tech's face as he heard the very processes and programs, he despised being read off the list. All the things he had fought hard against and refused to implement were looked at by his own leadership as amazing feats worthy of several thousand British Pounds Sterling. The look on his face was worth every hour I spent working on those projects and processes and after the ceremony was concluded I walked up to him to congratulate him on his award.

I extended my hand and told him "Congratulations, this is well deserved..."

He just shook my hand and did not respond.

I knew that he was aware that our team had been working on all those tasks without his assistance and he was also aware I gave him full operational leadership credit for it all. The performance award earned him about £5,000.00, or about $10,000, and since he had been employed at Lakenheath for nearly two decades not a single supervisor had ever submitted him for an award. He was overwhelmed by the gesture and came to my office after the ceremony to let me know that was the first cash award he had earned, and he thanked me.

His gratitude was the first positive thing he had ever said to me. Normally, if I talked, he made negative comments or contradicted my orders to the Airmen. This was a welcome start to what I hoped was a new beginning for progress in our section. I had found a motivator for the tech and from that quarter forward I continually submit him for awards that he always won hands down.

The team was gaining confidence with every milestone we completed. When I first took over the section, I had highlighted the tasks we were required to institute and gave a timeline for expected completion. The timeline was not set in stone, though I did hold anyone accountable for not meeting the original completion dates. This only took a few 7-day work weeks to get everyone on the same page.

I had learned early in my drill instructor tenure to using accountability to the set standards is an imperative that must always be upheld. If you set a realistic, attainable, and measurable goal then there is no reason the task cannot be met if the personnel are given the resources and support to do the tasks. The problem most people face is that they never map out a game plan for what they are trying to accomplish and attempt to make up the processes on the fly. This leads to inconsistency of standards for the jobs that are completed, or the team will lose focus and fail their objectives.

I made mentorship the cornerstone of my entire program and set aside times daily for each of the personnel that was under me. The Air Force mandated that supervisors conduct feedback sessions upon assignment to a section or rater, midterm, and follow-up after performance reports were completed, but the average Airmen who served would never receive these feedbacks as required. I only received official feedback sessions in my career when a supervisor wanted to document some deviant performance to justify why they were going to mark down my performance reports. This was the most common practice and supervisors would even threaten that if they had to write out an official one the ratee would "be sorry they asked".

My mentorship program was more involved, and I gave weekly feedback that was informal and monthly official feedbacks about how the personnel was meeting the set standards. This gave them the opportunity to improve any deficient areas and add some additional recommended tasks that I would highlight that would separate them from their peers. The goal was not to make their performance reports better because the reality was that no matter how much anyone sucked, the leadership would force the rater to give them an "exceptional" rating. The goal was for me to have the required data to ensure they were submitted for recognition every quarter if they were exceeding standards.

The year I implemented my mentorship program our small section earned nearly 50 monthly, quarterly, and annual awards. The effect on the team was astonishing. The more success they earned the more we were able to accomplish as a team. I was not even considered for a single award during this entire year because my supervisor was the Senior who despised me. He did not consider me a good performer even though my team had earned more than half the entire available awards for the entire squadron we fell under. When my team earned the Squadron and the Group level "Team of the Quarter" awards the credit was downplayed for my efforts. He went so far as to ensure I was not present when the award presented.

My team was coming together extremely well and the level of performance they were reaching led to more than just awards. The biggest recognition the team would receive was from an initiative the re-classed SrA I had traded for recognized as a process that could be improved. We created a LEAN process improvement initiative that was adopted by the MAJCOM and was considered for the entire Air Force for our career field. Unfortunately the LEAN initiative was killed at the Air Force level because SNCOs who had no mechanical training and who were primarily POL troops who did not understand the dynamics of the merged career fields decided to keep the status quo.

I had trained the team to consistently look for methods to improve the efficiency of everything we did in the shop. We constantly talked about processes. I empowered the team to create new processes that would take the minimum standards and enhance the outcomes to be better than the status quo. The SrA was skilled in coming up with new ideas and used the gift to create an entirely new vehicle inspection process that saved 1,000s man-hours annually across the Air Force.

The entire team pitched in to give him the support he needed to create the new process. I managed the overall submission to the MAJCOM and did not allow the crab-logic from the other NCOs in our flight to interfere with our progress. The efforts paid off and led to a highly visible initiative that epitomized the leadership culture I was attempting to create. The team was rewarded for their efforts with numerous awards and personal recognition, though not everyone in the flight was excited about the new processes we had created.

I was not concerned with the politics of the flight and I knew that my mission was to build up stronger Airmen and NCOs to expand my programs that were creating successes individually. I was building up a very strong reputation on the rest of the base and every program I managed was rated as the top for the fighter wing. Senior NCOs outside of my unit loved me and requested I take a more active role in the base leadership by nominating me for positions in several base mentorship groups such as the Air Force Sergeants Association. I was well known on the entire base and at Royal Air Force Base Mildenhall which was our neighbor a few miles away.

My mentorship programs gained momentum and before long I was writing a weekly leadership motivational letter to over 2,000 Airmen around the world. I began the letter with a handful of Airmen I had trained and slowly grew it as I met new troops who wanted to learn and grow as a leader. I had completely stopped listening to the radio by this time and was only focused on listening to leadership content. I found the more I studied leadership the quicker I could make decisions in my normal duties and the more ideas I could accumulate for creating innovative new concepts.

The study of leadership was not to memorize the lessons or every detail of the concept. The purpose was to help your mind increase the number of situations that were recognizable. This would give your mind more tools to reduce the time required to make decisions overall. My peers all thought I was a know-it-all because no matter what the issue was, I could create rapid solutions or could fix complex problems quickly. The real secret was that all the books I had consumed were like tools for the mind where similar situations were studied. The solutions provided could be accessed for real-time problems. The more I read the more tools I had to access in my leadership toolbox. I was rising to the apex of my career. I was unaware that the end of it was about to abruptly come. As 2007 ended the group dynamics of my unit changed and it was not a good one.

The Higher You Climb The Farther You Fall

The leadership in my unit from 2006-2007 was mostly dismissive of my accomplishments overall. I was certified as one of the squadron Physical Training Leaders and Unit Fitness Program Managers. Most assigned members' interactions with me were me holding them all, regardless of rank, accountable to being in the best shape possible and being ready to go fight a war at any minute. The Squadron Commander had many times butted heads with me about the training sessions being too hard, but the sessions I hosted were the basic training workouts for zero week and first week trainees who were not even Airmen yet.

His argument was he felt like he was at football practice and I explained to him that the workouts were for people who had just entered the military and should be well below the abilities of full Air Force members. This was about the extent of our interactions and he left me alone to do my duties. Then he was given orders to leave the base and would be replaced with a female Lieutenant Colonel from the Pentagon who had never commanded. The outgoing commander's entire team received orders and the Squadron was set to have an entire changeover of leadership. The changes also included my supervisor and Flight Chief being replaced, and I thought this would be a welcome change as he was severely biased against me.

The year started off well for me as I was nominated for a base level award and won it making me the NCO of the Year for Lakenheath's Air Force Sergeants Association (AFSA) Chapter. I would be required to travel to Germany to compete for the US Air Forces in Europe (USAFE) level competition at the AFSA Division Professional Airmen's Conference. This would be my first ever professional development conference and I looked forward to the experience gained, though I doubted I would win the award because I was competing against the top NCOs from several dozen bases.

I attended the conference and learned a lot of interesting leadership and Air Force level information about enlisted lobbying efforts in Congress. I was also exposed to the top NCOs in all of Europe and gained notoriety for myself with other top performers. I had spent the first two years of my assignment in Europe fighting for changes and implementing new levels of performance into the status quo without being recognized. I had missed a lot of opportunities to spend time with the "best of the best" that the other top performers had earned through competition in the awards programs. Now I was exposed to another level of the Air Force and I fit in perfectly with the other performers.

I was very surprised when I was announced at the awards ceremony as the 2007 AFSA Division 16 (USAFE) NCO of the Year. This made me the number one performer out of over 35,000 personnel in the command. I had won small awards during my career and never thought it was possible to earn an award on this level. I was informed that I would be competing at the AFSA Professional Airmen's Conference (PAC) later that year.

The AFSA PAC is an annual conference where the top leadership of the entire Air Force meets for leadership development and to discuss Air Force current issues. The annual event is attended by a "who's who" of Air Force history with all the living Chief Master Sergeants of the Air Force, many former Chief of Staff of the Air Force, and the current top leaders from the Pentagon. All the NCO of the Year nominees were given mentorship by the strategic level leaders and developed to be future strategic leaders in the service.

The level of competition was very high, and I found myself sitting next to actual war heroes who had earned Bronze Stars with valor in the mentorship sessions. I felt more confident about my chances to win this time than I had at the USAFE event. I found that when you achieve a level of success you never thought possible then it awakens your mind to other levels of success that are possible. I knew my chances were slim, but I felt like I represented USAFE where 35,000 Airmen served, and many were as good as anyone in the competition, but I was the representative.

I was let down at the awards banquet when the Tactical Air Control Party NCO won the award. He was a true war hero who had called in thousands of pounds of ordnance on enemy targets killing hundreds of terrorists and earning him a Bronze Star with Valor. I could not realistically compete with a war hero and I was satisfied to be considered on the same level as him and knew it was the right decision.

My unit did not give me the warm welcome I thought I would get when I returned. The flight level just treated me like "I told you so" about my loss and the new Squadron Commander wanted to see me the minute I showed up to work. I assumed it was to ask about my experiences, but I was wrong.

I reported to the Squadron Commander's office as requested the morning I returned to work from the conference. When I walked into her office, I was aware that the welcome mat was not rolled out for me and I was ordered to sit at her conference table in her office. She then proceeded to officially, read me my rights and presented an Inspector General's (IG) complaint that had been filed against me for something that had occurred while I was on a Temporary Duty Assignment (TDY) prior to the conference.

The accusations in the IG complaint was that I had illegally used a rental car while deployed. I was being charged with fraud, waste, and abuse. My cloud of success that I was on from the conference exploded. I tumbled haphazardly to earth in disbelief. I was supposed to be at the apex of my career having finished in the top 3 NCOs in the entire Air Force. Now my career was in jeopardy. I was potentially going to be put in jail. I had to search my memories about what this was about. I narrowed the complaint down to two times I had used a rental car in the gray areas of the regulations.

Prior to the conference, I was sent TDY for several months to Nellis Air Force Base in Las Vegas, Nevada and then to Tyndall Air Force Base in Panama City, Florida. There were two trips I took then that could be deemed inappropriate. I waved my "right to

403

remain silent" and fully cooperated with the Squadron Commander. I explained both trips we had taken and the purposes as I saw them necessary.

The first trip was in Las Vegas. I had a SrA with my team that was having troubles being deployed and he was drinking heavily. He had a history of alcohol problems and after acting out one day at work I took him on a road trip to Los Angeles to get away from the craziness of Las Vegas for a short period. I took the time locked in the car with him to discuss his issues and help him work out his challenges ahead. We created a plan of action for him to not let his drinking cause him to get in trouble and overall the trip was an intermediate success as his drinking stopped and his performance improved.

The second trip was while we were in Panama City and this time, I paid for my team to go see the Jacksonville Jaguars play a game in Jacksonville, Florida. The trip was a reward for the team doing a very good job and I thought it was a good idea for us all to do some team-building activity. Everyone had an amazing time and, on the way back from the game we stopped at my father's home just outside Jacksonville and ate dinner before returning to our hotel.

Either trip could have been considered improper use of our assigned rental car per the Air Force instructions on the subject. I explained that I was not doing anything different than any other Airmen assigned to this TDY as other teams took rentals to drink at clubs and casinos, drove to do skydiving, and I personally was the designated driver for the group that included all the highest-ranking Senior NCOs and the TDY Commander more than one evening while in Las Vegas.

I was not in a good situation. The Squadron Commander was new and did not know me, therefore I had no performance capital with her to allow her to see my decisions were not per my normal behavior. She had also created her own bias about me from the outgoing leadership and the day she arrived I was assigned as her driver and she did not like me from her first impression. I informed her I was going to seek military defense counsel and fight the charges against me. She was not pleased and discontinued the meeting as I invoked my rights under Article 31 of the UCMJ. I had been read my rights at Lackland numerous times, and each time I always knew I had not done anything wrong making it not as stressful. This time I clearly had violated the rules and I was facing a potentially painful outcome.

The year 2008 had been very good up until that point. I had been promoted to Master Sergeant in June, led the deployment for several months, and competed for an Air Force level award. Now my career was over, and I did not know what to do to fix it. Everything I had worked for was lost and I would be screwed if I received anything less than an honorable discharge.

I reported to the Area Defense Counsel and my lawyer gave me instructions for what to do to fight the case. I followed his instruction exactly and wrote a rebuttal to the charges then turned a copy into the commander. After that, it was a waiting game, and several weeks passed without any word. Finally, the commander's secretary called my supervisor and told him to send me to her office promptly.

The drive a few short miles to the Squadron Commander's office was the most stressful period I had faced in my career. I was not certain that I would not be walking in free to be escorted by Security Forces personnel out of the building. I arrived and waited on her waiting area couch for what seemed like forever before being called inside. The Squadron Commander proceeded with all the formal processes she was required to do in cases like mine and then she gave me my sentencing. She had decided to give me a "Letter of Reprimand" (LOR) for my bad decisions and no other actions would be taken. She formally read the reprimand and I signed it then she kicked me out of her office. I had dodged a huge bullet and survived with minimal damage, minus a lot of stress, or so I thought.

The real reason I received the LOR was that in my rebuttal I named high-ranking people's names who had been aware of my trips and they would also be held accountable if they proceeded with my case. I was not given a pass because the commander wanted to be fair, I was given one because other people would be brought into the mess if she filed formal charges. I had engaged in the same activities as other members and it was not right, but the other commanders involved did not want to destroy their people's lives like my commander had no problem doing.

I had been given a short-term pass, but I was far from out of the Squadron Commander's sights. She would ensure that she made me pay for the loophole that saved me and it was not long before the first shots were fired in what would be a year-long war she waged against me. The first steps the Squadron Commander took to destroy me was she fired me from all my special assignments for the squadron. I had worked about 13 or more extra duties and programs for the Squadron or

Wing level since I arrived at the base. A few days after receiving my LOR, I was told I was no longer assigned to any of them. The reason was that the commander said I was incompetent, and she did not want me assigned to any special duties.

The accusations were unfounded and every program I managed was at the top of the Wing for performance. I could not fight it as she was the final approval authority for all duties assigned. I did not complain because I had been doing the work of many NCOs while my peers had no assigned programs. The work level inequality was very unbalanced, and I took the changes as a much-needed break. The attacks did not stop with the removal of the programs however and continued into other areas of my life.

I had been selected to appear in a Paul Greengrass movie featuring Matt Damon that was set to film in Morocco. The part was small, but the pay was more than I made in a year in the military for only 30 days on location. The opportunity was huge, and Paul Greengrass had personally emailed me to hire me which was an honor. I was required to submit leave paperwork, and this is when the attacks started. The Squadron Chief called me to his office for no reason one day and when I arrived, he began drilling me about the movie.

I told him about how I got selected and Paul Greengrass personally contactgvbing me as well as how excited I was to do it. He then threatened me that if I took the leave, I would face severe consequences from the Squadron. He continued that "my career would regret" the selfish decision to be in the movie because the Squadron Commander felt Greengrass was anti-military and would exploit me. I was very confused by the conversation. I discussed it with my supervisor. He made me aware that he was told if I left for the movie, I would regret making the decision. He did not tell me what that meant or why it was a big deal to be in the movie. The situation was completely blown out of proportions. The message was clear – I would be punished if I took the leave I had earned to do the movie. The Squadron Commander could not legally deny me my leave. She could make me aware that my career would be in jeopardy if I went. I was forced to contact Paul Greengrass to let him know my commander's views on the politics of the movie.

I was robbed of a huge opportunity to potentially have a very real career in the entertainment industry. There was no logic to the reason for the threats. I was still focused on overcoming the LOR I had just received at this point. I hoped that I could maybe deploy to get away. Then when I returned I would leave to another base. I had no idea the storm that was coming. Had I known no matter if I went to film the movie or not my career was already doomed I would have just gone. The bullying had barely even started. I would soon find out the extent of my situation at Lakenheath. I was nearing the end of my assignment there but to leave I required the Squadron Commander to "approve" my orders and allow me to move. I had just over a year remaining before I was set to move to my next assignment. This would prove to be too long to save my career.

The change of leadership in my unit in 2008 had shaken up the chain of command to include my Flight Chief, and my new supervisor was a "good ole boy" with a reputation for being an "old school NCO". This translated in POL-speak to "he played favoritism and should be treaded lightly around". He was a new Senior when he arrived and was still learning the new responsibilities of the job. He was a jock who at this late stage in his career was more concerned with the record of the softball team than the professional development of the Airmen assigned under him.

He and I never connected in any sense of the words. He resented the recognition that I had received from outside the flight and squadron because he believed that he should solely control the fate of "his Airmen", but my influence had grown well outside his circle of influence. He set forth to interject himself into all my outside connections and started by running as my Vice President for the Lakenheath AFSA chapter. The position of Vice President would mean he had no real responsibilities, but he could interject his will by way of his higher rank, into my strategic plans for the chapter. The position allowed him to take the credit for the good things we were doing without him personally having to put in any effort, and he was a master of using his rank over his laggard leadership skills.

The Senior rarely contributed anything of value to the AFSA chapter, but he did a good job of filling open positions with his "good ole boys" to increase his leadership influence over the group. I was the President of the organization, but I was soon surrounded by his cronies and was like a CEO without the support of the executive board. I had taken solace in the fact that I could escape the bullying of the squadron by engaging in AFSA activities and did not have people over me who were set on destroying my career. Now I had no safe place to get away from the people over me, and I was trapped.

The Senior began his bullying in the organization first in little ways. One time a Staff Sergeant, who was assigned as the recruiting NCO for the chapter, gave a presentation and he was very obviously distraught by public speaking. The Staff Sergeant's first language was Spanish, and he was very concerned about his English skills but soldiered on through his presentation. The Senior pulled me aside at the end of the meeting and ordered me to "ban that idiot Staff Sergeant from ever embarrassing him again" and told me that if I let him speak in front of a group again he would deal with me personally. The Senior's leadership philosophy was very clear at that moment. He was not a leader. He was more concerned with his own personal reputation than creating opportunities to help the junior NCOs develop their skills.

The AFSA opportunities were designed to help younger NCOs develop skills outside of their technical or supervisory positions in their unit. The purpose of assigning the young leaders to special positions was to give them opportunities to gain experiences in public speaking, leadership, project management, and any other tasks that would help them improve their abilities to build better leaders in their own organizations. The AFSA model worked well and helped young NCOs and Airmen develop without the formal judgments of the official chain of command.

The Senior's selfish leadership beliefs did not meet the AFSA model that I had been brought up within over the past 12 years at that point. He believed that the organization was an extension of his reputation and he forbid anyone to "embarrass" him and therefore he set forth to rid the organization of all younger members serving in leadership positions. Before long the entire AFSA chapter was full of laggard Master Sergeants who were unmanageable and lazy but were loyal to the Senior and met his approval only. The tensions of his attempts to dominate me in all aspects of my life grew by the day. He knew the Squadron Commander did not like me and he could exploit that to gain his next promotion. I was just a pawn to sacrifice and he despised me enough to not even blink when he did it.

The time between the Squadron Commander's first attempt to destroy me and her next attack was only a few weeks, but the next attack was not due to any mistake I made, it was a direct attack on my character and influence. The catalyst for the incident started at a squadron "Top 3 Meeting", a strategic planning meeting for the top three enlisted ranks where we discussed squadron business for the upcoming quarter. The big topic of discussion at this meeting was the lack of support the Squadron Commander was getting and the lack of participation she was receiving at events she hosted.

The top squadron Senior NCOs had a lot of inputs on why they believed the Airmen in the squadron were not participating in the Squadron Commander's programs, but none of them were telling the truths from their people. I decided to pull the Squadron Chief Master Sergeant aside after the meeting and let him know the truth from the lowest level, and we discussed the issues for about a half-hour. I explained to him that the average Airman in the ranks saw and heard about how the Squadron Commander was hammering people at all levels to enforce her policies. She refused to gain any buy-in or support from the people under her and all the Senior NCOs had witnessed how she had destroyed a half dozen very solid leaders for not agreeing with her. This had included several Chief Master Sergeants that she had fired from the Senior Enlisted Advisor position.

I explained that I had dealt with her concerning a serious issue and found her to be fair in her treatment of me, but that was an exception to the rumors or actual documented cases of abuse of power she was creating across the entire squadron. The people in the ranks feared to deal with her because she seemed to take pride in destroying enlisted member's careers and had zero empathy for anyone under her command. I clarified that her need to control everything surpassed any logical leadership practices and it was clear her management style was only the directing style where she wanted to make 100 percent of every decision for every flight level program under her. She seemed to lack trust in her leaders, and this was the real reason no one in the squadron felt like participating in anything she created.

The Squadron Chief asked me a few questions and then ended our impromptu feedback session. He told me he would attempt to address the issues I brought up with the Squadron Commander and thanked me for my candid feedback. We then parted ways and I put the conversation out of my mind. Then all hell broke loose in the squadron and I was oblivious to the storm I had created. The Squadron Commander called "emergency rank tier calls", a meeting with her broken into the ranks of E1-E4, E-5-E6, and E7-E9. The purpose of this type of meeting is to allow each rank to speak candidly if required without supervisors being present to seek retribution if someone speaks up about something the supervisors felt should not be talked about.

I was told that I was not allowed to attend any of the tier meetings because I needed to manage the flightline operations. I had to juggle the schedules of all the Airmen and NCOs that were required to attend and ensure the flightline operations were all met without delay. I easily created a plan to meet the requirements and proceeded with my day as required. I did not think anything about missing the meetings or the purpose.

The next day I had scheduled a Thanksgiving celebration for my troops and all the NCOs brought in different traditional dishes for our Airmen as thanks for them working extremely hard this year. The NCOs covered all the flightline operations while the lower ranking troops enjoyed a day of feasting and socializing. Everyone had an amazing time and I felt a sense of pride at how well everyone worked together to show their appreciation to the lower-ranking troops. I was unaware that this would be the last time I ever felt anything good about the Air Force and this would be the last mission I ever lead as an NCO as my world was about to be destroyed forever.

The Thanksgiving celebration ended as a success. The flight went back to normal operations. The Airmen took over flightline operations later in the day. Then the NCOs took their time to warm up some leftovers and relax. Then a call came into the Fuels Control Center that a fuel truck had crashed into the gate at our parking area. I let the supervisor know immediately. He gathered the Flight Chief and the Flight Commander to go out with us to investigate. The crash was minor, but the Airman did manage to damage the gate keypad that is required to enter the parking area. We called in an emergency work order to the contractor who serviced the gate. The issue was closed from the operational side. I would still have to take actions against the Airman, to which I delegated to his immediate supervisors on his shift.

The group of flight leadership that had gone out to investigate the accident then started the walk back to the main building when the Flight Commander came up to me to chat.

He asked. "How is everything going TSgt Franks?"

I replied, "Today was an amazing day, all the Airmen got a chance to enjoy the Thanksgiving celebration, all the NCOs supported the flightline without complaint to let us do it, and minus the accident everything was perfect…'

The Flight Commander then turned to the Flight Chief, the Senior, and asked, "…hey do you want to go ahead and get this over with now since we are all here?"

The Senior replied, "Yeah I think that is best…" then told me to follow them to his office.

When I arrived at his office, I was completely ignorant about the purpose of their impromptu meeting. I assumed it was something to do with the accident but was shocked when I attempted to sit down and was scolded to "stand at attention!!!" by the Senior.

The bewilderment must have been obvious on my face as the Senior began reading me my rights from a card he pulled from his pocket. My mind raced to think of what the hell I had done now, but I could not find an answer in my mind. The reading of my rights seemed to take an eternity and I do not remember any of the words coming from the Senior's mouth due to the pace my mind was racing.

He completed his mandatory drama before asking me, "Do you know why you are here?"

I was very confused and still thought this was some joke.

Maybe they were promoting me. Maybe I won some award. Maybe one of my troops was being promoted. My mind could not grasp what was happening.

I replied, "I have no idea what this is about..." and stared concernedly at the Senior.

The Flight Commander, a young First Lieutenant who had very little military experience stood to my left lazily leaning on the bookshelf. My immediate supervisor, a very experienced Master Sergeant stood behind me quietly reading the situation. The Senior stood behind his desk attempting to portray an imposing figure of authority as he played the part of the inquisitor.

He then formally read me the charges against me. He explained that I was being charged with "maltreatment of the Airmen placed under my supervision" and that he had "credible evidence" that I was guilty of the accusations.

I stopped him right there and laughed out loud asking, "You are joking right?"

He assured me that he was not joking, and the allegations were credible and serious. He explained that the Squadron Commander's tier meetings had uncovered several Airmen and NCOs that "feared for their lives" because of the "bullying culture" I had created in my duty section. He stated that due to these serious allegations my "NCO responsibilities where thereby removed" and I was "not allowed to engage with any NCO or Airman without proper supervision being present…"

He was essentially telling me that without a trial or official punishment that I had been accused, judged, and sentenced to losing the NCO authority and responsibilities that I had earned. My mind rejected this, and I immediately demanded that I be court-martialed for a jury of my peers to convict me. I knew the Squadron Commander would just destroy my career without any due process.

Finally, the severity of the situation I faced was real and I broke down in tears. I had been reassigned from my smaller duty section to manage a much larger one and I was building a leadership culture with my team of nearly 100 Airmen. I knew that we had a long road ahead due to the number of laggards that were assigned, and I had led the team fairly and given even the worst NCOs hours of my off-duty time mentoring them on improving their personal performances. The impact I had made in the short time I was the leader had resulted in many early promotions and awards for the team. I had engaged in this mentorship with the best of intentions and gave myself fully to the team. Nothing I had done was illegal, and I knew it, but the Squadron Commander did not care as she shunned leaders and I was her next victim.

The Flight Commander inappropriately began to speak and though I forget his words I do know that he was making light of my tears and poking fun at my situation.

I responded forcefully, "I would watch your next words if you know what is good for you Lt."

The room got very quiet as the anticipation of the response from the Lieutenant was cut short by the Senior yelling at me to "be respectful" and something about "this is exactly why you are in trouble…"

Here I stood, the fittest, strongest person in the room and I was a very highly competitive black belt martial artist and they assumed that I would become violent with them about this issue. Instead, all I could do was cry in my hands as they mocked me and took pleasure from my brokenness. My strength was leading people to become better than they believed they could be and now I had nothing. I was an empty shell of an NCO with no influence, no voice, and no one had my back. I could sense the pleasure the Senior took in breaking me, and it felt like he was growing more confident the more I broke down. Not a single person attempted to console me. They just stared at me and made further accusations to further push me over the edge.

I was informed that I was removed from my positions in all my duties and assigned to another Master Sergeant who would babysit me every day until I left the base. I had over a year to go until I was eligible to move, and I could not see anything but darkness in my future. I had no hope and no support. I was alone and publicly humiliated when the Senior told the entire flight about my issues and how I officially had zero authority and no Airman had to listen to anything I said. This was not legal and there was still nothing I could do to change it.

The bullying I experienced was a daily occurrence. I would nearly have panic attacks driving to work because I knew I would face a day full of being yelled at in front of the lower-ranking troops for little to no reason at all. The typical day would have me report into work and the Senior would come into the hallway in the center of the office where everyone could see and hear him before he publicly mocked me. He would scream loudly at me and tell me how I was a "piece of shit who did not care about anything…" then retreat to his office to let the humiliation set.

The Squadron Commander ordered him to ban me from being submitted for any awards in or out of the squadron regardless of my performance. I was also removed from every duty I was assigned leaving me with no purpose in my career. Outside my squadron, I was still viewed as a superstar and was sought for many projects that required the best person. However, inside my squadron, I was a criminal and was treated like I had murdered people. I had no privileges of my rank and had no authority. I could not even execute my very basic assigned duties because I was not allowed to speak to any Airmen alone without a supervisor present to monitor me.

All I could see was blackness around me. I felt like the Senior was trying to get me to commit suicide to justify why he bullied me daily. I still believe that he wanted me to kill myself for him to have a sad story he could tell others about the NCO he tried to save but could not and make him the victim. I noticed throughout my career that the Air Force leadership would create the very chaos that pushed people to kill themselves. Then the leadership would spend weeks feeling sorry for themselves even though they are the reason the Airmen did it. Supposed leaders bullied many Airmen across the service for various reasons and then claimed the victim status for the very incident they caused. There was no real leadership for the Airmen that killed themselves. There was no real teamwork, but there was a lot of selfishness. The person who killed themselves were chastised for their actions and condemned because they did not seek help, when in fact if they did no Air Force leader would step forward to assist them.

I know this because I attempted to seek help through formal and informal leadership channels and was told: "stop being a cry baby" and do my job.

I contacted the Air Force Inspector General's office and was told: "this is not worth my time…"

I contacted the Area Defense Counsel lawyers and since I was not officially charged there was nothing they could do.

I contacted the Lakenheath Wing Commander's hotline and reported the on-going bullying in the squadron and did not even receive a return message.

I contacted every leader I served with, Senior NCOs and commanders, asking for help and every one of them told me "sorry, your situation is not worth risking my career..." The locally assigned Senior NCOs all stated that they knew what I was dealing with was illegal, but I was not worth them facing the same treatment if they helped me. I was utterly alone, in service with over 350,000 people not one of them would help me. If I was not a strong person, I would have killed myself at this point. I loved the Air Force and it had saved my life. Now I was found not worthy of being a part of it and no one valued all the sacrifices I had made at the Air Force's last-minute requests for over 12 years. If they needed someone to do something hard that a fraction of one percent of the service qualified to do I always did it, and at huge personal sacrifices.

I was in a hopeless situation and I had several years left on my enlistment making the situation untenable. My only course of action would be to get out before I was in prison for no reason. I made the decision and I went to the separations NCO to file for voluntary separation. The separations NCO explained to me that once I signed the paperwork there was no turning back and my career would be lost. My promotion to Master Sergeant would be lost, and I would not be able to return. I had two choices at this point, kill myself or separate. Those were the only options I saw in front of me and therefore I chose to leave the Air Force.

I signed the paperwork and only required a signature from the Squadron Commander to make it official. She was more than happy to oblige me and kick me out without having to do any paperwork. She had won. She got to take my Master Sergeant stripe without fabricating reasons why and got to kick me out of the service without having to create the paperwork required to show how horrid I was when my performance for 12 years showed otherwise. I made her case and closed the deal for her.

She signed my voluntary separation orders the fastest I had ever gotten anything approved by her in the months I had known her. I returned the papers to the separations office and my clock began to count down instantly. I asked for six months to give me enough time to save money to be able to afford the separation and loss of income I would be facing. If I had been smarter I would have left that day because I thought the bullying would end once I surrendered my career, but the weakness the Senior and Squadron Commander sensed was too tempting to not exploit and they set forth to push me to the other option I previously mentioned, suicide.

Throughout the time I was contemplating the separation option I was still the President of the AFSA chapter and people still thought of me outside of my squadron as a superstar performer. I was submitted for another award outside the squadron, against the orders of my Squadron Commander, and once again I easily won the award for the wing and was set to compete in the USAFE competition again. The Squadron Commander was livid about me earning the award and even though I invited her to the awards ceremony, and she attended, she chose to ignore me and shook all the other winners' hands but not mine.

She did make a comment as she was leaving, "if you were only as useful in your job as you are in extracurricular activities…" then walked away.

Her remarks were ironic because the common belief in her command was that she was the tyrant who could not do her job because she was too busy destroying Airmen's careers. The stories about her abuses of power were abundant and included rumors that she had fired or deployed all the squadron leadership that did not agree to her illegal actions against Airmen. She had also created a complete leadership shut down within the ranks because no one other than herself could make mundane decisions and all the SNCOs feared to make any decision because she could end their careers.

Also, I knew that I had done exceptional things as an NCO and changed people's lives while serving under her command. The list of Airmen that I had improved the performance was long and included many Airmen that the other NCOs were following the commander's lead by bullying these troops. The section I led had about a hundred assigned members and many of the "good ole boy" NCOs had created a culture of favoritism before I assumed control of the section.

I immediately had assessed the status of each Airman we had assigned and figured out their strengths and weaknesses. I found out that there were Airmen the NCOs had outcast in the section because they "did not like them". I took a different approach and met with each of them to determine the root causes of their troubles. The common complaint was that no matter what they did the NCOs treated them like they were trash, and each one of them had given up.

I was able to completely turn around each one of these Airmen's lives by mentoring them and holding them accountable. The NCOs assigned were also informed that the culture of favoritism was over and everyone in the flight would be treated the same or the NCOs would be held accountable. The conversation was not met without complaints as the NCOs attempted to resist these changes.

A TSgt that was a laggard complained that leadership was not found in a book, but when questioned about his philosophies about leadership his points were incoherent. He was an NCO that was on the laggard path and he was nearing twenty years of service but had just been promoted recently to E6. He resented my promotion to MSgt since I had served nearly ten years less than him. Still, I was the ranking individual, the positional leader, and my vision was the one that dictated the changes required. My program had been resisted heavily before we began seeing results.

My mentorship of the outcast Airmen led to one Airman self-identifying as an alcoholic. His poor performance was due to his illness. He had been hiding the causes of his poor performance for years. He ended up being voluntarily admitted to a treatment facility and got the help he needed. His career was saved because I did not allow the NCOs to torment him and required them to mentor him until he confessed about his issues. He would make huge improvements with his performance and would finally separate to become a commercial pilot. He wrote to me a few years after I had left the service to thank me for not giving up on him and pushing him to improve.

Another Airman who was bullied by the NCOs also improved his performance with the support of his supervisors. He was promoted to SSgt and did an exceptional job managing our fuels bulk storage facilities. His efforts were recognized when he was selected as Airman of the Year for the entire Fighter Wing and competed at the United States Air Forces in Europe competition where he finished in the top three out of nearly a dozen nominees.

A third Airman was a TSgt who had a career field-wide reputation as a laggard. He turned his career around under me. He started working for me as a very old SSgt with no ambitions. I spent hundreds of hours of my time mentoring him and his performance steadily improved. His old unit had called our base to condemn him before he was given a fair chance and due to his reputation, he was assigned to me. The changes he made in his life led to him being a catalyst for our team creating the LEAN program that saved thousands of man-hours across the service and saved millions of dollars. He would later retire from the service as an MSgt, a rank he told me he never would have attained if he had never met me.

Even the SSgt that was told he was "the same as me" when I first arrived contacted me to thank me for showing him a better path in his career. He had received the STEP promotion to TSgt and then was handpicked to fill an Air Force level Fuels Management job where he finally earned the rank of MSgt. He told me that he did not understand the lessons I was attempting to teach our team in the beginning, and it had all resonated several years later when he was promoted to SNCO. Emails or letters like his were nearly a daily occurrence for me at this point in my career and was a testament to the impact I was making in many Airmen's lives.

The commander selectively dismissed any performance from me that created these life-changing events for my Airman and was dedicated to fitting me into the beliefs she held about me. This is a common leadership error that immature leaders make because they will prejudge people they do not like and then set forth to find only the facts that support their beliefs. The commander had decided from the beginning that I was useless and then she set forth to find the needed issues required to condemn me.

She had created the entire thing with the help of her First Sergeant who also had a reputation as a poor leader. They did it as retribution for me talking to the Squadron Chief and used two poor-performing NCOs' complaints about them being held accountable as justification for my expulsion from the unit. The two NCOs were not credible in their accusations and both were known across the career field as substandard performers. Neither one of these NCOs could be placed in charge of deployment taskings for their rank because our management team knew they were too incompetent. Now they were star witnesses against me in the commander's inquisition.

The first was a TSgt who had served about 20 years. He had been a problem for the flight throughout his four years assigned due to his inability to perform at the level required for his rank. He also was very obese and was never deployable due to failing every fitness test he took for over two years. His weight was extremely out of regulation because his waist measurement exceeded 45 inches.

He had complained that I was not nice to him and that I would not allow him to hold any official position in our section because of his incompetence. He failed to mention all his negative influences on the troops assigned where he consistently attempted to circumvent the set standards by ignoring lawful orders he was given. He also attempted to align the younger Airmen under him to stand against having to meet the minimum standards. His goal was to get rid of having anything more than just show up to work.

He had no actual complaint but vaguely told the commander I was too tough on people and he did not like me. Ironically, three days before I separated from the service he came to my desk where I was inspecting folders to apologize for his role in my firing. He stated that he realized after I left how much I had done for them all and how I took his own recommendations for an idea he had, and I got it implemented. No one in his career had ever taken anything he said seriously. He admitted he never gave me a chance out of jealousy for my promotions and he intentionally tried to cause me issues because of it.

The second accuser was the TSgt's troop and was a 16-year SSgt who idolized his mentor. This SSgt had a nearly identical career to the TSgt's where he was too incompetent to be allowed to hold a position or be deployed in his positions equivalent to his rank. He also was in poor physical shape and constantly failed his fitness evaluations. His complaint to the Squadron Commander was that I had ripped up an EPR he had turned in and posted it on the NCO's bulletin board.

He failed to mention the reason this occurred. The reason was that the EPR was past due and when he turned it into me it was not correctly formatted, written unintelligibly, and would have poorly reflected the Airman's accomplishments he supervised. He also failed to tell her that I had spent about four hours of my off-duty time mentoring him on bullet writing and have given him all the changes that needed to be made. After our mentorship session, he only was required to type out the bullets we had worked on and print the report.

When he turned the EPR in he did not make a single change. He decided to print the original version and give it to my supervisor, per the TSgt's advice, to attempt to circumvent me in the process. The result was my supervisor yelling at me for allowing this behavior and counseling me about the poor writing skills of the SSgt. I did rip up the EPR, posted it on the board, and recalled the SSgt on his off-duty time to fix it. His complaint was retribution for this incident, but I had done nothing wrong.

The Squadron Commander used these laggards to fulfill her inquisition requirements. Her desire to destroy me led her to accept any complaint as valid regardless of the source. Incompetent leaders tend to seek only the answers they want and not the truth, and her consistent behavior fit this model. The truth leaders must understand is that people will live up to or down to the expectations you have for them. Your goal should not be to punish poorly performing workers. It should always be to improve their performance or find the root causes of their deviant behaviors. She had no intentions of either option or was seeking revenge for me questioning her authority to the Chief. Now that I had won another award that she desired to strip from me, she was not pleased at all.

She became extremely annoyed after the awards ceremony when the wing leadership funded my travels to compete in Germany at the USAFE competition and she could not deny my attendance. I took the trip as a much-needed respite from the squadron and it knocked off a full week that I would not be treated poorly of my remaining time in the service. I did not think much about winning the award as I was done with the Air Force and just wanted to leave. I went through the motions and had no expectations at the awards banquet when suddenly it was announced I had won a USAFE level award for the second consecutive year.

Winning awards at this level was normally a single occurrence in the best Airman's career and one that 99 percent of Air Force members never achieve. To do it two consecutive years placed me in a fraction of one percent of all Air Force members. The awards should have been my springboard to making Chief Master Sergeant, and instead, it was as worthless as a used Kleenex since I would be out of the service in a few short months.

Ellis Franks "Always Leave An Airman Behind: A Real Story of Surviving The Crab Leadership Culture

The normal procedures when someone wins a Major Command level award is the squadron lets the wing know and then they make a formal announcement on the wing website. I knew that my award would not be sent through the normal process. The only people who would know about it were the handful of AFSA members that attended the next meeting when the secretary covered the old and new business. I was lucky that the Command Chief Master Sergeant was in attendance and offered to cover the costs of my trip to compete at the Air Force level competition.

Once again, the Squadron Commander was livid. This time she set forth to figure out a means to stop me from gaining any recognition. The next few months between the USAFE and Air Force level competitions would be the most stressful of my life. The Squadron Commander would have me arrested numerous times for trivial issues. The most ridiculous one was when my dog jumped our fence and killed rabbits in the neighborhood.

The incident occurred when I was teaching a martial arts class on the base and I was not even present. My wife was getting ready for a big AFSA fundraiser we were hosting the next day. She had let the dog out into the backyard to get him away from the food she was prepping for the event. She had to deliver the prepped items to another location and left him in the backyard while she drove everything over to our staging area for the next day. While she was out the dog saw the rabbits and jumped the fence then proceeded to kill about three to four of them. I got a call on my mobile phone when I was headed to the fundraiser staging area and was ordered by the security police to report to my residence immediately. When I arrived the police officer was nice and talked casually to me about what had happened.

He then abruptly left me to take a phone call for a few minutes and when he returned his attitude had changed. He pulled out his service pistol and pointed it at me aggressively. He told me to turn around and get on my knees. I thought he was joking at first because he was very nice when we were chatting before his call. Whatever he was told on the call changed him because now he was treating me as a hostile suspect. Someone had told them I was a threat and he obliged the order to rough me up. The person who had driven me to my house tried to get out of his car because of the turn of events and was threatened with the use of force if he did not get back in the car and wait for further instructions. The officer's back-up arrived in a panic and put me in the dirt and handcuffed me leaving me face down while they discussed their next actions.

The handcuffs were so tight they cut into my skin and bruised my wrists. The new officers lifted me up by the painful cuffs and pushed me into the back of the police car then drove me to the police station. They kept me in the cuffs for the few hours that they had me in custody and my Senior arrived to take possession of me from the police. The look of disdain he had on his face was all I needed to know. Either he or the Squadron Commander had made the call to apprehend me and make an example of me. Someone told them I was a danger and needed to be treated harshly and the police were glad to do it. I had physically done nothing wrong and I was treated as if I was the one who had murdered my neighbors or some other crime. The entire situation was confusing and writing about the incident seems like a lie that a dishonest person made up, but it happened just as described because being arrested you remember every detail of the traumatic experience.

I was released from my jail cell to my Senior very late in the evening and was ordered to report in my service dress to the Squadron Commander's office first thing Monday morning. I still had a fundraiser to manage and not just any fundraiser as this one had turned into a competition with the Senior about the best items to sell to make profits. The AFSA planning meetings I had suggested and got approved to sell "agua frescas", a Mexican drink with water and fresh fruits that are very popular in the Mexican culture. The fundraiser was open to British locals and this would be a unique item that no other vendor would be selling. The Senior disagreed and argued we should sell hamburgers and sodas because that is what people know.

I shot down his request and then he used his cronies on the board to approve him to sell the burgers additionally to the drinks I approved of selling. He set forth to prove he knew better and invested nearly $2000 in products, as opposed to the $200 I invested buying the ingredients for the drinks. He was adamant to show me how his rank made him smarter and the entire fundraiser was tense anytime he was present.

This led to boiling over point when I was discussing getting more water for the agua frescas with my wife and the Senior thought we were talking about him. He started screaming at me, just like my daily berating at work, that "he knew we were talking about him and I better respect him or else…" My wife and I just stared at him confused because we were only talking about where to get a water source for more drinks as we had sold out multiple batches and used up all our water supplies. This was the first time my wife had firsthand witnessed how the Senior talked to me daily. She asked if he was always like that and I explained that his reaction was how he always addressed me. His disdain for anything I said or did was very apparent and she asked how I dealt with him every day, to which I explained I was just numb to it.

The fundraiser ended after over 20 hours of preparations and working the booth. I was exhausted from the night before being spent in jail and the work I did selling the products all day. The final totals were very lopsided as the $200 investment in the drinks earned over $2,500 in profits and the $2000 invested in burgers earned a net of about $300. The Senior was pissed and accused me of lying about the earning for each to make him look bad. I just blew him off because we had not lost money on either and increased the AFSA chapter's budget by about $3,000 in a single day, which was the goal.

Monday morning came too fast and I donned my service dress to appear formally before the Squadron Commander. She had called several of my peers and supervisor into her office to witness her reading me my rights and the entire drama of her telling everyone that I was a douche bag in a long-winded way. I was used to dealing with her dramatics by then and just invoked my Article 31 rights to shut her down and reported to the lawyers again. The scene was becoming laughable and the lawyers would even ask, "what did you do now…" before laughing at the ridiculousness of it all.

The next few weeks would be a repeat of this same scene, me reporting to the Squadron Commander to be paraded as the scourge of the squadron, and then reporting to the lawyers to report yet another made-up crime I committed. The charges were never official, and I was never given any paperwork for any of the made-up accusations. The entire drama was designed to punish me for whatever slight I had done to the Squadron Commander and my Senior who was now her partner in attempting to push me to kill myself.

Some of the charges were rougher than others as the Squadron Commander found new ways to embarrass me, and she was extremely annoyed when she could not get me kicked out of the competition I was due to travel for to compete for the Air Force level award for which I was nominated. Then one day I made an honest mistake that would give her the ammunition to put the nail in my coffin. I attended a barbeque with some of the people I worked with at a coworker's house off the base. The entire day all the other guests were drinking and eating, and for the most part, it was a good day. Then after about six hours of people drinking tequila and other hard liquors, I had one of my coworker's daughter decide to hit me in my crotch for no reason when she was passing by me in the house. When she attempted to do it a second time, I used a martial arts technique to sweep her off her feet, gently placing her on the ground, and told her that was inappropriate.

There was another NCO and my wife in the room that witnessed exactly what happened and they also told the girl that her actions were not acceptable. Her parents were outside shooting tequila and we went to let them know what happened. My coworker's wife, the mother, made a big scene and the father just said: "it is ok and be lucky she did not do worse since she is a kung fu student she could have hurt you severely…" The family all left right after that and the situation seemed concluded.

A few hours later, a hard knock at the door startled all of us who were still hanging out and the NCO who lived there answered. Standing outside was an entire team of British police officers ready to engage a hostile target. They ordered us to stay seated and entered the house before asking "do you know why we are here?"

The group remaining looked around at each other and collectively shook their head no.

The police leader informed me that a base official had contacted them about the incident with the girl and stated I was a dangerous person that needed to be arrested. The police did not ask me for a statement and just apprehended me in handcuffs and took me off to a British jail nearly an hour away.

The weekend at a British jail is full of idiots coming and going for various offenses, mostly drinking-related stupidity. I was processed into the jail and they stripped me of my shoes, belt, and all my other possessions before putting me in a completely pitch-black room that contained a metal toilet and metal bed. The room was extremely cold, and the police refused to give any blankets per their policy to protect against suicides. I was the first "criminal" put in a cell that day and throughout the rest of the evening, I got to hear all the other criminals be processed in and locked up. The roster included many guys who were arrested for drinking incidents, and the worst was a guy accused rape. I listened throughout the night as all the drunks were released on bail and before long the only criminals remaining were the rapist and myself. This was my new peer group, and this was a humbling realization.

I had no idea how long I would be held a prisoner in this facility and after two days of pitch-black darkness, with no food or water, the police released me without filing charges. I was just let go barefooted and told to get out of their building. I had no means of calling people and had no idea where I was at since they locked me in the back of the car and drove me there. I finally managed to make a call and got a ride, but I was forced to sit in the grass outside the jail for over an hour since I was so far away from my home. I knew the routine that would take place the next day at work and I mentally prepared for my public berating and humiliation that I would endure yet again. The scene was becoming so mundane I did not even get anxiety anymore. This was just how my life was for the next few months until my separation was official, and I boarded a plane to anywhere but there.

I reported into the Squadron Commander's office in my service dress and endured another humiliating hour. She called me trash and other low life level names before informing me that the wing leadership was notified, and they canceled my trip to Atlanta for the Air Force level competition that I was supposed to attend in a few days. She smiled as she delivered her rehearsed speech about how I never deserved to be nominated much less attend something at that level. I could see the satisfaction that she had finally stopped me from gaining outside recognition and her pride in knowing that the rest of the wing now knew what she always felt that I was a loser NCO that did not belong in the uniform.

I remember smiling as she talked, and I think I even laughed out loud because this was all like a dream that someone was telling me about, but it was lucid, and I felt every word of their story.

The Squadron Commander then called in my "new supervisor" to introduce me to her. When the door opened, I was astonished to see a Staff Sergeant enter the room. I was a Master Sergeant select, meaning I had been promoted to the paygrade of E7 but my turn to sew it on had not arrived yet, and all my duties were on the E7 level, but I got paid as an E6. It was illegal to force a higher-ranking person to report officially to someone their junior, and it was very illegal to do it just for the sake of embarrassing the offender. I went through my normal routine and answered the questions I was asked and finally, I invoked my Article 31 rights to stop the crazy soap opera unfolding in real-time. I proceeded to go see my lawyers again. When I arrived there was another Airman sitting in the waiting area and I recognized him from meeting him at the Mildenhall car wash a few months back.

At first, I asked, "what are you doing here?" then I recanted the question because no one went to see the defense lawyers unless they were in trouble.

He looked at me with the same confusion because he knew me as the AFSA superstar that won a lot of awards and was very involved with the base. We chatted for a while and I could see the despair in his eyes, the same feelings I had for the past year, and I offered to talk to him if he ever needed someone before giving him my personal mobile number.

The lawyer called me back to his all too familiar offices to discuss my case. He was amazed at how many times I was forced to see him over the last few months. I assumed he judged me as the source of my own troubles by the way he spoke to me. Military defense lawyers are not there to defend clients. They are just in an assignment to provide counsel for military members as to fulfill the appearance of justice. The lawyers are more like the Washington Generals, the team that always loses to the Harlem Globetrotters. They put on a show but roll over in the end to let the military win. Here I was again in my own personal version of "Groundhog Day", except in my version there was no chance to correct the mistakes of the past to move on to the best future possible. I was just stuck in a never-ending cycle of bullying and my freedom was more and more being jeopardized each time. The saddest part was that no one outside my squadron knew what was going on and the ones I had contacted for help did not even care.

This was the reality of the military justice system. Once you were labeled by a ranking person as a bad Airman the leadership would set forth to end your existence forever. The negativity attached to being part of this cycle only attracted more negativity and you found yourself in a dismal loop of despair. I knew I was not a bad NCO, but perception is 99 percent of reality in life and the perception the military lawyer had of me was that I was obviously the issue. His mannerism and tone gave him away.

I explained to the lawyer the details of the incident and how there were witnesses that were standing no more than a few feet away that saw the entire act unfold. The witnesses had told the police their versions of the story and it was not enough for them to not arrest me, but it showed that I was first assaulted by the kid and then I safely stopped her from trying to hit me again. The witnesses would also corroborate the father telling me I was lucky she did not hurt me worse because of her lack of self-control and kung fu training.

The lawyer informed me that he could easily defend the case if there was a witness and that I needed to file assault charges against the kid for initiating the assault. I told him I would only do that as a last resort because it was not the child's fault that her parents allowed her to act as she did. He agreed that he would hold that as a bargaining chip for the case if things looked grim otherwise. I also explained the Squadron Commander assigning me to a lower-ranking person and he agreed that it was illegal to force a higher ranking individual to do that per Air Force Instruction 36-2618, The Enlisted Force Structure and that the evidence for substantiating my bullying claims would be another weapon we could use to fight the commander. He told me to just do whatever I was instructed to do and not cause any trouble and he would do his part to get me cleared.

      I left the lawyer's office not feeling reassured that my case would not end well for me. No official military channel would help anyone who this commander had wronged. Her connections to high ranking officials from her Pentagon days was the most likely reason. The lack of any negative consequences towards her empowered her with every person she destroyed.

      I reported into my new office as ordered after meeting with the lawyer. The section was small with about 10 people assigned. The Staff Sergeant, who was my new supervisor, was not even the ranking person in the section, but I was ordered by the commander to report to her officially each day and this is what I did.

I walked up to her desk and stood at attention and replied, "Ma'am, TSgt Franks reports as ordered…"

She looked at me baffled with the situation.

I continued, "I was ordered to report to you like my new supervisor…"

She continued to look as if she did not know what to say, and the rest of the Airmen in the section also stared at me.

I was not familiar with the group of people who were assigned. They were not the exceptional performers that I usually associated with; they were just ordinary Airmen doing their jobs. They all knew me though and were confused by why I was reporting like a basic trainee to a lower-ranking NCO. I could feel their eyes on me and sense the confusion at the scene in front of them.

I broke the silence and stated, "I am here to work on whatever you need me to do. I understand the commander briefed you on my situation and I was told you were my new supervisor…"

She finally replied with an awkward tone, "Yes I was briefed and still it does not make it weird to have a Master Sergeant select as my subordinate, I have never even heard of it ever."

I addressed the group directly and explained that I had gotten into a situation that the commander was unhappy with and this was my punishment. I told them I just wanted to work and nothing else. I was there to fulfill my obligations until I separated in a few weeks and I would not cause any issues with their team. They all collectively eased up on their stares and went back to their duties. The SSgt then sat me down to give me my job task and put me to work. The commander decided I was best suited for "reviewing deployment folders" and at the desk, I was assigned was several thousand of them stacked and waiting for me to review.

I sat down and situated myself into my new reality. I took note of the stacks of folders and did a little math to determine the pace I should work to ensure this petty job would last until I was out of the military forever. The task at hand was very demeaning for someone of my abilities and rank, and that was the whole point. I decided at that moment that I would put on a smile and do my best. Many people who are facing this type of embarrassing situation will act out negatively and create a worse situation. I knew I was isolated, I had no friends, no supervision that would stand up for me, no former commanders who would stand up to say I was not the bad troop that I was being accused, and nowhere to turn for help. I was trapped like a king in checkmate, the commander had won and there was only acceptance that I could choose to make.

I summoned all my martial arts training and calmed myself, then got to work. I found the task I was assigned to be very monotonous, but my superior attention to detail learned as a drill instructor, safety manager, and in special operations made me well suited for the job. I found hundreds of errors that the squadron would have been penalized for if we had been inspected by the MAJCOM. Even in defeat, I was able to turn the bad situation into a positive one.

I was not capable of being a crab and being lazy. I craved constant challenges and industry in everything I did. I made those folders my mission and I completed the task at a level that the program may have never seen before. When I completed the several thousand high stacks of folders at the end of my Air Force career, they were 100 percent correct and I found a little pride in the work, even though it was not an effective use of my time.

The Squadron Commander made it a daily visit to come by our office to see her prized possession in action. I poured on the charm and smiled every time she entered to room. I greeted her warmly and asked about her day, and I could see the hate fill her eyes each time I did it. I did not take any of her bait that she threw at me with her snide comments or disdain and this made her even angrier. I have searched thousands of hours in my mind to find whatever reason I gave the commander to dislike me the way she did. I had always treated her with respect and if I disagreed with her I did it professionally, providing feedback only as a Senior NCO is required to do. I concluded that she was just a very sad person on the inside, and she projected her inner pain towards anyone she felt was succeeding without her approval. She was the type of control freak that hated to see anyone succeed that she personally had not pushed to the top. Her brand of leadership was control and favoritism. She was very similar to any murderous dictator that murdered his advisors because they did not tell them the facts they looked for and delivered only the truth.

The Air Force had decided nearly 20 years earlier to eliminate the leadership training concepts from the lessons taught to young leaders and replaced leadership with civilian management concepts that relied on metrics and data over leading people. I fully believe that the years spent indoctrinating these officers and NCOs led to a complete collapse of leadership for the commanders and Senior NCOs that were now leading the Air Force.

The tested system did not teach leaders how to lead their subordinates, the system counted the troops as metrics and assets to be assigned and deployed as the managers wished. The lack of leadership understanding led to a loss of compassion and created selfishness that rewarded individual achievements over team building and mentorship. The program led to serious issues where the Air Force consistently chooses the appearance of success over actual success. The result of the decision to eliminate leadership led to some of the major news stories in recent history such as Airmen accidentally sending nuclear weapons components that were highly classified to Taiwan, and essentially Communist China.

The Air Force got to that point because leadership was devalued for decades. The need for leadership was never lost and the people in leadership positions were forced to make it all up as they went. This led to a service-wide "pencil-whipping culture".

The Senior NCOs and officers pencil-whipped inspections, they falsified performance reports to make everyone exceptional, and they created a new leadership culture that lacked anything resembling leadership.

In 2009, on paper the Air Force was full of Elon Musks, all performing at the highest levels and everything was perfect. This was a confabulation created by the lack of leadership in the ranks. The average performer was not exceptional, yet if you pulled all the performance reports for decades before this year you would find at least 99 percent of them showed exceptional ratings. The truth was that over 90 percent of the service performed at the status quo level or lower, but the Senior NCOs refused to be honest unless they disliked the Airman then the ratings would be lower than reality.

The Senior NCO reports were even worse because the Air Force created an additional system of control to keep these ranks from doing the right thing. The system forced them to toe the line the commander dictated, whether it was right or wrong. Each Senior NCO was required to receive "Stratification" and "Senior Rater Endorsement" or they would never be promoted again, and many would be forced to retire.

The system was an excellent form of professional slavery because it tied the hands of any ambitious Senior NCO. The ranks were filled with a bunch of "dancing monkeys" who performed whatever dance the commanders wished on cue. This was the reason my Senior NCO peers told me that even though they knew I was being bullied they could not help me. Each one of the Senior NCOs feared our Squadron Commander and knew if they got out of line, she would not hesitate to destroy them. The commander would at the very least refuse to endorse their performance reports, essentially ending their careers where they stood. The system worked perfectly, and the Air Force suffered because of it.

The 2009 Air Force Professional Airman's Conference should have been another apex of my career. I was the USAFE nominee for 2008 Air Force Sergeants Association International Member of the Year. My mind wandered to the conference as I sat at my desk looking through the deployment folders. I was supposed to be there rubbing elbows with a "who's who" of Air Force leadership and making a name for myself as a prospect for Chief Master Sergeant of the Air Force in a few years.

I had been performing in the top 1% of the NCO ranks for several years at that point and the award I was nominated for was the fruit of thousands of hours of mentorship and team building that I had done. The award was the culmination of the time I spent developing my Airmen to be the best they could be and with every success they had it increased my level of success. The Lakenheath POL team had improved vastly since I arrived, and I had played a large part in that success. The unit was recognized as the top in our career field MAJCOM for numerous awards and we were consistently ranked in the top 3 units for the entire Air Force. The packages submit for these huge achievements contained a very large percent of my personal accomplishments and the accomplishments of my team. The secret of these successes was the foundational training I had begun the minute I walked into the unit and the momentum created would last only a small-time after I was excommunicated from the Air Force.

Instead of enjoying the fruits of my labors and receiving the recognition I had spent a lifetime working towards, I was sitting at a desk doing the work an E1 was more than capable of doing. The people in the office were unaware that I was even in competition for an Air Force level award. They only knew me now as the "bad Senior NCO" who was getting kicked out for an unknown reason. The Airmen in the section did not know I was not getting kicked out that I had quit the Air

Force. I did not correct them when they said it because it was mostly true.

I had seen myself retiring after 30 years serving and achieving the highest rank and position possible. I may never have earned the position of Chief Master Sergeant of the Air Force, but I was performing close as anyone to that level in my peer group. If I missed my goal, I would still find myself at the top of the service in many aspects. That was the dream, and that dream was dead.

My computer dinged with a message and snapped me out of my daydream of what could have been. The Squadron Commander had sent the Senior who hated me in my place to the awards banquet as another dig at me, and his email address was the one that popped up on my screen now. I opened the email and began to read;

Trey, I would like to be the first to congratulate you on being selected as the 2008 Air Force Sergeants Association International Member of the Year. The award is a testament to your hard work and leadership over the past few years. I was astonished by the reaction when your name was read, as the number of people who erupted in heavy applause showed the level of impact you have made across the Air Force. I had no idea the level of leadership you have created, and it was an honor to walk across the stage to accept the award on your behalf from the Air Force leadership…

His words stopped my heart.

I stood up and walked out the door to go to the restroom, overwhelmed with emotions.

When I walked into the restroom and saw myself in the mirror, I could not contain the emotions I felt. I had done it. I had earned an Air Force level award. I had earned an award although in my squadron I was being bullied and told I was not allowed to be submitted for anything. I had overcome the subjugation of being hated and the Air Force, a board with former Chief Master Sergeants of the Air Force had chosen me as the best out of 350,000 plus members eligible.

I wish I could say that I was happy, but I was not. I collapsed in the stall at the very end of the restroom on the dirty floor and cried. I cried, not tears of joy or accomplishment, my tears were of defeat. I cried unlike any way I had ever cried before in my life and I cried for a long time until I could pull myself off that floor and move forward.

I was not fully back to reality and felt separated from my body as I walked the halls back to my prison cell desk. When I walked in the door one of the lower-ranking members asked if I was ok and a responded in a mumble, "I just found out I won an Air Force level award…"

The entire room looked around at each other in disbelief. They were confused. How could I have won anything when I was a dirtbag being kicked out of the service?

One of them asked for clarification, "You won what award?"

I told them I had been selected as the 2008 Air Force Sergeants Association International Member of the Year, and explained I received an email from the Senior congratulating me. The group could not comprehend the situation. Their biased opinion of me had been formulated by the commander's biased words to them about me. There was no mention that I was up for anything other than a possible jail cell, and they could not understand how someone in my position could have overcome the hate the commander had for me to win an award for the entire Air Force. The situation seemed made up and all I could do was print the email and hand it to my SSgt master for her to tell the group I was not lying.

I was completely unproductive for the remainder of the day. The Squadron Commander had been on the same email I received but she refused to acknowledge the feat. It would be days before she mentioned the award and the conversation was not nice.

The Squadron Commander told me once again, "Too bad you are only good at outside the squadron, useless stuff..."

That was my thanks for a 13-year career worth of achievement. The award I earned was the culmination of years of work and study of leadership, success, and team building. I had earned an average of 3 significant awards each year I was in the military over my entire career. My sustained success included the "good ole boy club" intentionally preventing me from receiving awards and medals I had earned out of their personal bias against me. I had not had any clear mentors after my first duty station supervisors and I had no champion for my career to push me forward, but I achieved on every level I made it to and in the face of some of the worst mistreatment possible.

The worst thing about earning the award was that the Senior who bullied me for months and helped end my career was the person who walked across the stage to receive it. All the pictures of the moment had him receiving my award that he attempted to deny me. The moment was forever tainted and every time I see the trophy all I can remember is that fact. The entire effort was highjacked by the Senior and the Squadron Commander.

This was the last good thing in my career. I would board a plane a few weeks later and fly back to Georgia with an uncertain future. I would never again earn another award in my life and I would never again be called "sergeant", which was a title I wore with much pride. I would leave with so many lost opportunities and failures behind me. I would leave a completely different person than the scared civilian that had flown for the first time from Atlanta to San Antonio for an unknown journey that would end up lasting 13 years, 352 days.

Looking back I wish I could have done many things differently. I wish I could have not taken the tough road I chose, because I have peers who never did anything hard who were rewarded with promotion after promotion who will retire at the top enlisted rank. I wish I would have stepped back to enjoy the successful moments I had earned instead of looking past them to the next big thing. I wish I would have spent my career-making connections with people and creating a network of success instead of leaving the service without a single person who had my back.

Those wishes are just the crab mentality attempting to take away from what I was able to accomplish because I know for certain that the path to success is never found down the easy road. People may achieve promotions and ranks, but without failures, there are no true successes. If you find any person whose life was easy, and their resume lacks failure then they have not challenged themselves. Failures can only occur when you are on the outskirts of your comfort zones, and the value of these learning opportunities cannot be duplicated.

Aftermath

On 1 December 2009, I was officially a civilian. My career had ended like the Space Shuttle Challenger mission, in a ball of fire. I was now faced with the uncertainty of what the future would hold. I was also facing a tough road ahead because little to my knowledge the US economy was in shambles when I separated. The task of finding a job was nearly impossible. Many businesses had signs posted for job seekers to not come into their offices.

My plan for transitioning was to file for my Department of Veterans Affairs (VA) benefits to start school and to get a part-time job to offset my living expenses while I took classes. I visited the VA Regional Offices located in Decatur, Georgia immediately when my separation date had passed. I filled out all the paperwork required to receive my benefits and to also start my medical appointments to receive any disability payments I was eligible to receive. The reception at the VA offices was not good. Most of the employees acted like all the veterans in the office we bothersome.

The VA manager that I met with that day was a sharp-looking man who was wearing an expensive suit. He paid little attention to anything about my paperwork.

He even referred me as "Frank Ellis" which showed how little he valued my presence in his office. He sat down and looked at my paperwork. Then within a minute told me that he could not approve my package and that he deemed that I was not eligible for VA benefits.

I argued with him that I had served my country and that I received an honorable discharge which meant that I had "earned" the benefits. He responded that he would not approve my package, stood up, and opened his door for me to leave. I was astounded by his dismissal but could do nothing about it. I decided to go online to fill out paperwork for my benefits and I left the VA to go do it.

I drove home annoyed at the lack of customer service the VA had shown and was determined to get my benefits to submit past the dismissive gatekeeper at the VA offices. The paperwork was simple online, and I filled it out in a short amount of time. Then I was required to wait for the VA to decide the outcome for my paperwork. I set forth on my job hunt.

I spent weeks sending out 100s of resumes a day and never got a response. I applied for any job available and would have accepted any position offered. The reality was that there were no jobs and no prospects for finding one in the US. The only opportunities available ended up being scams that took advantage of people. I worked for two separate businesses that refused to pay, was sent checks that were fake to set up home offices, and other fake job offers created to get your personal information. The state of the economy was not good. I was forced to seek assistance through the unemployment offices in Georgia.

The state officials for Georgia were overwhelmed with people flooding their offices daily. When I arrived at the offices in Marietta, Georgia the line to enter was several hundred people deep. The wait was an entire day to be seen and then sadly I was told by the unemployment representative that I was not eligible to receive any unemployment benefits.

The state employee explained, "I am sorry, but you are not eligible for receiving unemployment because you quit your job in the military."

I was baffled and explained that I had successfully served my country for 14 years and earned the right to not reenlist for the final time to receive my retirement benefits. I had done more to earn these benefits that I was seeking that most of the people in the room. I was not seeking them to fleece the government as many of the laggards in her office did. I just needed help until I found employment.

She replied, "Perhaps you should go back to the military..." then called the next person without helping me at all.

I was stunned that this was the treatment that veterans received in Georgia. The denial of benefits to veterans who had honorably served in the military did not make sense. A lazy civilian could be fired to get government assistance but a veteran who serves honorably is not allowed to make the same decisions. The system was totally messed up and left me in a dire predicament. I was quickly running out of money and had to make drastic decisions to survive.

The VA paperwork that I filled out was not being processed quickly and this was adding to my dilemma as I was counting on the housing stipend that I would receive when I started school. After a long wait I was approved for my educational benefits from the online system. The system sent me a check to start my school. The only problem was the Atlanta VA office was still refusing to give me the benefits I had earned. When my package came through their offices for the benefits the manager that I had met with filed collections against me.

He claimed I was not eligible for the benefits I had received from the online system and denied me any further benefits. There was no reasoning behind his actions, but this left me with a large debt to the government for the benefits I had received already. The VA would use this debt to seize all my tax returns for the next 5-6 years.. They also intentionally destroyed my credit with the collections they submit to all the credit bureaus.

I was quickly learning that the VA was not a veteran-friendly organization. Also, my medical paperwork to start my evaluations for receiving disability benefits was left pending for five more years. I would not receive any appointments to be seen for my VA evaluations until late in 2013 after I was briefed by someone to go online to a new system the VA was using that was created because the VA had dropped the ball or intentionally sat on veterans' disability packages to save money. The issue this caused was that when I finally did receive the disability ratings the VA scandalously changed my file date to the later online date. They stole over $100,000.00 in back pay they owed me due to their indolence. The people in the VA were very petty and the back pay I did finally receive was paid at the single rate saving the VA thousands of more dollars. This was another intentional error because every record I had in their system clearly showed I was married. I have no doubt the VA stole $100 millions of dollars from veterans using these insidious methods and the organization is also responsible for the suicides of thousands of veterans that they intentionally left without benefits or earned disability payments that the VA stole just like they did to me.

I was saved at the last minute by being offered a position in Afghanistan managing one of the United Service Organizations (USO) centers in the country. I quickly accepted the job offer I received after several interviews and I was off once again to a foreign country. The position I had been selected for was very lucrative compared to my military pay and I received an ID card with the rank of Department of Defense Civilian GS-13. This was equivalent to the rank of the toxic commander that I had dealt with in England and was a huge positional promotion from the MSgt stripe that I had lost by volunteering to leave the Air Force. The only problem was the location sucked and I would be away from my wife once again after promising her that I would not have to deploy ever again.

Karma is always there to fix you when making proclamations, but life has other plans for your path. I learned this when I had joked the commander wanted to put me in jail, but I was smarter, then ended up continually being arrested at gunpoint for nonsense. In this case, I had joked that all my deployments were over forever when I left the military, and now here I was on a plane back to Southwest Asian war zones.

The job was a blessing because the day I got paid I was traveling overseas, and I was down to my last $0.20 in our bank account and family members we had asked for help told us they "didn't feel comfortable" helping us out. When I started traveling I had spent my last few dollars on overpriced sandwiches at the airport that I was planning on rationing until payday, but the janitor quickly threw my food away when I was getting a drink, and now I was stuck with no food or cash to get anything else for the unforeseeable future. Somehow, I got paid immediately instead of the month-long wait many companies take to cut first checks saving me from this dilemma.

The financial issues were now subsided, and I just had to ride my time in Afghanistan until my wife was hired in a good job and I could return home. That wish would take several years to come true despite her substantial credentials and after a year in Afghanistan I felt like I needed to be somewhere else, I just did not know where. I made the decision to return home and before long I was once again searching for my purpose in the world.

The experiences of my military career had forever changed my understanding of what was possible. I had traveled the world and visited nearly every country in Europe, most of the Middle East, and Asia. I had just left my first job where I had earned over $100,000 annually, raising my expectations for my professional value. I was not the same lazy person that joined the Air Force in 1995, and now I was looking for a break to showcase my high-level performance. I did not value myself at that time and I had very low standards for what was possible.

Before I joined the Air Force, I was working dead ends jobs for tips and made minimal sums. I had valued my efforts at $7.50 per hour plus tips and thought if I could just make $20 per hour, I would have made it. I never saw myself traveling the world and meeting people who most Americans only see on CNN, but I had spent time with many high-ranking people over my career. I was now looking for my real place where I my skills were not detested, and my motivation was rewarded for all the labors I put into my work.

The day I returned from Afghanistan I started immediately sending out resumes to companies and applied to a job about video games. I was surprised when I received an immediate response to an interview the next day. My experience with the job market was that it took 10,000s resumes to get a single response if any, and now I had one business reply immediately to my resume. The job seemed like something I could do while I found a real job. I interviewed and was offered a position as a driver of video game trucks, hosting parties for kids all over Atlanta, Georgia. The job was not on the level I wanted but seemed easy and fun, and I humbly accepted their offer.

I did not know at the time that I would go on to create a new industry in the market and after several months I would invest everything I had into owning my own business. I had never considered owning a business because no one had ever shown me it was possible. I quickly learned that the impossible was never as it seemed, and if you expose people to opportunities, they will be awakened to other opportunities they never could see due to the barriers they had placed in their own way.

Growing up I consistently had to overcome the barriers of being poor and being exposed to the lowest quality people that my drug addict mother associated. The difficulties of living in poverty creates intellectual bondage over you that keeps you from seeing any opportunities in life. Joining the military allowed me to break the cycle of poverty and grow as a person. The discipline I gained from the military allowed me to commit to changing myself and engage in years of professional development that I still consistently do today.

Discipline is a foundational trait that is the cornerstone of any success and is a challenge for many people. If this trait is not developed, then no success is possible no matter how much effort is given. Discipline was the most important trait that led to my many successes in the military and was pivotal in helping me through some of the most challenging times of my career.

The next important factor that contributed to my successes was developing a personal set of core values. The Air Force assisted me in this aspect, and I adopted the core values the service promoted that included integrity first, service before self, and excellence in all we do. I took these core values to heart and learned them by consistently studying and teaching the lessons in the Air Force's "Little Blue Book" that was at one point a mandatorily issued item that all Airmen. Every Airman was expected to possess the book and to learn these values until the Air Force leadership decided it was asking too much of the personnel. This book broke down each core value into many traits that I would use in every part of my interactions with my subordinates.

Any person can develop their own core value systems, and the process does not have to be elaborate. The development of core values should follow the same concept of creating goals where the values are specific, attainable, and measurable. This will allow the individual to create core values that they can adapt and implement into every aspect of their success plans. When a person has core values, they will always be aware of where "true north" is located when making decisions. I can attribute surviving over a year of intense bullying to my dedication to my values. I knew that no matter what dirt was thrown at my character I had made every decision in my career, good and bad, for the right reasons.

Former Chief Master Sergeant of the Air Force (CMSAF) Sam Parrish once gave me excellent mentorship advice when he told me, "If you always do the right thing, for the right reasons, then no matter what people think of your actions you are on the correct path, and to hell with what people think."

Additionally, I learned success is only found through engaging in constant professional development. There is no finish line for studying the craft of success. Every lesson you study is a new tool for you to use to create something exceptional in your life. The process requires each person to take the same approach that professional athletes do when training to be the best in their sports.

Michael Jordan, Kobe Bryant, Tom Brady, David Goggins, and other champion level athletes engage consistently in personal development to be mentally, spiritually, technically, and physically ready to constantly push their successes to higher echelons. Each one of these champions also found mentors that pushed them past their mind's limitations to reach the next levels. My experience from being a part of the special operations culture is that there is always another level in every aspect of life, and we referred to this as your "second wind" or "additional gas tank". Every champion understands that to develop this next level requires constant growth in all aspects of life.

Lastly, I believe that taking massive actions towards your goals is crucial to individual success. Today's culture is not one that promotes action, and this is an advantage for the top one percent that wants to be the best. I once read a leadership metaphor from a Greek philosopher that stated every organization tended to follow the pattern of performance called "10-80-9-1". The philosopher stated that ten percent of people in an organization do not belong and should be fired, 80 percent of the people will do the minimum or less, nine percent will produce the majority of the positive outcomes, and the top one percent will be the visionaries who push people path their comfort zones to ensure mission success. An indication you are on the correct path towards being "The One" is when your massive actions make people tell you to stop being so "gung-ho" or call your activities "insane". This means your level of activity makes them uncomfortable because you are challenging the status quo and you should continue that path if the actions are aligned with your goals.

Taking massive actions should not be confused with being busy. The two things are not the same. The massive actions you should engage in are only things that move you closer to your goals. If you are an entrepreneur, then massive actions will only be the things that are money-making activities or ones that increase your business assets both physically and digitally. Too many people talk about being "too busy" but never produce anything of value for their efforts.

This was my success plan and it allowed me to achieve more than I ever realized I was capable of when I first started on my journey. However, my Air Force career will more than likely be judged by many who read this book as a failure. This would be a limited view of the life moments I discussed in each chapter. I started out as a homeless young teen with no direction and over the course of 14 years in the service, I had achieved things that many other people who have served for the past 100 years never accomplished. I am one of less than 50 people to earn the final award I received in my career out of millions of Airmen who joined the Air Force over that period. I continuously took massive actions towards goals I set, and many times engaged in activities that caused me extreme discomfort and fear.

I initially feared being forced to be disciplined because I had never been given a proper example of what that looked like in my life. The fear I felt on the flight to basic training was real and the uncertainty of what was to come in my life from that point was scary. My best friend failing to graduate could have been my excuse to leave the service too, but I faced the fear of being alone in the training and made the best of it.

The personal conflicts I dealt with throughout my career was also me facing my fears as I was not a person who wanted conflict when I first joined. Growing up with violent drug addicts always around me made conflict scary because I had seen the worst of people throughout my young life. Then I learned the conflicts I faced in the military was due to the status quo being challenged and pushing others towards improving the ideas of what was achievable was uncomfortable. I did not always win those battles because in the military the rank structure does not cater to lower-ranking people influencing organizations, but I found ways to inject my own standards by excelling at military boards, maintaining extremely high standards of personal appearance, and always challenging the "good ole boy" mentalities when I could.

My three times failing to become a Combat Controller was also a testament to my desire to conquer my fears and the desire to be part of the highest performing organizations possible. I entered the Air Force not being able to swim and three times took the PAST test to attempt to become a Combat Controller, failing two times and passing it on the third. I was deftly afraid of being underwater and I overcome this fear and can still do laps in a pool underwater. I was also afraid of heights and easily graduated from the Army Airborne School, and made many paratrooper jumps in my career.

Each failure I had in my career was preceded by me taking massive actions to qualify to be found worthy of these achievements. The number of people who attempted the things I did was very small, and the percent that could even qualify to be in my company is a long fraction of one percent of every Airman that has ever served. I learned that to hit home runs, you must take a lot of batting practice, and understand you will strike out a lot if you swing for the fences.

In the end, my life was forever changed when I took the video game truck driver position. I had trained for an unknown opportunity my entire life and I found it by happenstance. My leadership development had allowed me to see an opportunity, my dedication to taking massive actions allowed me to dominate the market, and my core values allowed me to build a business that I have earned a life that I would have never imagined when I was a homeless teen.

The failures all fit together to teach me lessons I would need to understand fully to be a successful entrepreneur. Had I not been pushed out of the service by the bullying I would have still been on active duty when the game truck opportunity was available, and I would have missed the chance to control my own financial future. Also if I had retired from the military I would not have been in a desperate position and would more than likely not had the internal fire required to create a business from scratch, in an industry no one knew existed, and probably would have accepted some mediocre job with a company that limited my potential.

The paths we take cannot always be the ones we desire, and sometimes life pushes us towards our real opportunities when we are just accepting the existences we fell into by chance. I would have never imagined I could have the life I have today, and I am here now telling others about my journey to success after a hard road that many would have quit a long time before now. I was never given support or handouts, even when I should have been given unemployment I was denied and having to succeed on my own was the biggest success I achieved. Your story no matter what you are facing today can be even more unbelievable than mine if you find your path and get to work as I did.

From The Ashes

Never accept the status quo. There will be times in your life when others will try to convince you that you are doing too much. My detractors told me I was too "gung-ho" constantly, and you must have the integrity, specifically the trait courage, to continue your path. You may find yourself face to face with the people who are supposed to have your back that will attempt to limit your potential, and you must have the courage to take the steps towards the unknown in order to achieve real success. People can be like the crabs in a bucket and pull everyone down to their level where they have given up on their dreams, and it is your choice to fight or quit yourself.

Success is always just past the barriers that you and others place in front of you. I was a poor, homeless teenager at one point in my life and I could have quit on myself to become a low life like the poor role models I saw every day. Instead, I chose to change myself, starting with my mind, and I took on challenges that pushed me past my fears. These decisions led me to experience opportunities that many of the Airmen I served with considered insane. The opinions of these Airmen were based on their own fears that they projected to my situation and because they could not see themselves doing the things I did they dismissed them as crazy.

This is the place you will have to live within if you want to be the best. You will have to do the things that other people fear and just past that fear of the unknown you will experience a breakthrough that will be more rewarding than you can imagine. I experienced these situations many times in my life, and none more intense than when I decided to start my first business. The status quo minded people I knew, especially family members, gave me tons of unsolicited advice about "what they would do if they had a business..." The advice was about how dumb I was for investing everything I owned into an unknown market, about how they would market the business, about how I should run processes, and a million other interjections that did not apply to my success.

When I launched my first business, I was mostly broke, renting a house, and doing any kind of odd jobs that would help me pay the bills. I worked as a sales rep, dressed as an elf to serve rich people hot cocoa, bartended, sold firewood, and anything you can imagine. My family all told me I needed to take the "smart path" and that I just needed a "good job" like Home Depot.

The Home Depot is a company that advertises about how they support veterans, and they hire thousands, but it is a dead-end path to working six days a week for part-time pay and benefits. This type of opportunity is a trap and will keep you from achieving the success you can reach. I was extremely humbled when I was in my original job search and would have worked anything I was offered, but the economy was very bad, and no company would even interview me. This ended up being a blessing as I was forced to figure out my own way without enslaving myself to someone else's dream.

I took the path that had the greatest risk, and when I succeeded, I ended up with more than a job. I refused to fail in this opportunity and applied every ounce of what I had learned in those hard lessons in my career to become the best in an entire industry that I had created from scratch in the market. I never was afraid of failure because I was creating something of my own and I knew that once I got past the hard times from the startup, I would have a different life. Then within the first three years of owning my business, I had created the new market, became successful enough to build my own home only from what I created from my efforts, and created a life that opened me up to a multitude of new opportunities.

Contrarily, the family who gave me the sage advice are all still living paycheck to paycheck, renting, and reporting for work five to six days a week for minimum pay. Their advice would have pulled me to their lower level, and this is very common with the people who are closest to you. You must accept that to overcome the status quo you will be required to do the very things the people you love fear and will do anything in their power to prevent. If you want success you have to perform like "The One" and set the tempo for everyone else to follow always.

I attribute my success to the core values I learned that guided me in my journey to overcome the status quo, and you can create your own set of values because everyone's situation is unique. The values you choose, as previously mentioned, should be;

1) Specific

2) Attainable

3) Measurable

The purpose of the core values is to give you a foundation for directing your decisions you will be required to make to become successful. If your core values are not specific, then you will leave yourself open to interpreting them and fail to gain the value of having a foundation that grounds you in your purpose. The effectiveness of core values is the fact that they will become your personal moral compass that will ensure you stay true to yourself. I used this principle to guide my life and my values kept me from falling for the negativity the crabs interjected into my journey. Now I live the life they dream about with a two to three-day work week max while earning many times more than in income than what is considered successful in traditional "job paths".

The values must be realistic and attainable because many people attempt to make up elaborate plans that they can never achieve as a personal barrier to justify their situations. You will find through your awakenings in leadership that most of the time you are the very reason you are not achieving success in your life. You cannot make bold claims of what you will achieve and then give yourself unrealistic timelines to do it. The reason this mistake is made is to justify why you will eventually fail and to allow yourself a pass to blame the systemic barriers in the world such as race, gender, economic backgrounds, sexual preference, or any of the other excuses people allow to limit their capabilities.

The success does not lie in the societal "canned excuses" that social media feeds you to justify failure.

The success lies in your actions, your character and how you present yourself to the world, and a constant hunger for improvement. If you truly want success you will have to evaluate all the information you put into your mind and the relationships that you hold dear because in your self-evaluation you may find that the influences you currently cannot live without are the very things holding you back from success.

Lastly, the values must be measurable to ensure you can always understand where you stand in relation to your foundation. Every sport has a scoreboard, and your success should be no different. This scoreboard should not be used to dissect all your failures or create excuses to create personal barriers. The scoreboard is created to let you always know where you stand in relation to your set goals.

Your core values will create your personal habits which will change your character. When your character changes the world will view your completely different from how you are today. When I embraced the Air Force core values, I was still that dumpy, lazy loser who lacked confidence and by the end of my career, everyone viewed me as overtly confident in everything I did. This was a result of changing my values.

The first awakening I have found in most of the people I have mentored is that when they begin the journey of professional development, they outwardly project themselves in misaligned ways. I have seen people change 180 degrees in the way they speak, dress, and carry themselves. Their core values improved their inner confidence and in turn, they outwardly became a different person. The only way to reap this benefit is to always measure your real-time decisions against a set of core values before you make decisions, ensuring you are at a minimum aware if you are measuring up to the person you wish to be.

Always reject mediocrity. I took two oaths in my career that required me to reject mediocrity in my personal performance and the performance of the Airmen I led. The first was the oath I took when I sewed on my SSgt stripes and I became an NCO. This was my first step towards seeking to be a mentor to others and changed the mediocre path I was taking.

Mediocrity is the actions taken by people to target hitting the status quo. It is the bare minimum expected to be performed to not lower the performance outcomes and not improve them. It is the target most workers strive to meet, and many times by aiming this low they fail to meet the minimum acceptable levels resulting in mission or business failure. When I was in

Combat Control training, they pushed our understanding about what was possible on every aspect of life to a point where we believed anything was possible. Every Airman that started the training was physically fit, but we had placed barriers in our training called repetitions, and the Special Tactics operators training us taught us that the evaluation standard reps were the status quo then forced us to complete a lot more than that minimum.

      The lesson was profound because the Air Force Special Operations leadership set the status quo totals for all exercises required to be eligible to enter and graduate the Air Force Special Tactics pipeline, but the seasoned operators who had completed the training knew what the real world operations were like and trained us to a superhuman level well above it. They would also do this with operational training if a checklist called for a single item, they would tell us to make it two, or if it was three, they would tell us we needed six. Their reasoning was that it was insane to show up to a battle with a single battery, only to find out it was dead and now the Navy SEALs you were charged with providing "Close Air Support" for are gravely endangered behind enemy lines because you chose to do the minimum. Mediocrity gets people killed in wars and gets leaders fired if they fail to provide the proper example for their team.

A leader must use their core values as the moral compass of the organization to ensure the teams under them understand the vision of the organization and then take appropriate actions to ensure the system is improved at all levels. If the leader allows mediocrity to be prevalent in their system, there can be no success for their teams. Mediocrity is cancer that infects teams if the leader does not create this vision adequately and fails to instill it within their people.

Mediocrity is the easy path and attracts the masses if there is no system that rewards exceeding goals. The Air Force fell into mediocrity because at some point SNCOs or commanders decided that everyone should be rated as "exceptional" unless they were a "troubled Airman" to be fair to everyone, and the practice spread across the entire service. This decision led to there being no incentive for Airmen to exceed the minimum requirements for their jobs because everyone would be rated "exceptional" if they just showed up. The concept is like the scene from the movie "Office Space" where the main character gave up on trying to please his bosses and did nothing at all but got promoted while others who were working hard got fired. Only the Air Force case was not a fictitious story and the unwritten policy of the Air Force has deterred motivation for several decades.

The results of this policy was a catalyst for all the major news stories from the Air Force over this period from the nuclear components being "accidentally" sent to Taiwan (essentially China), the Air Force Basic Military Training sexual assault scandals, and an increase in Air Force active duty and veteran suicides to a point where the Air Force was required to shut down all non-combat operations to address the issue. These can all be traced back to the Air Force's decision to accept mediocre as exceptional.

There was no incentive to do anything more than just show up to work when scheduled because working harder than the person next to you would earn you the same result of an "exceptional" rating on your performance report. This also allowed the incompetent members of each rank to be promoted because they were not realistically evaluated on their performance and were given ratings well above it to be "fair" nullifying the additional points the highest rating should have given top performers. The decision killed productivity dropping to the status quo or less resulting in leadership chaos. Mediocrity was the culprit behind all the major problems of the service and will not be fixed until the shortfalls addressed in this book are met.

The job of a leader is to push their people past their comfort zones and tap into their full potential. The secret to succeeding is to create a system that identifies the minimum standard for failure and then clearly define the expectations for each task performed. The team must understand not only what is expected, but they should also understand that there will be rewards for achieving set milestones. This creates your team's scoreboard and will promote competition against the standard as opposed to competition against other team members.

Rewards must be, just like the core values—specific, attainable, and measurable to ensure each member can make a personal choice in the efforts they choose. The scoreboard must also include the penalties for deviating from the minimum standards, and if a team member deviates then they must be held accountable to the set punishments. The most important aspect in the process is communication about the expectations. I have found that mediocrity is sometimes created because the leader left the team to individually determine the standards or goals. This is a leader's responsibility, not the team members', because the leader sets the vision, goals, core values, and culture then is required to communicate it to the team. Failure to communicate this will create standards that are subjective, not measurable, and lead to a degradation of performance.

In the end, you are the master of your destiny. You can choose to exceed or meet your full potential.

There is no magic spell to create your personal success. The secret is consistent professional development, a desire to be better tomorrow than you were today, and the motivation to take massive actions towards a goal. There is no barrier in your path regardless of what the news or social media tells you because success does not care about your skin color, gender, age, sexual preference, bank account balance, or anything else. Success only requires you to take massive actions towards a passion you have until you make it to the next level, one level at a time, and you make other people better in your journey.

Success is infinite and with the right plan every person living today can achieve their full potential, which should be the only goal for which to seek. In the end, it is your personal choice to be the crab in the bucket or a leader that determines your own destiny.

Acknowledgments

This book was completed thanks to the thousands of Airmen I had the honor of serving with during my 14 years of military service. The young leaders I was able to mold into successful leaders was the fuel that kept me fighting forward even in the face of the toughest challenges I faced. Knowing you were looking to me for the proper example helped me to achieve everything I did in my career.

I would especially like to thank my wife for standing by my side through the turmoil of my military service including the long deployments, long workdays, and the thousands of hours she volunteered to help me achieve my successes. I know you sacrificed a lot to support me and many times should have walked away but you never did. I appreciate your loyalty and support.

Thanks to all the agents who refused my work because my story "did not speak to your portfolios". Your rejections hardened my resolve to complete this entire book and get it published. The best motivators are the people who do not believe in you, and this book was your loss.

About the Author

Ellis Franks has dedicated his life to helping top performers achieve the highest levels of personal and team performance. He is an avid student of leadership and has personally mentored over 3,000 performers to reach their full potential. His experience has been obtained from over 14 years as a military leader and top performer where he was selected for multiple special duties open to only 1% of the total 350,000 active members. His performance was recognized by some of the highest performance awards attainable and his teams consistently earned service level recognition. He was honored to have received personal mentorship time with all the living Chief Master Sergeants of the Air Force (highest enlisted member & enlisted liaison to Chief of Staff of the Air Force), multiple Secretary of the Air Force & Under-Secretary of the Air Force, and numerous other high-ranking leaders during his career.

His military experience includes over 5,000 platform teaching hours in various subjects to include Anti-Terrorism Force Protection, Combat First Aid Skills, and Basic Military Training Instructor Trainer. He began his journey as a leader teaching basic trainees the skills needed to become excellent team members and future leaders. He excelled at the mentorship of his troops by incorporating the lessons of John C. Maxwell's "21 Irrefutable Laws of Leadership" & " 17 Indisputable Laws of Teamwork" into every lesson he taught. He directly impacted the lives of thousands of new Airmen, many of which continually contact him to say thanks for changing their lives.

Ellis has continued to excel in the civilian market pursuing numerous entrepreneurial opportunities to include starting new markets from concept, creating nation's largest adventure sports brokerage firms, launching digital advertising start-ups, and numerous sales consulting ventures. He has created highly skilled sales and marketing teams for numerous industries including inbound call centers & door-to-door direct marketing teams culminating in millions of dollars in sales for multiple industries. His secret to success is providing core value-based sales approach to his clients by always following the three core values that were ingrained within him in the US Air Force - *Integrity First, Service Before Self, & Excellence In All You Do*.

Now his career has come full circle to pass on the knowledge he has developed over a 25-year career in leadership, team building, and business. He believes anyone can become a self-made success by always displaying a high energy level and refusing to accept mediocrity in any form. These traits paired with the foundational training from the top leadership and sales mentors in their perspective industries are the basis for all training programs that have been developed to make your team the best in your industry.

AWARDS & RECOGNITION

•Published Author: "Always Leave An Airman Behind"

•Certified John C. Maxwell Leadership Coach February 2016

•Certified Google Partner July 2012

•Selected as CEO largest adventure sports network in the world—10K websites nationally & $40M revenues

•Created Game Cave Atlanta—successfully hosted over 6,000 events in metro Atlanta September 2011

•Recognized #1 Salesperson Video Game Truck Sales in US -Volume & Per Unit Sales May 2011

•2010 Kuk Sool Won World Championships Bronze Medalist (3 medals total)

•Founded Kuk Sool Won of Bagram, Afghanistan (Non-Profit) June 2010

•Co-Founded Zepol Optimized December 2009

•2009 Kuk Sool Won European Champion Medalist & 3rd Place Team—4 medals total

•2008 Air Force Sergeants Association International Member of the Year

•2008 United States Air Force Warren R. Carter Daedalian Silver Award—European Command winner

•2008 Air Force Sergeants Association Division 16 (Europe) Member of the Year

- 2008 Air Force Sergeants Association Chapter 1669 (Royal Air Forces Lakenheath) Member of the Year

- 2008 Kuk Sool Won European Championship School & Gold Medalist

- 2008 Kuk Sool Won United Kingdom Championship School & Gold Medalist

- 2008 Kuk Sool Won Scottish Champion Gold Medalist

- Graduated Air Force Senior Non-Commissioned Officer Academy (Strategic Leadership) Aug 2008

- 2007 Kuk Sool Won European Championship School & Gold Medalist

- 2007 Kuk Sool Won United Kingdom Championship School & Gold Medalist

- 2007 Kuk Sool Won Spanish Champion Gold Medalist

- 2007 American Petroleum Institute Fuels Management Silver Award

- 2007 United States Air Forces in Europe Golden Drum Winner--Best in European Command

- 2007 Air Force Sergeants Association NCO of the Year International Finalist

- 2007 Air Force Sergeants Association Division 16 (Europe) NCO of the Year

- 2007 Mission Support Group Team of the Year

- 2007 Fuels Management Flight NCO of the Year

- Kisling Non-Commissioned Officer Academy Distinguished Graduate May 2007

- Mission Support Group Team of the Quarter Jan-Mar 2007

- 48th Logistics Readiness Squadron NCO of the Quarter Jul-Sep 2007

- Air Force Commendation Medal 2006 (Meritorious Service)

- Selected Special Duty: US Air Force Special Tactics, Combat Controller

- Certified DoD Anti-Terrorism Officer October 2004

- Earned Military Training Instructor "Black Rope" (Instructor Mentor & Trainer) September 2004

- Selected Air Force Active Duty Baseball Team—competed nationally against NCAA teams (4-year starter)

- Military Training Instructor School Distinguished Graduate May 2002

- Selected Special Duty: Military Training Instructor

- 347th Supply Squadron NCO of the Quarter Apr-Jun & Jul-Aug 2001

- Navy Commendation Letter 2001 (Operation Southern Watch)

- Air Force Achievement Medal 2001 (Operation Southern Watch)

- Air Force Achievement Medal 1999 (Meritorious Service - Korean Defense Campaign)

- Air Force Achievement Medal 1998 (Meritorious Service)

- 1997 Supply Squadron Eagle Leadership Award

- 1997 Fuels Management Flight Airman of the Year

- Selected 37th Fighter Wing Honor Guard Jan 1997

- 1996 Fuels Management Academic Achievement of the Year

- 37th Fuels Management Flight Airman of the Quarter Apr-Jun, July-Sep, & Oct-Dec 1996

- 347th Supply Squadron NCO of the Quarter Apr-Jun & Jul-Aug 2001

- Navy Commendation Letter 2001 (Operation Southern Watch)

- Air Force Achievement Medal 2001 (Operation Southern Watch)

- Air Force Achievement Medal 1999

- Air Force Achievement Medal 1998

- 1997 Supply Squadron Eagle Leadership Award

- 1997 Fuels Management Flight Airman of the Year

- 1996 Fuels Management Academic Achievement of the Year

Made in the USA
Coppell, TX
28 August 2023